2017 Serial True Crime Anthology
Volume IV

By True Crime Writers

Peter Vronsky
RJ Parker
Michael Newton
Sylvia Perrini
JJ Slate

2017 Serial Killers: True Crime Anthology
Volume IV

By True Crime Writers

Peter Vronsky
RJ Parker
Michael Newton
Sylvia Perrini
JJ Slate

Copyright and Published by
RJ Parker Publishing, Inc.

Published in United States of America

12.15.16

ISBN-13: 978-1987902174
ISBN-10: 1987902173

Thank you for purchasing *SERIAL KILLERS: TRUE CRIME ANTHOLOGY, Vol. IV* (2017). Please take a moment after reading this book to write a brief review. Your consideration would be much appreciated. Thanks again for your support.

RJ Parker

Peter Vronsky

Sylvia Perrini

Michael Newton

Jennifer J Slate

Contents

Acknowledgements

We would like to extend our deepest gratitude to the following individuals for their help with this book:

Linda H. Bergeron
Marlene Fabregas
Kathi Garcia
Darlene Horn
Lee Knieper Husemann
Robyn MacEachern
Bettye McKee
Ron Steed

INTRODUCTION

Why are we so fascinated with serial killers and calculated murderers? Is it the pure madness of their killing streaks that intrigues us? How the paths they took in life are in stark contrast to our own? Or is it genuine disbelief in the types of acts they commit? Do you ever find yourself wondering what sort of things trigger such violence in killers? Were they born with some sort of "evil" gene? Maybe we're all born with these capabilities, but those who turn violent are simply taught how to be cruel from their parents, their peers, and their society? Maybe our fascination with these killers is a combination of all these things.

Whatever it is that intrigues us, there is no shortage of serial killers to examine. In the United States alone, it is estimated that there are approximately 25 to 50 active serial killers at any given time. And that is a conservative estimate.

Each year, a group of bestselling true crime authors gets together to collaborate on this Serial Killers Anthology. This year, for our fourth volume, we have ten terrifying stories for you. The stories are as dark as they come—from traveling recluse truck-driving murderers, to cousins that enjoy preying on innocent women, to charming serial killers that hide in plain sight. These bone-chilling true stories are a constant reminder that murderous monsters lurk everywhere, even today.

Chapter 1
KEITH HUNTER JESPERSON
The Happy Face Killer
By JJ Slate

As he repeatedly punched and bashed in twenty-three-year-old Taunja Bennett's face in the house of his ex-girlfriend, surely Keith Hunter Jesperson must have wondered how things had culminated in such a violent conclusion. In his thirty-four years on this planet, he'd never killed another human being before. What had brought him to this dark place where his deepest instincts pushed him to commit violent murder?

A Childhood Outcast

On paper, Keith Hunter Jesperson's life seemed pretty normal. It's hard to pinpoint exactly how a sweet, quiet boy like Keith could grow up to be a violent serial killer.

Born in Chilliwack, British Columbia, to Leslie (Les) and Gladys Jesperson in 1955, Keith was the middle child of two brothers (Bruce and Brad) and two sisters (Jill and Sharon). He often felt overlooked and left out as a child. His birthday fell on the same day as his big brother's, and his parents often held joint parties for the two boys, which always left Keith feeling less than special. His brothers didn't include him in their activities and Keith always felt his father favored them over him. As a result, he spent most of his childhood feeling lonely and unattached. As a young boy, he thought of animals as his only friends, and his chocolate brown Labrador retriever, Duke, whom he got around age five, was his best friend. Duke went everywhere with Keith, and even slept under the covers in his bed with him at night, in the same room he shared with his younger brother, Brad.

One time, Keith rescued a raven he'd found with a broken wing. He gently splinted the bird's wing with a Popsicle stick and made a makeshift nest for it in a box with rags, hoping to nurse it back to health. But after school one day, Keith's older brother, Bruce, took the box to a friend's house, where they dumped the injured bird on the ground and threw knives at it until it died. This enraged Keith. His brothers and neighborhood friends were always killing small animals. They would use firecrackers to blow up sparrows and robins. They'd nail small animals to boards and stick needles and nails into their skin. Sometimes they would tie two cats together by the tail and hang them over a rope, watching them claw and bite each other to death. Even his dad was known to put stray kittens in a sack and drown them. Sometimes, Keith would help his dad control the feral cat population by bashing kittens to death in their barn. To Keith, hurting small animals soon became something of the norm. He began to participate in the animal torture with the neighborhood kids, but he always left Duke at home, just in case any of them started to get ideas.

At school, Keith struggled to make friends. His teachers thought he was slow, and he was almost held back a grade before someone realized he was having trouble seeing the blackboard and just needed a good set of glasses. His grades improved somewhat after that, but not by much. He'd outgrown most of the other boys by the time he'd entered grade school, and his growth spurt showed no signs of slowing down. The other kids would call him names, ridiculing his size and his slow, lumbering walk. Even when he participated in animal torture with other kids in the neighborhood, he never really felt close to anyone but Duke.

Les, Keith's father, was a fan of the drink and would often be drunk by noon each day. Keith would later recall how he always seemed to be the one who'd get the brunt of his father's beatings, usually with the belt, but sometimes with his fists. To the media later, Les would emphatically deny ever using his own fists to punish his son and swore he only used the belt for punishment, like his own father did when he was a boy. But much of Keith's writing about his own childhood seems centered around this tortured relationship he had with his father.

Keith had two vicious fights as a young boy, before the bullies really started ganging up on him. When he was ten years old, he became friends with a neighborhood kid named Martin but soon learned he was a troublemaker. Martin was always getting into something he shouldn't be and blaming Keith when they got caught. One day, Keith felt he'd had enough. He jumped on Martin and began whaling on him. By the time his father pulled him off the kid, Martin was unconscious. Looking back on the incident many years later, Keith claimed he would have killed the boy if he hadn't been interrupted. He was just so sick of taking the blame for someone else's mischief. About a year after that incident, he held a boy's head underwater at the city pool in retaliation for the kid doing the same to him at Cultus Lake weeks earlier. He claimed the boy had held him underwater for a few moments, let him come up for a gasp of air, and then pushed him back under. He did this for nearly ten minutes, and Keith later claimed he'd nearly died that day. At the swimming pool, Keith felt he needed to stand up to the bully and held his head underwater until a lifeguard separated them. It seemed Keith had decided he was no longer going to be pushed around. He was ready to take matters into his own hands.

Despite his father's drunken rages and condescending tone, Keith longed for his father's approval. At a young age, Les instilled the ethic of hard work in his three boys. He put them to work for him, cleaning nuts and bolts in his workshop or baling hay. At age eleven, Keith got a job delivering the local newspaper, the *Province*. He began to look forward to his paper route, feeling good about keeping busy and making money for himself.

When Keith was twelve, the family moved from Chilliwack to Selah, Washington, for Les's job. The year was 1967 and the Jesperson family was doing quite well at the time. The family moved into a six-bedroom house with a four-car garage. His father even built the kids a miniature log cabin in the backyard. But Keith was not happy about leaving Canada. The kids in Washington really let him have it—they teased him about the way he spoke and his lumbering stature. They nicknamed him "Tiny," to be funny, but that was soon followed with "Sloth," "Monster Man," "Igor," and "Hulk." Keith just couldn't fit in anywhere.

As he grew into adolescence, Keith got in trouble for shoplifting and fighting back when the bullies challenged him.

When the boys were old enough, Keith's father opened up checking accounts for them and taught them how to balance their checkbooks. He paid them $1.50 an hour to help him in his workshop, where he manufactured special clips for hops growers in the beer industry. Les told the boys they needed to pay him room and board, $30 a week. After six months, Keith angrily went to his mother, complaining he'd just found out his brothers hadn't been paying. When he demanded a refund, his dad just laughed and told Keith to consider it a learning experience, something he often told his son when things didn't go his way.

In high school, Keith experimented briefly with alcohol, but he didn't like the feeling of losing control it gave him. After growing up in a house with an aggressive, drunk father, he knew how out of control booze could make you feel. He much rather preferred to be the sober one at the parties, feeling like he was the only one in full control. He didn't experiment with drugs for the same reason.

Girls were another mystery to Keith. His father had never taught him about sex, and by the time he entered adolescence, he barely spoke to his brothers. He had exactly zero information about how to act around a girl and what to do if one wanted to kiss him. Sometimes his flustered attitude scared potential dates into thinking he was threatening. He knew he liked girls, but didn't know how to make a move. When he was fourteen years old, he had his first sexual encounter with a girl. She took him completely by surprise and, in later writings, he described the encounter as if he was a victim of rape. He soon began fantasizing about overpowering and raping girls, but he was confused about what that might make him. All he wanted was to fall in love and have sex, but he couldn't stop combining his thoughts of lust with thoughts of power and control.

At age sixteen, Keith came home one day to learn his dad had shot his dog, Duke, his only true companion for the past eleven years. Keith had grown up with Duke. He'd even started tenderly carrying the old dog to bed with him when Duke let him know he couldn't jump up anymore. When Keith learned of his father's actions that day, he was never the same. He considered his father an evil murderer for what he'd done.

More than anything, Keith wanted to become a member of the Royal Canadian Mounted Police. He dreamed of sitting tall as a Mountie, impressing women in his uniform and position of power. But he knew he needed to work hard to get there— one of the requirements of becoming a Mountie was running ten miles, something Keith still could not yet do. He joined football to get into shape, but when he found that wasn't for him, he began wrestling. In senior year, during wrestling practice, he finally climbed to the top of the rope climb for the first time, but his jubilation was short lived. The rope snapped at the top and he fell hard on his head, side, and foot, tearing ligaments in the arch, which would go undiagnosed for months. Eventually, he had surgery to alleviate the pain. But his Mountie dreams were shattered for good.

College was out of the question, too. In fact, it was never even brought up. Despite the fact that his siblings all went on to earn degrees, his father didn't believe Keith was smart enough to attend college. Out of 174 students in his high school class, Keith graduated ranked at 161 with an IQ of 102. It seemed Keith's only option after the rope-climbing accident was to help his father out with the family business after high school. His father had decided to turn some of their land into a trailer park by then, so Keith resigned himself to a life of working for the man who never seemed to think he was good enough to do anything. Keith's father sued the school over the rope-climbing accident and they eventually won a settlement of $33,000. His father talked him into investing all the money into the new family business.

At age nineteen, Keith met Rose Hucke. They met at a burger joint and quickly hit it off. Less than a year later, they were engaged to be married, but Keith wondered if he was making the right decision. He later recalled how he'd gone to his father to ask him what he should do.

"Two weeks before the wedding, I said, 'Dad, I can't marry Rose. I don't really love her.' He says, 'I've already invited the relatives. Don't disgrace your family, Son.'"

For a while after the wedding, Keith and Rose lived on his father's property, and things seemed to be going well for the family. The newlyweds soon learned they were pregnant, and before long they had three children, two daughters and a son.

At Rose's urging, Keith finally found a new job away from his father. He began driving long-haul trucks for a living. Keith loved driving trucks. He felt powerful and important driving his big rig and making real money. He would often work longer shifts than was legally allowed to pull in more money and enjoyed the feeling of providing for his family. Whenever he came home, he'd scoop his children up into a bear hug and let them climb all over him on the floor. He felt like he was a good dad.

But the time away from Rose eventually drove a wedge between them. While he was gone, she sometimes received mysterious phone calls where the caller would hang up as soon as she answered. Rose began to suspect Keith was cheating on her, and she was right. Keith eventually told her he'd found another woman named Roberta who really made him happy. Fourteen years after they were married, the couple separated. Rose packed up her three children and moved to Spokane, Washington, over 200 miles away.

Keith moved in with his new girlfriend in Portland, Oregon. Roberta had two of her own children from a previous marriage. She liked to accompany Keith on his long-haul trips in the big rigs and even drove for him on occasion when he needed to get some rest. Whenever he was in the area of Spokane, Keith would stop in to visit his family, often bringing gifts and taking the children out food shopping when he saw how bare the family's cupboards were. He tried to be a good dad to his three children, but he sometimes felt like they took advantage of him when he came around.

One day, Roberta had enough of their bickering and left for Knoxville, Tennessee. Keith remained in Roberta's home for weeks while she was away, feeling sorry for himself after getting dinged with one too many driving violations, causing him to lose his job. On the afternoon of January 23, 1990, he drove to a local watering hole to drown his sorrows. It was there he met Taunja Bennett.

The First Murder

Twenty-three-year-old Taunja Bennett lived with her mother in Portland, Oregon. She'd suffered oxygen deprivation at birth, leaving her mildly mentally disabled. She was a petite brunette with piercing dark eyes and an impulsive personality. She loved meeting new people and would often greet complete strangers with a contagious smile and a hug.

Taunja Bennett

Keith was just finishing up a solo game of pool at B&I Tavern when he noticed Taunja. She was flirting with two other men at one of the nearby pool tables. When she noticed Keith's wandering eyes, she immediately walked up to him and gave him a welcoming hug, catching him off guard.

A waitress quietly let him know that Taunja was a nice girl, but she was a little off. Deciding to cut his losses for the night, Keith decided to head home alone.

He didn't stay there for long. He couldn't get Taunja's pretty face out of his mind. About two hours later, he headed back to B&I Tavern, hoping she was still hanging around. As he walked toward the door of the bar, Taunja was walking out.

Keith spun on his heel and followed her into the parking lot. He struck up a casual conversation with her and offered to take her out to get a bite to eat. Taunja agreed and got into his car.

Once in the car, Keith made up a story about being low on cash. He had to make a quick pit stop at his house to grab some money. As he pulled into the driveway, he suggested she come inside while he used the bathroom. Taunja complied.

When Keith got Taunja into Roberta's house, he immediately tried to push himself on her. They struggled a bit, and Taunja immediately tried to run for the door. But Keith caught her and pushed her down on a mattress that was lying on the floor.

Perhaps sensing she was out of options at this point, Keith later claimed Taunja stopped fighting back and let him kiss and grope her. But something about her lack of enthusiasm enraged Keith. He snapped and punched her as hard as he could in the temple.

Instead of being knocked unconscious, Taunja looked up at him with a blank stare.

Keith hit her again. Then again. And again. The more he hit her, the angrier he got. She never responded to his punches— she just lay there with the same blank stare on her face. Keith hit her close to two dozen times, until her face was completely unrecognizable.

When he finally stopped, she began wailing. Her eyes were swollen and bloody, and her jaw was clearly broken. Keith knew he couldn't let her leave the house like that. He'd be arrested for assault. So he leaned in, grabbed her throat with his hands, and squeezed.

Each time he let go, Taunja gasped for breath, still alive. Finally, after several attempts and one final squeeze, Keith removed his hands and she didn't take another breath. This man, who had never raised a hand to a woman in all his years on the earth, had just brutally killed an innocent woman.

Cover Up

Keith might not have been college smart, but he liked to consider himself street smart. He watched all those court TV shows and knew the first thing he needed to do was establish an alibi.

Keith thought about all the things he needed to do to make sure he wasn't caught while he drank a cup of coffee. As he went over the list in his head, he stared at Taunja's body. The first thing he wanted to do was to make sure she was really dead. He tied a nylon rope around her neck and cinched it as tight has he could. Eying the button fly on her jeans, he worried police might be able to lift his fingerprints from the metal, so he cut the fly from the fabric and tossed it into the fireplace.

He cleaned himself up and made sure his clothes were free of any blood spatter. Leaving Taunja on the mattress, Keith drove back to B&I Tavern. He drank a beer at the bar, purposefully speaking to the same waitress from earlier that afternoon and chatting casually with a few of the patrons. He made sure they watched him as he left the bar alone.

Next, he headed to a gas station to fill up his tank and check his brake lights—he didn't want to run out of gas or get pulled over for a blown light with Taunja's body in his car! He headed home and backed into the driveway, cutting the lights as he pulled in.

He pulled Taunja's body out of the house by her feet and stuffed her into the passenger seat with her head leaning against the window. Thinking ahead, he walked back inside and grabbed a second pair of sneakers to change into after he ditched the body. The last thing he needed was for his shoe prints to match those taken from the dumpsite.

Keith drove around for a while with Taunja crunched up next to him in the car. He made sure to stay under the speed limit and slowed down at yellow lights. Finally, he found an area with a steep embankment off the side of the road and pulled over. He yanked Taunja out of the car and tossed her in the direction of the ravine, watching her body tumble down the embankment like a ragdoll.

Keith paused for a moment, wondering if he should cover her up with brush but decided it was best to hightail it out of there before another car came upon them. He drove for a while before tossing his shoes out the window into the night and ditching Taunja's Walkman along a main stretch of road. He threw her purse into a blackberry patch along Sandy River Road and headed home to begin the long process of cleaning Taunja's blood from Roberta's home. Later, he confessed, even after steam cleaning the rugs, washing the walls, and painting the ceiling, he was still finding tiny specks of blood spatter in the oddest places. Then, Keith sat back and waited for the police to come and find him.

A Confession

Taunja's body was found the next day by a biker. Imagine Keith's surprise when, just a few weeks later, he read in the papers how a woman had confessed to the murder and implicated her boyfriend in the crime. The two were taken into custody and it wasn't long before charges were filed. Keith was baffled. Someone else had confessed to his crime? How? Why? He knew he'd done a great job at getting rid of the evidence, but he didn't think he'd been able push the guilt onto someone else!

The couple in question, fifty-seven-year-old Laverne Pavlinac and thirty-nine-year-old John Sosnovske, were picked up after Laverne went to the police and confessed to helping her boyfriend dump Taunja's body after he'd killed her in a blacked-out drunken rage. She even produced a button fly cut from a pair of jeans she claimed matched the victim's and led police to the approximate area where Taunja's body was found. When investigators pointed out the fly did not match the pair of pants Taunja was wearing, Laverne produced another one, and then finally admitted she'd cut the fly from her daughter's pants but insisted she was telling the truth.

Her boyfriend, John, vehemently denied the accusations and refused to confess to a murder. Weeks later, Laverne recanted her statement, too, but the police felt the evidence was damning.

At trial, Laverne stood by her recanted confession, claiming she'd only gone to the police in an effort to escape her abusive boyfriend, John. She'd heard about the murder details from a friend familiar with the case and thought she might be able to pin it on her boyfriend. She thought if she could convince the police that John had killed Taunja, for sure she would get immunity for helping them put a killer behind bars and she would be free from his violent behavior. Unfortunately, that plan backfired on her when she told police she'd helped with the killing and disposal of the body. After hearing her original confession to police, a jury of her peers found her guilty and she was sentenced to life in prison. Shortly after her conviction, John pleaded no contest to murder in an effort to avoid the death penalty and was also sentenced to life in prison.

Keith followed the case in the news religiously. He was impressed with his ability to keep the police off his trail, but part of him wondered what would it take for someone to notice him? He'd been flying under the radar, so to speak, his entire life. His siblings had all exceeded him in their life endeavors, his father didn't respect him, and his wife wanted nothing to do with him.... Why was he so invisible? Getting away with murder was both exhilarating and infuriating at the same time.

A few months later, at a rest stop in Livingston, Montana, Keith wrote a note on the wall of a bathroom stall. "I killed Tanya Bennet [sic] January 21, 1990 in Portland, Oregon. I beat her to death, raped her and I loved it. Yes I'm sick, but I enjoy myself too. People took the blame and I'm free." He signed the note with a happy face.

Two months later, he left another bathroom rest stop note, this time in Umatilla, Oregon. "Killed Tanya [sic] Bennett in Portland. Two people got the blame so I can kill again. (Cut buttons off jeans—proof)." He signed the note with another happy face.

Leaving these notes made him feel powerful and untouchable. It was as if he was taunting the police. *Come and get me.*

Another Murder

Two-and-a-half years had passed since he'd killed Taunja Bennett and Keith thought about her every day. He remembered how it had felt to kill Taunja—like killing a gopher or a cat, only better. He'd had a few violent encounters with women since then, but he hadn't killed anyone. One woman had sprayed mace in his face, and another called police on him and had him picked up on assault charges. But he'd managed to talk his way out of that rap, which only fed his huge ego.

One summer day in San Bernardino, California, a cute woman named Claudia approached him at a truck stop. She asked for a ride in the direction towards Phoenix, or anywhere in the area, and climbed right into his truck. Keith was amazed at her lack of hesitance and instantly knew she would be his next victim.

They drove to a truck stop in Coachella, where they ate and went back to the truck. When Claudia told Keith she'd only have sex for money, he forced himself on her. She resisted at first but then pretended to get into it. At the next truck stop, they ate again and she demanded he buy her some new clothes in exchange for the sex. When Keith refused to give her money, she threatened to call the cops and have him arrested. That was all it took for Keith to see red.

He locked the doors to the truck and threw her in the back of the sleeper. Using duct tape he'd hidden underneath his pillow, he taped her arms and legs together and then taped her to the side vent. With her secured in the back, Keith continued driving along his route, stopping periodically to rape Claudia whenever he pleased.

He began to play a game with her, squeezing her neck until she nearly lost consciousness. Each time he let go, he'd wait patiently for her to regain awareness and tell her to count to ten, when he'd choke her again. The next time, he told her to count to nine, then eight, then seven.... He liked this game. It gave him power. He was in charge.

Keith played his death game until he choked the life out of Claudia. Then he casually walked into the truck stop and ordered himself an iced tea.

He drove miles with Claudia's body in the cab of his truck before pulling off the road in a desert town called Blythe, near the Arizona border. There, he dragged her body into some brush and covered it up with some tumbleweed.

As he drove on to pick up his next load in Phoenix, he couldn't stop thinking about how easy it was for him to kill and get away with it.

Highway to Murder

About a month after Claudia's murder, a pretty blonde girl approached Keith's truck, soliciting herself. She was very cute, but Keith was tired and would later say he turned her down. He'd already fallen asleep when the same woman barreled into the passenger door of his truck, possibly running from someone else.

He grabbed the woman and slammed her down on the bed, quickly wrapping his hands around her throat and squeezing as hard as he could. Only a few moments passed before she

stopped breathing. Angry with himself for killing her so quickly, Keith used zip ties and duct tape to restrain her, just in case
she wasn't dead. He needed to get out of that rest stop before
anyone came knocking, and he didn't want the woman to wake
up while he was driving away.

He drove for miles before pulling over at another rest stop
and taking another look at the girl. Sure enough, she was dead.
Keith thought maybe when she'd approached him earlier that
night she'd said her name was Cynthia, but he couldn't be
sure.

He removed the zip ties and duct tape from the body and
carried Cynthia over his shoulder to the corner of the parking
lot near a large pile of trash and tumbleweeds. He flipped the
body facedown into the trash and covered it with tumbleweeds. He drove as fast as he could to Fresno, to make sure he
couldn't be reported in the area where her body was found.

For weeks, Keith thought for sure the police would close in
on him soon. He worried about patrol cars that drove near him
on the highways. He fretted about who might be watching him
at rest stops when he pulled in to get some sleep. He even
monitored the CB radio frequencies, convinced someone
might turn him in. But nothing happened.

Approximately a month later, in November of 1992, Keith
struck again. He met up with a prostitute named Laurie he was
familiar with in Wilsonville, Oregon. He'd used her services
several times before and was always satisfied after meeting up
with Laurie. This time, he paid $40 up front, but when they
were finished, she asked for $40 extra. Keith refused, but she
threatened to call the police on him if he didn't pay up.

Enraged, Keith grabbed her and threw her down on the
bed. Looming over her, he stared into her eyes as he pressed
his fist into her throat.

He later claimed just as she lost consciousness, he'd yelled,
"You're number four that pushed your luck with me, bitch!
Now you're dead!"

Laurie didn't die right away. She slowly regained consciousness only to realize her killer wanted to play with her. Keith spent nearly an hour choking the life out of her, reviving her, and starting over. Finally, when she didn't open her eyes again, he laid back, satisfied with his work.

Keith pocketed the $240 he found in Laurie's pockets and thought about where he might be able to leave her body. He ended up driving over an hour to get to the GI Joe's parking lot in Salem, Oregon, where he left Laurie's body next to a fence, covered with leaves.

He had now killed four women, three of them in the last four months.

In March of 1993, Keith spotted a young girl at a truck stop diner in Corning, California. Her hair was soaking wet and she looked lost, hungry, and down on her luck. Keith watched her as she sat by herself, sipping a cup of coffee.

The urge was too great to pass up. He knew he was going to take this woman.

Keith gestured his waitress over and told her to ask the woman to order whatever she wanted and put it on his check. Gratefully, the woman ordered a huge meal and scarfed it down before coming over to thank her savior. She said her name was Cindy and she wondered if he might be headed to Sacramento next. She said she had a sister living there and would love to be able to meet up with her. Keith invited her along.

After several hours of driving, the two eventually climbed into the back of the sleeper for a little fun before getting some sleep. Keith turned on her almost immediately, raping her and playing his little death game. Cindy floated in and out of consciousness several times before Keith finally choked the last breath from her lungs.

He disposed of her body behind a pile of rocks along Pacheco Pass Highway. Her body wasn't discovered until three months later.

During the summer of 1993, Keith met a blonde woman named Julie Winningham at a truck stop in Oregon. There was something different about Julie—he didn't want to kill her. He wanted to get to know her. They talked for hours the first night they met, and he invited her on one of his long-haul runs. She quickly agreed, and soon they were on their way.

Eventually, Keith introduced Julie to most of his friends and family as his girlfriend. He even met her family. It seemed the only obstacle the couple faced (besides the obvious problem that he was a violent serial killer) was Julie liked to smoke pot and take drugs, but Keith did not. In fact, he wouldn't stand to be around it. The two were hot and heavy for about a year, and Keith would often visit her whenever his route took him back to her area. He eventually broke things off when he suspected Julie was sleeping around, but that wouldn't be the end of their story.

Happy Face Emerges

After he broke up with Julie, Keith started thinking more about the couple in prison for his first murder. He wondered why no one had ever reported the notes he'd left in the rest stop bathrooms for the police.

He decided to write a new letter and mailed it to the Washington County Courthouse. He signed the letter with a happy face. The uncorrected letter reads:

I killed Miss Bennett Jan 20, 1990 and left her 1½ miles east of Lateral Falls on the switchback. I used a ½" soft nylon rope burnt on one end—frayed cut on the other—and tied it around her neck. Her face her teeth protruded from her mouth. Death was caused by my right fist pushed into her throat until she quit moving. Threw her Walkman away. Her purse $2.00—I threw into the Sandy River. I cut the buttons off her jeans. I had raped her before and after her death. I left her facing downhill and her jeans down by her ankles. I did not know any of them.

When there still wasn't any response from police, Keith

took a different approach. He wrote a new note and mailed it to the Oregonian. At the top of the letter, he drew a happy face.

I would like to tell my story! I am a good person at times. I always wanted to be liked. I have been married and divorced with children—I didn't really want to be married but it happened. I have read your paper and enjoyed it a lot. I always have wanted to be noticed like Paul Harvey, Front Page, etc. So I started something I don't know how to stop. On or around January 20th 1990 I picked up Sonya [sic] Bennett and took her home. I raped her and beat her real bad. Her face was all broke up. Then I ended her life by pushing my fist into her throat. This turned me on. I got a high. Then panic set in. Where to put the body? I drove out to Sandy River and threw her purse and Walkman away and I drove the scenic road past the falls. I went back home and dragged her out to the car. I want [sic] to know that it was my crime. So I tied a ½" soft white rope cut on end [sic] and burned on the other—around her neck. I drove her to switchback on the scenic road about 1½ miles east of Lateral Falls. Dragged her downhill. Her pants were around her knees because I had cut her buttons off. They found her the next day. I wanted her to be found. I felt real bad and afraid that I would be caught. But a man and a woman got blamed for it. My conscience is getting to me now. She was my first and I thought I would not do it again, but I was wrong.

Shortly after sending this letter, he sent another one with additional information:

My last victim was a street person. It was raining in Corning, California. She was wet and I offered a ride to Sacramento, California. I stopped at a rest area near Williams and had her. I put her body on or near a pile of rocks about 50 yds. north of highway 152 westbound about 20 miles from Santa Nella.

It was getting hard to trust my inner self. I kept arguing with my conscience. I had to get away from long haul trucking. Victims are too easily found. So I quit and found a good job driving where I am in the public eye and out of harms way. The truck has a bold name on the side so it is easily recognized. I got away from what became easy. I do not want to kill again and I want to protect my family from grief. I [sic] would tear it apart.

I feel bad but I will not turn myself in. I am not stupid. I do know what would happen to me if I did. In a lot of opinions I should be killed and I feel I deserve it. My responsibility is mine and God will be my judge when I die. I am telling you this because I will be responsible for these crimes and no one else. It all started when I wondered what it would be like to kill someone. And I found out. What a nightmare it has been. I had sent a letter to Washington county judges criminal court taking responsibility, to [murder] #1. But nothing has been in your paper. This freedom of press you have the ball. I will be reading to find out. I used gloves and same paper as last letter "no prints." Look over your shoulder. I may be closer than you think.

Keith also started reading up on the psychology of serial killers. He learned about the Macdonald triad—three telltale childhood behaviors typically engaged in by soon-to-be serial killers: animal cruelty, fire setting, and bed-wetting. He knew he fit two out of three of those symptoms, but he wasn't sure what that meant. Then he wondered if setting fires might alleviate his hunger for killing. For many months, Keith Hunter Jesperson was the cause behind several massive forest and brush fires. He believed his fires were actually saving women he might have killed.

But the fires grew boring and Keith finally put an end to that. In fall of 1994, he picked up a woman named Suzanna near Tampa. She was hoping to hitch a ride to Lake Tahoe. Keith promised he could get her as far as Reno, but that was it.

Before getting into his cab, she asked, "You're not one of those serial killers, are you?"

Keith feigned a laugh and told her not to ask him stupid questions.

Like the others before her, Keith raped Suzanna and choked her to death. He deposited her body in some brush somewhere along Okaloosa County and continued his way back west.

In January of 1995, Keith met a younger woman named Angela Subrize in Spokane. They spent the night together in a hotel and she contacted him soon after to ask if he could get her from Spokane to Denver, where she could visit her father. About halfway through the trip, she changed her mind and instead asked Keith to take her to Indiana, to see an ex-boyfriend.

Angry and feeling taken advantage of, Keith told her to find her own ride there. Angela cried and begged him to take her. An idea began to formulate in his mind as they got back into the truck.

By the time they'd hit Nebraska, Keith was ready to play his games. He choked her and revived her several times before she died. At this point, he wasn't quite sure what to do with her body since she'd been with him for over a week and she'd used his credit cards to make personal calls to her father and boyfriend. He didn't think dumping the body in his usual way would be very smart.

Around three in the morning on January 23, Keith carefully duct taped Angela's hands in front of her and tied her by the ankles to a crossbar under his truck. He placed her facedown on the pavement so her head and torso were hidden by the rear tires. His gruesome plan was to drive several miles down the road, dragging her body onto the pavement to grind off any fingerprints and leave her face unrecognizable.

Keith drove for approximately twelve miles before pulling off the highway to check his work. Angela's face was completely gone—it was ground down to her ears. A leg and both arms were also missing, her chest had opened up and her insides had disappeared. He figured other drivers might see her body parts in the road and assume it was road kill.

Keith dragged what was left of Angela down a steep embankment and dumped her body in some tall grass.

The End of the Road

A few months after killing Angela, Keith ran into his ex-girlfriend Julie Winningham. They spent a few days together and Keith started to think he might actually be in love with Julie. When she asked him to marry her, he decided to play along and say yes. He soon believed Julie was just trying to keep him happy in an effort to get him to pay off her recent DUI fines and buy her drugs, cigarettes, and alcohol. They spent several weeks together before Keith killed her.

He strangled her unconscious during sex one night in his truck. Before she woke up, he duct taped her arms behind her back and taped her legs together. He also put tape over her mouth. He then began to drive.

She woke up at some point and Keith pulled his truck off the road. Keith raped Julie over and over and continued to play his choking game with her throughout the rest of the night. As he played, he told her about the seven other women he'd killed. With each story he told, Julie gave up a little more. Finally, just as he drove his fist into her neck for the last time, he told her, "You're number eight. And, yes, I *will* get away with it." Those were the last words she heard.

Keith threw his fiancée's body down a fifteen-foot embankment along the Columbia Gorge. As he drove away, he wondered if Julie might be the one that got him caught. Nearly everyone in town knew they'd been engaged for that brief moment in time, and her mother knew she'd been staying with him. What would they think when she turned up missing?

Less than a week later, police came around looking for Julie. Two detectives from Clark County, Washington, picked Keith up in Las Cruces, New Mexico, while he was working on one of his trucking runs. Keith learned that they'd found Julie's body the day after he'd dumped it. He lied through his teeth and denied knowing anything about what had happened to her. When police asked why he didn't seem surprised or upset that his fiancée was dead, he told them she was into a lot of drugs and nothing surprised him about Julie anymore.

After several hours of questioning, Keith began to wonder why the police hadn't arrested him yet. They hadn't even read him his Miranda rights. He began to suspect they just simply didn't have enough evidence on him.

The detectives nodded toward Keith's arms and asked why he was so dirty. He told them he'd been folding tarps from his truck earlier that day. They told him that Julie's body had been dirty, too, and suggested he might've wrapped her body in one of those tarps before dumping her down the embankment in Washington.

Keith shook his head and told them they had it all wrong. The last time he'd seen Julie was after they'd fought about him paying her DUI fines. Maybe one of her junkie friends had killed her, but it certainly wasn't him.

Realizing they weren't going to get a confession out of Keith, the detectives knew they had to eventually let him walk. They had him photographed, fingerprinted, and took blood and hair samples before they took Keith back to his big rig. There, they seized his tarps and his trucking logbook before letting him drive away a free man.

Over the next several days, Keith tried to kill himself multiple times by overdosing on Tylenol and cold medicine, but each time, he woke up hours later, covered in vomit or feeling like he'd been run over by his own truck. He couldn't seem to get the dosage right.

On March 24, 1995, he wrote a letter to his little brother, Brad, and dropped it into the mail, knowing he was sealing his fate.

Hi Brad—

Seems like my luck has run out. I will never be able to enjoy life on the outside again. I got into a bad situation and got caught up with emotion. I killed a woman in my truck during an argument. With all the evidence against me, it looks like I truly am a black sheep. The court will appoint me a lawyer and there will be a trial. I am sure they will kill me for this. I am sorry that I turned out this way. I have been a killer for 5 yrs. And have killed 8 people. Assaulted more. I guess I haven't learned anything.

Dad always worried about me. Because of what I have gone through in the divorce finances, etc. I have been taking it out on different people. We pay so much of child support. As I saw it I was hoping they would catch me. I took 48 sleeping pills last night and I woke up well rested. The night before I took two bottles of pills to no avail. They will arrest me today.

Keith

The next day, Keith called one of the detectives who'd interrogated him in New Mexico and told him he was ready to confess to Julie's murder.

Keith was arrested in Arizona and extradited back to Washington, where he learned that Brad had immediately turned the letter over to authorities after he'd received it.

Realizing there was nothing left to do but admit to it all, Keith began confessing to murders left and right. But first, he told authorities, he wanted to right a wrong—he'd been the real killer of Taunja Bennett back in 1990, not Laverne Pavlinac and John Sosnovske, who were still serving out their life sentences in prison. But police didn't want to hear it—why would a woman admit to a murder she didn't commit? And how could she possibly know so much about it if she didn't have anything to do with it? As far as the Oregon prosecutor's department was concerned, they'd nailed the two people responsible for the crime years ago, and they weren't interested in hearing Keith's story or admitting they might have wrongly convicted two innocent people.

Jesperson's booking photo.

Eventually, Keith sent a letter to a reporter, which contained a diagram where he believed he'd thrown Taunja's purse after the murder. Taking a search team out to the area, the reporter was stunned to find a purse in a blackberry patch with Taunja Bennett's license still tucked inside.

On November 2, 1995, Keith was convicted of Taunja Bennett's murder. He was sentenced to life in prison with a minimum of thirty years before being eligible for parole. Days later, a judge freed Laverne Pavlinac and John Sosnovske. Keith, who was still communicating with the news outlets (even signing many of his letters "Have a nice day, from Happy Face"), told the Associated Press that he'd cried on the day he learned they'd been set free. "I started crying. I couldn't help myself for about ten minutes. I lost total composure," he wrote. "I was just very overjoyed. Basically my feeling is God bless them."

In December, Keith was sentenced to life in prison again, this time in a Washington courtroom, for the murder of Julie Winningham. He'd pleaded guilty to her murder in October.

He was also convicted of Laurie Ann Pentland's murder after investigators linked him to the crime using his DNA, earning him an additional life sentence in Oregon.

In June of 1998, Keith agreed to plead guilty to the murder of Angela Subrize in Wyoming, but only if authorities promised not to seek the death penalty. He was given another life sentence, which would run consecutively against his others. If he ever receives parole in Oregon, he'd have to serve his life sentence in Washington and then another life sentence in Wyoming.

In all, Keith Hunter Jesperson is linked to eight murders across California, Florida, Nebraska, Oregon, Washington, and Wyoming, though he was only convicted of four. It is unclear if he will ever be tried for his remaining crimes. He remains in the Oregon State Penitentiary to this day as inmate number 11620304. His earliest release date from Oregon would be March 1, 2063, just one month before his 108th birthday.

Chapter 2
JOSHUA WADE
The Alaskan Killer
By RJ Parker

Joshua Wade

In 2007, the otherwise quiet municipality of Anchorage, Alaska, witnessed the biggest manhunt organized within the state that led to the arrest of Joshua Wade. Life in the town of Anchorage came to a halt on the day that the Alaskan killer was finally taken into police custody. The Federal Bureau of Investigation (FBI) along with the Anchorage Police Department led a huge manhunt in search for the dangerous killer who was wanted for his involvement in the murder of Mindy Schloss.

Mindy Schloss was a nurse psychologist and a model citizen. At fifty-two years of age, she had recently moved into the quiet neighborhood of Sand Lake. Her sudden disappearance became a cause of concern for family and friends, who immediately notified the police. The police started searching for her and soon enough discovered that Joshua Wade was Mindy's neighbor.

His name raised a few red flags, as Wade had been on the

authorities' radar for quite some time. He had been taken into custody almost seven years earlier regarding the murder of a woman named Della Brown. At that time, the Anchorage Police questioned him, and he was subsequently charged with murder, assault, and evidence tampering. However, due to lack of evidence and witnesses, Wade was acquitted by a jury on all counts, except evidence tampering. He was released and moved into the house near Mindy Schloss soon after.

Background

Joshua Wade was a resident of Anchorage, Alaska, and was known for being an angry, violent boy since a young age. At nineteen, it was alleged that he was involved in a number of aggravated assaults and hard crimes in the area. However, it would not be proven until much later.

Near his twentieth birthday, Wade became a person of interest in the Della Brown murder case. The police were able to uncover his violent history and soon became convinced that he was the person who assaulted and murdered her. Unfortunately, the evidence was circumstantial and nothing could be proved during trial.

After he was caught and convicted for the murder of Mindy Schloss, he gave a confession statement admitting that he had murdered Della.

But that's not all he confessed to. The police got a surprise when Wade gave another statement claiming that he had committed three more murders. In a press conference, the authorities announced that they were looking into the names that Wade had brought forward and would soon find out whether or not it was true. Joshua Wade claimed that he had victimized three men before he killed Della. He confessed to brutally murdering these men and gave their names to the authorities.

Experts and officials believed that he did it as part of his violent nature and that he derived a sick pleasure from all the brutal acts that he committed. In a statement that Wade gave after his sentencing, he claimed that he was no 'serial killer'; however, all the signs indicated otherwise. He was remorseless and disturbed. The agents who had brought him in were convinced that he had all the makings of a serial killer and realized that they had just removed an extremely dangerous man off the streets.

After he was arrested for his involvement in the murder of Mindy Schloss, the investigating officials ran an extensive search on the man they had just captured. However, at that time they were not able to uncover anything of consequence.

The authorities had already put him on their watch list after the Della Brown murder case. Wade had been twenty years old when he was initially taken into custody for being involved in Della's murder. The police had no evidence to see the case through; hence, Wade was acquitted on murder and assault charges.

During all this, the police officers tried to find some concrete information and evidence that would indicate that Wade was indeed an aggressive and violent killer, but to no avail. Joshua Wade's attorneys overturned all the claims and ensured that he walked away with an acquittal.

According to the officers who brought him in at the time, Wade was a dangerous man who deserved to be locked up. They had figured out that something was wrong with him and that the man could be a danger to society. Experts and analysts tried to present possible motives and objectives behind the brutal murder, but it proved quite difficult.

Questions were raised about his state of mind, behavior and who he actually was. He didn't have many friends or acquaintances within the area. Even the residents of the neighborhood did not know much about him and the house that was next to Mindy's. When the investigation for Mindy Schloss was underway, the police officials and FBI agents went around inquiring more about her next-door neighbor; however, nothing tangible turned up.

Della Brown

On August 31, 2000, nearly
seven years before the murder of Mindy Schloss, Della
Brown, 33, was reported
missing.

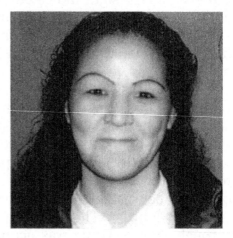

The police launched an
investigation and started
canvassing the area where
her last known location was
detected.

Della Brown was a lively
and very friendly girl who
had been raised by her
grandparents. Friends and colleagues recalled her fondly and
praised her ability to always be polite. Upon investigating, the
authorities learned that although she had struggled with drugs
and alcohol earlier, she had recovered from all that and was
settled in her job.

Brown held a steady job as a Bingo hostess and was well
liked among her colleagues, as well as customers. The police
found out that with the exception of an ex-boyfriend who had
been charged and arrested for displaying aggressive behavior
towards her, she had no bad history with anyone.

A report was filed against him stating that he had beaten
Della up and was known to be temperamental. He became a
prime suspect in the investigation initially, but the police were
soon able to rule out his involvement in her case.

On September 2, 2000, the police officials discovered Della
Brown's body in a hidden shed situated within a rough neighborhood of Anchorage. The place where her body was recovered was already known around the area as being a hideout for
drug abusers, gamblers, and prostitution rings. The police
knew that if the tracks led there, it could not mean anything
good.

They were not wrong. When Della's body was found, the place became a crime scene and was cordoned off by the investigating officials. The police officers who discovered the body knew that there was little chance of them getting any evidence or tracking down the murderer from that place. It was a dark shed that was well hidden by bushes and trees. There was no chance of anybody seeing or hearing anything that went on at the time of Della's murder.

Police officers were able to conclude that Brown had died from extreme blunt force trauma. There were several indications on her head and face that pointed towards the use of force to subdue her. It appeared that she had been beaten up badly and that it had led to her eventual death.

Upon further investigation, it was revealed that Della Brown had also been sexually assaulted before her murder. The officers on scene started looking around the area searching for clues. Some of them believed that any of the rocks around the shed could be the murder weapon. However, at the time, the canvassing and search yielded little results.

Della's mother and family were spared the horrific details of her murder at the time. Her near and dear ones were told only that she had been killed. All other details were kept under wraps by the police and investigating authorities. The officials ensured that nobody was able to obtain the details of her murder till after the investigation was over and the case went to trial.

The disappearance and murder of Della Brown proved to be very harrowing for the police department and authorities. According to one of the police officers on the case, this could mean something very bad for the town of Anchorage. At that point in time, investigating authorities and Anchorage police department were already looking into three or four murders that had occurred over the past few months. They feared that Della's murder was another one that could be connected to the other murders.

Police officers were wary of the possibility of a serial killer on the loose, but they did take it into consideration. The previous victims had also been found murdered at outdoor locations with signs of assault and injuries. The lead detective on the case stated that he had found five or six bodies in similar circumstances as Della Brown's.

At that time, the police had very little to build a case on. They still did not know whether one person was committing all those murders or if there were multiple killers on the loose. The evidence recovered was not substantial, and the police were organizing comprehensive searches to find out more about Della Brown's murder.

Soon enough, the detectives learned that Della's ex-boyfriend had been previously arrested for beating her up. He became the focus of the investigation, as the police believed that he could be the suspected culprit in this case. However, after thorough, extensive questioning and investigation, the authorities were able to rule out his involvement in the murder.

The police officers were struggling to prevent the case from going cold, as they practically had nothing left anymore. All the leads that were followed led nowhere, and it looked like the killer would continue to walk around freely if something didn't turn up.

By a stroke of luck, in a few days, the Anchorage police department received a surprising tip. It came from a person who had seen Della's body before the officials found it. In fact, the witness had been taken to see the body even before the police had received the incident report. The officers were told that that the witness might have been taken there to see the body by the person who had perpetrated the crime.

It was believed that Della's murderer took the witness to see the body right after she was murdered.

The police followed up on the tip and came across the group of informants who claimed that they had all seen Della Brown's body following her murder. The informants claimed that twenty-year-old Joshua Wade told them he had spotted the woman passed out on the road. It seemed that she might have been rendered unconscious due to alcohol consumption or drugs.

Instead of helping her, Wade carried the unconscious woman to the hidden place and killed her brutally. After that, he approached these witnesses and took them to see the body. According to one witness's statement, Joshua turned up all of a sudden and seemed out of breath. He appeared excited, agitated and even had blood on his shirt.

None of the people there could figure out what he was doing there until he asked them to come to the shed to see something. That was when they found out that he had murdered Della Brown and hid the body in the shed.

This tip proved to be very helpful for the investigating officials. Nearly a month after Della's body was discovered, the police were able to arrest Joshua Wade. On September 30, 2000, Wade was taken into custody and charged with murder, sexual assault, and evidence tampering.

He was sent to jail pending trial. Della Brown's mother, along with many other people, awaited justice. When court proceedings were initiated, everyone was already sure that Wade was going to be convicted on all charges. However, that did not happen. He had two of the best defense attorneys in the state on his side, and they put forth strong arguments against his involvement in the murder.

The argument stated that Wade was not the actual perpetrator of the crime, but that he had accidentally come across Della Brown's body. In order to make an impression on his friends and appear tough, he'd admitted to murdering her.

The testimony of the people who had informed the police about him did not help, as Wade recanted everything that he had confessed to during the trial. His attorneys insisted that Wade had only been bragging about himself, and none of what he'd said was actually true. Their defense was aided by the fact that no substantial evidence implicating Wade in Della Brown's murder had been presented. The little that was recovered from the crime scene was of no help. Police learned that the semen within the victim's body did not belong to Wade, a fingerprint that had been recovered was not his, and a few pubic hairs found near the body were not a match either.

All of this helped strengthen Joshua Wade's defense and was enough to raise reasonable doubt. His attorneys also suggested that there could be other killers who might have committed this heinous act. They cited the serial killer running loose around the area and even pointed towards Della Brown's ex-boyfriend who had already been arrested for beating her up once before.

The case started looking weak, and it seemed that the unthinkable might happen. As the trial progressed, the witnesses came forward with their statements. These informants testified against Wade, but to no avail. During cross-examination, their own rather murky pasts came to light. All the informants were believed to be involved in a number of incriminating activities and had a rough history. It looked like they might end up facing charges themselves.

By the end of it, the police and authorities became convinced that Joshua Wade was going to get away with murder. The jury deliberated on a verdict for several days, and when they finally came to a decision, everyone's worst fears were confirmed. Since there was no concrete evidence and reasonable doubt had been established, the jury acquitted Joshua Wade on all charges except evidence tampering.

Out of the thirteen charges brought against him, he was sentenced for only one. He got served with jail time for six-and-a-half years since he had been accused of tampering with the evidence around a crime scene.

It was a dark day for everybody. The police and investigators later went on record to say that when they heard the verdict, they knew something terrible had happened. One of them even stated that he absolutely "felt sick to his stomach." Della's mother was very disappointed and admitted that it was one of the worst days of her life.

Despite all this, nobody could actually do anything to overturn the verdict. There were no witnesses and no evidence to indicate that Wade was anywhere near Della that night.

After his acquittal, Wade appeared to mock the Anchorage police department and seemed completely non-apologetic. He thanked the jury for being "fair" and not convicting him of all the "false" charges. Wade reiterated that he was not guilty, even though everyone believed that he was. According to him, his only fault was that he did not alert the police immediately after stumbling onto the woman's body.

Wade was taken to jail where he had to serve out his sentence for evidence tampering.

He was released from jail on December 31, 2006, after serving time for more than three years. Just a few weeks later, he moved to Mindy's neighborhood.

Confession

During his guilty plea in 2010, Wade confessed to murdering Della Brown and admitted that the jury had made a mistake with his acquittal almost ten years earlier. He stated that he had indeed killed Della Brown and left her body in the shed after assaulting her.

In that plea statement, he also revealed that he had killed Della by hitting her hard with a rock. The authorities could not substantiate that with proof, but all the signs indicated that Wade might have actually done that. He also stated that while driving through Spenard with a group of people, he came across Della Brown. Wade claimed that the people with him at that time were the ones who had testified at his earlier trial in 2003.

According to him, he saw her passed out and drove by. However, just a few hours later, he went back with the intent of robbing her. Once he got to her and saw that she'd fallen unconscious due to either alcohol or drugs, he dragged her over to the shed. This was when he not only robbed her, but also raped and brutally killed her.

After abandoning her scantily clad body in the shed, he went to the group of his acquaintances and brought them around to show them what he had done.

Wade's confession brought an end to the murder case of Della Brown that had been lingering on since 2003. Earlier on, he had been acquitted and cleared of murder and assault charges, but this time there was no getting away. The authorities and police ensured that they had a rock solid case and enough evidence to put the man away for good. In fact, for some time, it had seemed likely that Wade would be put on death row, but he made a plea arrangement and confessed to all his heinous acts.

The confession helped him avoid the death penalty, but he was sentenced to life without the possibility of parole. His sentence was to be served out in the maximum-security prison of Alaska.

Later on, when he was finally taken away for good, some of the jurors who had acquitted him in Della Brown's murder were contacted for a statement. They admitted that while the verdict made them uneasy, there was little that could have been done at the time. There was no implicating evidence and Wade's attorneys had managed to instill reasonable doubt.

Many people also felt that had he been sentenced and convicted earlier only, Mindy Schloss's murder could have been prevented.

Mindy Schloss

A hardworking nurse psychologist, Mindy Schloss was fifty-two years old when she was found ruthlessly murdered. She had recently moved to Anchorage and commuted every other week to Fairbanks, where most of her work was based. On August 4, 2007, it was reported that she had gone missing from her home.

Schloss was staying in for the weekend and had just finished emailing a few friends and colleagues from work. A few hours later, it seemed as if she had disappeared into thin air.

Mindy's longtime best friend called her several times and was worried when she did not answer. In a statement she made later, she said that she used to go stay at Mindy's and take care of her cat while she was away at work. Her friend was concerned when, despite several calls, Mindy did not pick up her phone. Then a few days later, she tried calling again and failed to get through because Mindy's voicemail was full with unanswered messages. This was not like Mindy at all. According to her friend, Mindy was particular about these things, and it was a rare instance when she left voicemail messages unanswered.

The following day, her friend went to the house to check on Mindy. She saw that the door lock had become a little loose and there was something wrong with it. When she went inside, she found an empty wine glass and a few bills that were scattered across the table. Everything felt different. Mindy was known for being meticulous and would have never left her house like that.

Her friend felt uneasy about the situation and called up her supervisor to ask about Mindy. The reply she got was not very encouraging. Mindy's boss said that she had not come in to work that morning, nor had she left any message. This was quite surprising for both of them, since Mindy Schloss hardly ever missed work.

It wasn't just her friend who was worried, even her boss realized that something was not right. Her supervisor also knew that Mindy would never skip work, especially if she had patients coming in that day. Hence, her boss called up the Anchorage police department to report that her colleague may have gone missing.

Police officials conducted a routine search around Mindy's house. After looking around for a bit, they found that there were no signs of any kind of forced entry that may suggest kidnapping or robbery.

Mindy Schloss missed work again the following day, which prompted her supervisor to call the Anchorage police again. This time, a homicide detective was called in to look into the suspicious missing person. Immediately, the police officer realized that there was much more to this case. Upon profiling Mindy Schloss, the police officials learned that she was a responsible, reliable person who was fully committed to her job. There was no way that she would be out of contact for this long and miss work without a reason.

Police started their investigation by going through Mindy's house and searching everything there. While the detectives searched the house, Mindy's friend also showed up. She pointed out some things that did not seem right to her. For instance, she found the apron that she had made for Mindy and gifted to her as a birthday present in the trash. Mindy held that gift very dearly and would have never thrown it away. Additionally, her friend told the detective that Mindy's car should be in the garage, but it was not there.

Her friend was extremely worried and wondered where Mindy could possibly have gone. For some time, she even considered that maybe Mindy had gone to look for berries, her favorite hobby, and suffered physical injury doing that. Nothing seemed to make sense.

The police looked into flight records and found out that Mindy Schloss had not boarded a plane that day. They were convinced that this was not just a missing person case anymore, and something more sinister had happened to the woman. The lead detective on the case did not believe that Mindy Schloss was coming back.

Investigators expanded their search and started looking through every single aspect of Mindy's life. The police officials extensively examined all her bank records to find a clue to her possible location. According to the detective's statement, they were trying to determine if there was anything unusual going on in Mindy's life.

Upon careful examination of all her bank records, the detective was able to point towards some suspicious activity. It was discovered that there had been two cash withdrawals of five hundred dollars from different banks within the same day. Furthermore, the money was taken out early in the morning the day after she went missing.

The police and authorities pulled out surveillance footage from both the banks where the money was withdrawn. Upon closer look, the detective's suspicion was confirmed. The person withdrawing the money was not Mindy Schloss. It was in fact a man who was heavily disguised to avoid being identified through the surveillance cameras.

Anchorage police officials were sure that Mindy Schloss was in danger and something had happened to her. The lead detective knew that the search for Mindy had to be expanded and time was of the essence. Thus, the FBI was called in to help.

Since the only lead that the authorities had was the bank surveillance video, the FBI officers began by looking through those. The first bank transaction indicated that the man in disguise was trying to get some money out of Mindy's bank account. He had been in and out of the ATM almost four times. Officials discovered that before withdrawing the money, the man had checked the account balance and found that it held almost twenty thousand dollars.

He tried to withdraw cash, but the ATM card got stuck in the machine, which was why he kept on coming back for it. The investigating officials were unable to recover a clear picture of the man. The only thing that stood out about his appearance was the bandana that he had used to cover his face.

Luckily, one of the FBI officers was able to locate a witness on video in the other ATM machine that he accessed from a different bank. The witness had most probably seen the suspect going in and withdrawing money.

However, finding that one witness who had been present

during the ATM transaction was not an easy task. It would take a lot of time and resources. If there was any possibility of recovering Mindy alive, the authorities and police had to act fast. They could not afford to spare any more time.

The FBI officials started questioning everyone who was related to Mindy Schloss. They went through family, friends, neighbors, and anybody who could have a motive for hurting Mindy. Through the process, the authorities came across Mindy's boyfriend and brought him in for questioning. The authorities let him go when he proved that at the time of her disappearance, he was actually in another city. Soon enough, they learned that Mindy was also looking through contractors, as she was planning to get some remodeling work done.

In fact, just before she disappeared, she had been going through her kitchen remodeling plans. The court documents stated that Schloss was also preparing to start her own business and had been emailing her friends about that.

Investigators questioned all known associates, including the workers who were set to remodel her house. They discovered that Mindy had met one of the workers on the very same day she disappeared. This meant that the worker could have been the last person to see Mindy alive. Apart from this, the authorities also discovered that another man working on the remodeling plan with Mindy had a criminal history.

They began investigating each possibility. However, before any conclusions could be derived, there was a breakthrough in the case. One of Mindy's friends spotted her red car while driving to the airport. The FBI and team were called and, sure enough, they saw the license plates matched the number of Mindy's car. It was parked near a cargo facility near Anchorage International Airport.

Upon looking through the surveillance footage, the officials discovered that Mindy's red Acura was driven to the facility by a man who parked the car there and then walked away. The cameras were able to catch glimpses of the man, as he was in full view and was not attempting to hide. However, this lead also proved futile, as the suspect was walking very far away and it was almost impossible to get any identification.

The police's only hope was to find something concrete inside Mindy's car. The officials were able to recover most of her belongings, including a purse, house keys, and wallet. Everything was there except her ATM card. In order to look for more clues, a forensic team was deployed to lift fingerprints and check for DNA inside the car. The authorities were trying to find anything that could help them identify the man who had stolen her debit card and driven her car to the facility.

The FBI team knew that it would take a lot of time for forensics to come up with the results. Hence, to speed up their search, the officials requested scent-detecting dogs. The headquarters obliged and agreed to assist the Anchorage police department.

Scent dogs were sent to aid the officials in the search for Mindy Schloss. While one team looked around with the help of the dogs, another one began questioning everyone in Mindy's neighborhood. The Anchorage police canvassed the entire street. Police officers went door to door to inquire if anything out of the ordinary had happened the night Mindy disappeared.

Everyone they questioned pointed them in the direction of her next-door neighbor. It turned out that the house right next to Mindy's had raised a lot of suspicion. People in that area did not actually know who lived there, except its tenants were very loud and a lot of youngsters visited the place frequently.

When the investigators finally got to the inhabitants of the house, they could not get any clear answers from them either.

The investigators became highly suspicious at the evasiveness of the people. They started to search through the place extensively in order to find out who lived in the house next door to Mindy Schloss.

Another one of Mindy's neighbors got caught in the midst of the investigation when suddenly Joshua Wade turned up at her house. At that point in time, the authorities had not yet questioned her, so she did not know what exactly was going on. Wade showed up at her doorstep and seemed frantic. She recognized him as her neighbor and stepped out to see him. He asked her if she had spoken to any police officers about him.

She told him that nobody had been to see her yet and she hadn't said anything to the police about him. Soon afterwards, a police officer came to see her and ask a few questions. By that time, the neighbor was really scared and aware that she was being watched by Wade the entire time. Hence, she did not answer any of the detective's questions properly and told him that she knew nothing. Wade had told her that there was a warrant out for his arrest and if she said anything to the police, he would know.

Terrified that Wade would act out against her, she sent the detective off without giving any information. However, sometime later, she called up the Anchorage police department and left a message for the detective saying that she was scared of her neighbor and wasn't able to talk because of him. She also asked to be interviewed somewhere outside and far away from her neighborhood.

Later on, she found out that Wade had been watching her closely. He even came up to her house and looked around for a few minutes before walking away.

When the police got the woman's message, they took immediate action. Joshua Wade's house was put under surveillance and the officers diligently monitored everyone who went in and came out. Soon enough, the authorities were able to identify who actually lived there. They found out that twenty-seven-year-old Joshua Wade had moved to the area a few months back.

Police were convinced that he knew something about Mindy's disappearance that night. It had been almost two weeks since she had gone missing, and the chances of her being discovered alive were looking rather slim.

The FBI forensic team came to Anchorage and brought the

hound dogs with them. The dogs were taken to the ATM machines where the suspect had withdrawn money. Both the hounds were able to single out the scent and followed it to Mindy Schloss's neighborhood. The investigators observed closely as the hounds led them up to Mindy's house and then on to Wade's. This confirmed the police's suspicion that Joshua Wade had information regarding the incident.

They looked into Wade's past and discovered that he already had been in trouble with the law before. Della Brown's case was examined and investigators discovered that Wade had narrowly avoided conviction with that.

Police and FBI officials increased their efforts to search for Mindy. The authorities had realized that there was little chance of her being alive anymore, and even the hopes of her family and friends were fading away.

Investigators knew that the only way they could find something was to go through the entire case extensively. Officials questioned everybody again and ruled out possible suspects. Mindy's friends, associates, and those who were remodeling her house were investigated comprehensively. Nothing turned up.

The police just had one person of interest left, and that was Joshua Wade.

Since he had already been involved in one murder and disappearance, the police suspected that he might have something to do with this one as well. Further investigation depended on whether the witness at the ATM machine would be able to recognize Wade as the man in disguise or not.

Within a week, the investigating authorities were able to track down the witness. However, all that effort was rendered useless since the witness was unable to describe the man properly. It was too early in the morning; nothing seemed clear at the time he had gone to the ATM.

With one of their last leads going cold, the officials became increasingly frustrated. The only thing that they knew for sure was that Joshua Wade was connected to Mindy Schloss's disappearance. The hound dogs had picked up the scent from Mindy's car and led the police towards Wade's house again. It was a clear indication that he was somehow involved and was hiding crucial information from the police.

By that time, it wasn't just the officials who were suspicious of Wade. Even the people who knew him felt that something was wrong. One of the residents of that area had a daughter who was an acquaintance of Joshua Wade. She became concerned that her daughter was spending time with him and even giving him occasional lifts in her car. Wade's behavior had seemed odd to her at times, and for her daughter's safety, she kept a close watch on their activities.

She soon discovered that two weeks after Mindy's disappearance, Wade had asked her daughter for a lift to his house. However, when they got there, he saw the police cars surrounding his place and started to panic. He told the girl to keep on driving and take him somewhere else. The girl immediately became suspicious, but she did as he asked and drove away.

Meanwhile, the police and FBI had secured a search warrant for his house and were canvassing the entire place. The Anchorage police detective, Pam Perrenoud, and FBI officials looked through all of Wade's belongings and came across some highly incriminating evidence. A jacket was discovered and it appeared quite similar to the one that the suspect was wearing in the surveillance video. The officials took his shoes and some clothes in order to confirm the scent that the dogs had picked up from Mindy's car.

Apart from this, a woman's watch was also found hidden in Wade's belongings. Later on, one of Mindy's closest friends confirmed that it was most likely hers.

The authorities had realized that Joshua Wade was a threat to everyone in the neighborhood and should be put away as soon as possible. However, the evidence they had was not enough to bring him in on murder charges. They had to come up with another way.

FBI officials suggested that they could charge Wade with bank fraud and identity theft on account of the incriminating evidence recovered from his house. He would be sentenced to at least two years in jail for that. This would give the police enough time to gather evidence and build a strong murder case against him.

However, the authorities could not act on their plan since Wade seemed to have gone into hiding. Almost three weeks after Mindy's disappearance, the state issued a federal arrest warrant for Joshua Wade. On August 29, 2007, the Anchorage police department and FBI officials organized the biggest manhunt that the town has ever witnessed.

During that time, Wade's family had also been contacted. In fact, his father even made a public appeal asking his son to turn himself in.

A startling discovery led to the eventual arrest of Wade. The girl who used to give occasional lifts discovered that he had left his backpack in her car when she had dropped him off. She immediately informed the authorities that she had found it. The contents of the backpack included bank receipts and a cellphone.

However, before the police could get to her, Wade showed up at her apartment. He asked her to drive him somewhere for work, but she refused. Once inside her apartment, she called the Anchorage police. By that time, Wade had fled to a nearby apartment building. He knocked around on a few doors asking to use a phone. When he got no response from anybody, he forced his way into an apartment where a brother and sister lived.

He let the boy go but took the sister as his hostage. When the police cornered him, he told them to stand down as he had a hostage with him inside.

The police, FBI, and SWAT team surrounded the entire area. Authorities were able to evacuate the building and get everyone else out safely. A suspected murderer had taken a girl hostage inside her own apartment, and the situation seemed to be getting tenser with each passing moment. Police officers were able to block off all the roads and, within minutes, the entire neighborhood was shut down.

After a tense standoff with the authorities, Wade decided to surrender and released his hostage. The authorities moved in quickly and arrested him.

He was taken in for questioning first and the FBI officials asked him about Mindy's disappearance. One of the agents, in his statement, said that Wade's behavior at the time made him realize that Mindy was not going to be found alive.

On September 11, 2007, Wade was taken into a correctional facility and indicted for fraud. Mindy Schloss's body still hadn't been discovered, which meant that there was not enough evidence to build a murder case.

Nearly a month after her disappearance, Mindy's body was discovered in the woods situated north of Anchorage. A man had been walking through the place when he came across what looked like a woman's body. Authorities rushed to the scene and found the female body, which was difficult to identify since it had been burned almost beyond recognition.

Dental records proved that the body belonged to Mindy Schloss.

Sentencing

The police had enough to build a strong murder case against Joshua Wade and ensure that this time he would not get away.

When the murder trial began, more facts came to light. It was established that Wade was a violent and disturbed man who was upset over his job, had no money, and was looking for a way to let out his frustration.

He picked his next-door neighbor as his victim and broke into her house in the middle of the night. Although there were no signs of sexual assault, there were injuries that indicated Wade had tried to physically subdue her. In his statement, he said that his intent was robbery and he only tied her up so she would give him her ATM card and PIN number.

However, he did not stop there. He shoved his victim into her own car and then drove to the woods. The area was completely abandoned and nobody heard or saw anything. Wade shot and killed Mindy, burning the body after she had died.

Wade was tried in federal court, and it became evident that he would be sentenced to the death penalty. On February 17, 2010, Wade entered into a plea agreement to avoid a death sentence. He gave a confession where he not only admitted to killing Mindy Schloss, but also accepted responsibility for Della Brown's murder.

The judge sentenced him to life in a maximum-security prison without the possibility of parole.

Sometime after his sentencing, Wade made another revelation. He asked for a transfer to another prison in exchange for more information. He confessed he had also killed three men. John Michael Martin and Henry Ongtowasruk were declared dead in 1994 and 1999 respectively.

Martin's cause of death was a gunshot wound to the head, while Ongtowasruk was found dead under mysterious circumstances. His body was discovered in a motel by a maintenance worker.

Wade claimed that he had killed the third man at the same time as Della Brown.

The authorities announced that they were looking into his confession and investigating all his claims in light of the new information. It was also revealed that Wade would be transferred to another correctional facility for some time.

Chapter 3
ORVILLE LYNN MAJORS
Angel of Death
By Michael Newton

There is something doubly reprehensible in crimes committed by medical personnel against those entrusted to their care, and thus placed at their mercy. The routine offenses— overcharging, faulty diagnoses, needless tests, botched surgery—all pale before the spectacle of care providers, physicians and nurses included, who stalk their patients as a hunter tracks game, to kill and kill again. One such is Orville Lynn Majors, and the final tally of victims still remains unknown, nearly two decades after his conviction in a court of law.

Majors was born in Clinton, Indiana, on the Wabash River in southern Vermillion County, on April 24, 1961. At the time of his birth, Clinton had fewer than 6,000 residents, declining to 4,893 by 2010. Orville's father was a coal miner transplanted from Greenville, Kentucky, even smaller than Clinton with 3,198 citizens in 1960. Caring for his aged grandmother seemed to awake a sympathy for senior citizens in Majors, prompting him to study nursing after high school, in Nashville, Tennessee.

Majors emerged from that program a licensed practical nurse (LPN), distinguished from registered nurses (RNs) by a shorter course of study—normally one year, versus three years for RNs—and requiring supervision by a registered nurse. Returning home, Majors found work at Vermillion County Hospital—a small facility with 56 beds, four in Intensive Care— subsequently leaving briefly, then returning permanently in spring of 1993. A lifelong bachelor and reputedly bisexual, he threw himself into his work, but not with the result most nurses normally expect.

***

Medicine is risky business. No one needs a nurse or doctor on the best days of their lives. They seek help only in extremity, and if they wait too long, or if their injuries are too severe, they die. Death is a daily fact of life in hospitals, particularly where the aged are concerned.

And yet...

While Orville's performance evaluations at VCH depict a compassionate, caring nurse who doted on his patients, deaths at the hospital increased dramatically when he was hired. Between 1990 and 1993, when Majors took his full-time post, patient deaths at VCH ranged from 24 to 31—an average of 26 per year. In 1994, although admissions showed no increase, the mortality figure jumped to 101 patients, with Majors on duty for 79 of those losses. Statistically, with Majors at work, a patient died every 23 hours on average: roughly one out of every three patients admitted. When he was absent, on vacation or whatever, that figure decreased dramatically to one death every 552 hours.

The strange "coincidence" was not lost on other VCH nurses, who would later tell police they joked about the rising toll of deaths on Majors's shifts. Some even placed bets on which patients would die the next time Majors worked. When Majors transferred to working weekends, the high death rate shifted accordingly.

Nurse Marilyn Alexander was the first to note the apparent link between Majors's work schedule and deaths at Vermillion County Hospital, in October 1993. A year later, in October 1994, Nurse Debbie Sollars expressed concern about the rising death rate to her nursing supervisor. That same month, male nurse Bill Balla undertook a private study of the hospital's log, noting a correlation between patient deaths and the times when Majors was on duty.

In March 1995, twenty-two months after Majors started working full-time and hospital deaths began to skyrocket, Indiana's State Department of Public Health confirmed 153 deaths at VCH since May 1993, most caused by sudden respiratory failure. Fifteen corpses were exhumed for autopsies, and law enforcement officers spent nearly 90,000 man-hours investigating the case, finally concluding that Majors might be responsible for 130 fatalities. True or false, it hardly mattered. Those statistical studies were barred from introduction when Majors faced trial in 1999.

***

Finally, Majors was accused of killing only seven victims. In each case, he was the only nurse attending patients when they died, and forensic evidence indicated death was caused by lethal injections of potassium chloride and epinephrine.

Potassium chloride (or KCl) is an odorless metal halide salt with various medical and industrial uses, probably best known as the heart-stopping part of a "three drug cocktail" frequently used for lethal injections in prisons. Epinephrine, aka adrenalin, conversely, acts in an opposite way when injected, producing shakiness, anxiety, sweating, an accelerated heart rate and high blood pressure. Either drug—or both, in combination— may prove fatal to humans, depending on the individual's medical condition and the dosage introduced.

The first "official" victim charged to Majors was 89-year-old Luella A. Hopkins, a longtime Vermillion County teacher and librarian, retired since 1967. She was admitted to the hospital on December 24, 1993, for examination and treatment of pneumonia-like symptoms. Hopkins died on January 8, 1994, with her death certificate blaming a "cerebrovascular accident"—that is, a stroke causing sudden death of brain cells due to lack of oxygen when the blood flow to the brain is impaired by blockage or rupture of an artery to the brain. However, patient Georgia Hobson reported that Orville Major entered the room she shared with Hopkins on the afternoon of January 8 and told Hopkins, "Honey, I'm going to give you a shot now." While a drawn curtain screened Majors and Hopkins, Hobson heard a gasp, and then Majors fled the room shouting, "Code blue! Code blue!" Police exhumed Hopkins on May 13, 1996, her autopsy listing cause of death as being from "administration of a foreign substance into her body which would cause a suppression of her heart's electrical activity" (probably potassium chloride). Records showed her physician had authorized no injections.

Next in line to die was 75-year-old Cecil Ivan Smith, operator of a Rockville gas station and delivery service, admitted to VCH for apparent heart problems. Smith died on April 3, 1994, from what his death certificate described as an acute myocardial infarction (heart attack). His fatal lapse was unexpected, occurring just three minutes after his doctor moved Smith from Intensive Care to a regular hospital room. Exhumed three years later—on April 29, 1997—his remains told forensic pathologists a different story. According to their report, "His hypertension tachycardia [elevated heart rate] and EKG changes are consistent with injections of substances in the nature of epinephrine and potassium." Orville Majors was at Smith's bedside when he expired.

Number three on the indictment list was 80-year-old Dorothea L. Hixon, a former licensed practical nurse at Vermillion County Hospital, who died at her former place of employment on April 23, 1994 (some published reports claim April 25). Hixon had been hospitalized 20 different times since 1992 with symptoms of congestive heart failure, but she had always pulled through in the past. On her last visit, Hixon entered VCH to have fluid drained from her lungs. Her two daughters were present when Orville Majors entered Hixon's room, gave her an injection through her IV line, and said, "Everything is going to be all right now, Punkin," then kissed Hixon's forehead. Once again, her doctor had authorized no shots. Moments later, Hixon was dead, with congestive heart failure named as the cause. Exhumation on August 27, 1996, revealed that radical changes in her final electrocardiogram were consistent with a potassium chloride overdose.

The fourth murder charged against Majors was that of 69-

year-old Mary Ann Alderson, admitted to VCH at 10:30 p.m. on Saturday, November 5, 1994, suffering chest pains after a meal of pizza and beer. Following a few hours of observation in the hospital's Intensive Care Unit, physicians transferred Alderson to a room on the medical-surgical floor, where nurses reported her sleeping and breathing normally. On Monday, Alderson's doctor told her she could go home the next day, but that afternoon—November 7—Majors was alone with Alderson when he called a Code Blue alert for respiratory failure. Nurse Nadine Skonk arrived to find Majors cranking down Alderson's bed with his right hand, holding a hypodermic syringe in his left. Alderson's death certificate blamed ventricular tachycardia—an elevated heart rate that may produce fatal ventricular fibrillation. Authorities exhumed her corpse on November 1, 1995, finding the cause of death was consistent with a needless and unauthorized potassium chloride injection.

Fifth in line to die was 64-year-old Derek H. Maxwell Sr. of Universal, in Vermillion County, admitted to VCH with apparent heart problems on November 14, 1994. Maxwell's heart stopped once, with Orville Majors standing at the head of his bed, but doctors restarted it with a jolt of electricity from a defibrillator. Derek's physician told wife Kathryn Maxwell that he was stable, and she visited his room periodically throughout that night. The next morning, November 15, Mrs. Maxwell found Majors at the head of her husband's bed once again, holding various tubes in his hands that transmitted medicine and fluids to the patient. Seconds later, she said, Majors "ran across the room in front of me and into the nurses' station. All the machines they had [Derek] hooked up to started making noises. I looked at him and I sank. He was gone." Once again, exhumation and postmortem reexamination suggested death by an unauthorized injection.

Next came Margaret A. Roland Hornick, age 79, born to Italian immigrants, a widow suffering from Alzheimer's disease and admitted to VCH with a broken hip. After surgery to repair the damage, doctors moved her to Intensive Care, where she died nine minutes after arriving, on November 25, 1994. Hornick's physician found her alleged death from congestive heart failure suspicious, and he told police that the attending nurse—Orville Majors—never called him to report her changing condition, although such a call was noted on Hornick's medical chart. Police exhumed Hornick's remains on June 3, 1996, whereupon autopsy results blamed her death on potassium chloride.

The last count filed against Majors involved 56-year-old Freddie Dale Wilson, lost at VCH on February 16, 1995, to what his death certificate called pneumonia. Pathologists refuted that diagnosis after exhuming Wilson on June 18, 1997, attributing his end to yet another lethal injection.

***

As to *why* Majors might have killed seven patients—much less 130—investigators were torn between conflicting motives of spite and "mercy." He acted sympathetic to patients and their families, prompting aged women in particular to compliment his bedside manner. Speaking privately to other nurses, though, he seemed to despise the elderly, calling them "a waste," opining that they "should be gassed," while he branded their relatives "white trash" and "whiners." Those most likely to die on his shift, coworkers said, were the most demanding patients and those who added to his workload. One hospital employee testified to seeing Major seated at the bedside of a senior who was sitting up and seemingly alert. When asked what he was doing, Majors replied, "I'm just sitting here waiting for the woman to die." And a few minutes later, she did.

Two peculiar deaths at VCH prompted Nursing Supervisor Dawn Stirek to find out which nurses were working when the patients expired. As numbers multiplied, reaching 147 deaths during Majors's tenure at the hospital, Stirek said, "I saw that I had a pattern, that there was one person present a majority of the time." She passed that information on to Indiana's State

Board of Nursing, which moved against Majors in March 1995, suspending his license for five years on charges of giving unauthorized injections, failing to apprise doctors of altered patient conditions, and exceeding his authority by increasing a patient's prescribed oxygen supply in one case. Suddenly at loose ends, Major took charge of a pet store and florist's shop in his hometown, Clinton.

State police began investigating Majors a month later, compiling a list of 165 deaths at VCH between May 1993 and March 1995. Of those cases, Majors was on duty for 89 percent—a total of 147. Information passed to the State Attorney General Pamela Lynn Carter spawned a report linking Majors to 26 deaths, though detectives privately spoke of a number five times that size. Officers obtained search warrants for a home once occupied by Majors and a van he often drove, owned by his parents. Those searches turned up vials of potassium chloride and a box containing empty vials of epinephrine—neither of which Majors was authorized to own, nor to administer without a doctor's direct supervision. Exhumations and fresh postmortem testing proceeded, leading officers to arrest Majors on December 29, 1997.

Majors staunchly denied all wrongdoing, but prosecutors charged him with six counts of murder. Suspension of his nursing license turned into a permanent revocation. He had no coherent explanation for the drugs collected by police, but mother Anna Bell Majors stood by her son, telling reporters that Orville's commitment to health care dated from his grandmother's death. "Lynn would never harm anyone," she insisted.

Majors made his first court appearance on December 30, represented by attorney Irving Marshall Pinkus from Indianapolis. Majors pled not guilty to six counts of murder (the seventh was added later, in December 1998) and requested a jury trial, before his judge denied bail. Kinfolk of the victims seemed disappointed with Vermillion County Prosecutor Mark Greenwell's announcement that he would not seek the death penalty, leaving Majors eligible for a 65-year prison term on each count, if convicted.

Leaving court in handcuffs and shackles, Majors faced jeers from relatives of his alleged victims. Those shouting, "Be a man!" and "Tell them what you know!" included Carol and Marjorie Doran, daughters-in-law of VCH patient John Doran, who died at age 76 after Majors gave him an unexplained intravenous injection on October 31, 1994. Robert Doran, who also witnessed the injection, snapped at Majors, "Own up to what you did!" While not among the victims with whose deaths the state charged Majors, Doran's mysterious passing would spawn a civil lawsuit.

Lawyer Pinkus scored a victory on January 21 at a pretrial hearing when Clay County Circuit Court Judge Ernest Yelton barred admission of the State Nursing Board's incriminating report on Majors from 1995. While suggestive of murder, postmortem results were couched in terms of "consistency" rather than proof, thus excluded in the interest of a fair trial for the defendant. More specifically, Pinkus argued that evidence presented by Vermillion County authorities was outdated and the prosecution's epidemiological studies—analyzing patterns, causes, and effects of health and disease conditions in defined populations—were critically flawed.

Even before that victory, Pinkus had won his first move by obtaining a change of venue for Majors from Vermillion to Brazil in Clay County, 40 miles southwest of Newport. Furthermore, jurors would be drawn from Miami County, with 1,400 prospective veniremen packing a high school gymnasium, each filling out a 145-question survey to narrow the field. Given the level of media coverage devoted to Majors and his crimes, it was the best Justice could do.

***

Majors and his counsel had to wait for trial through 1998 and into 1999, while exhumations of 15 corpses and further postmortem testing proceeded. Meanwhile, relatives of patients who were not included in the state's indictment fumed and sought some kind of closure on their own. Sixty-five other families joined the furious Dorans in a class-action lawsuit against Vermillion County's Board of Commissioners—which hired hospital administrators—alleging wrongful death and negligence. Their case was buttressed by a report from Washington epidemiologist Steven Lamm, saying that VCH patients were 43 times more likely to die with Majors in attendance than when he was absent. Irving Pinkus scoffed at such findings, telling reporters, "Not a witness saw Lynn do anything wrong. I call that circumstantial suspicion." Majors won again when a panel of judges dismissed the civil case, ruling that the Board of Commissioners had no day-to-day control over hospital operations.

Russell Firestone Jr. disagreed, emphatically. On December 12, 1994, he personally saw a male nurse jab a hypodermic syringe into his father's chest, moments before Russell Sr. expired. "I want some answers," he insisted, even though his father—while exhumed by state police in September 1995—did not make Prosecutor Greenwell's official list of victims.

Judge Yelton ultimately chose 18 jurors—12 regulars, with six alternates on standby in case illness or some other difficulty whittled down the starting lineup. Each of those selected heard advance warnings of a "huge sacrifice" ahead, in the name of their civic duty, spanning an estimated three months with testimony from 300 witnesses. All were ready in Brazil on August 30, 1999, when the trial began at last for the man reporters called Indiana's "Angel of Death."

One thing was certain: if convicted, Majors could not qualify as any kind of angel.

While Prosecutor Greenwell and assistant Nina Alexander sidestepped statistical analyses of the deaths at VCH, their opening statements summarized evidence that Majors administered unauthorized injections to the seven listed patients soon before their deaths. Irving Pinkus countered that nurses everywhere routinely gave shots without doctors standing at their sides, further noting that some VCH employees considered Majors hardworking and sympathetic to his ailing charges. Indeed, prior to trial, Dr. John Albrecht, in charge of Vermillion County's tiny ICU, had already testified twice in depositions that he believed Majors was innocent.

At trial, the prospective witness list was trimmed back from 300 to 79, including nurses who recalled Majors's insulting remarks about elderly patients and police who retrieved deadly substances from his home and van. On cross-examination, the state's lead investigator, Detective Frank Turchi, admitted performing a background check only on Majors, while ignoring all other nurses and doctors at Vermillion County Hospital. Likewise, Turchi considered no one else at VCH while obtaining blood and fingerprint samples from Majors. Irving Pinkus made the case for a skewed investigation, which ignored other potential suspects.

On Tuesday, September 21, prosecutors announced plans to rest their case by Friday. Jurors received their final instructions from Judge Yelton on October 14 and deliberated for nine hours that day, without reaching a verdict. Debate continued, interrupted by sporadic prayers for guidance to the truth, until the panel returned its verdicts on Sunday, October 17. Jurors convicted Majors on six murder counts, failing to reach a verdict in the case of Cecil Smith.

Afterward, jury foreman Duane Flaherty of Macy, Indiana, described the panel's methodical considerations. "It actually was just looking at all of the evidence," he said. "We didn't pick any one thing or any item that we felt was the big key to unlock the door." Juror Pamela Gritzmacher of Bunker Hill agreed, crediting prayer in part for the panel's arrival at partial truth. "We felt good about what we had done," she told reporters. "There'll never be a time that any of us will ever look back and say, 'Did I miss something?'"

With no prospect of execution impending, Judge Yelton sentenced Majors on November 15, 1999. The final tab: 60

years in prison on each of six counts, to be served consecutively—a total of 360 years, with theoretical eligibility for parole in the year 2179, assuming Majors survived to the ripe old age of 218 years. At the hearing's conclusion, Yelton told the court, "At long last, may the souls of Mary Ann Alderson, Dorothea Dixon, Luella Hopkins, Margaret Hornick, Freddie Dale Wilson, Derek Maxwell and Cecil Smith rest in peace."

Relatives of Majors continued to support him, stubbornly insisting he was singled out and framed to cover up shoddy medical practices at VCH, and perhaps because his bisexual lifestyle left him "demonized" in small-town Indiana. Irving Pinkus announced his intent to appeal the verdict.

First, however, the defense filed a petition for a new trial, based on allegations of juror misconduct. Specifically, juror Ronda Baldwin—after voting with the rest to convict Majors—belatedly complained about two picnics held at the home of Clay County Sheriff Rob Carter, attended by jurors and state police officers, where those present imbibed free alcohol and, at least in Pinkus's opinion, improperly discussed details of the trial in progress. Ronda Baldwin felt "uncomfortable" about those outings, saying, "This wasn't to hurt anybody or cause anybody any pain. I was telling the truth, what I experienced." Foreman Flaherty said of Baldwin, "She feels guilty for having found him guilty, and she is trying to find a way out of it." Judge Yelton dismissed the defense bid in March 2000, defending the right of jurors to enjoy reasonable diversions during a lengthy trial. His decision said the panel deserved some consideration, rather than being subjected "to the security of unemotional British Beefeater guards."

Next, Pinkus carried his appeal for Majors to Indiana's Supreme Court, rejected on August 14, 2002. Today, Orville Majors remains inmate #995992, incarcerated in the state's maximum-security prison at Michigan City, where he ranks as the state's most prolific caged killer. With time off for "good behavior," prison records online list his "earliest possible release date" as July 1, 2177, at age 216.

***

The case was not finally settled with Orville's conviction. On August 30, 1999, Indiana's State Health Department fined Vermillion County Hospital $80,000 for negligence and various code violations. VCH was subsequently renamed and leased to Sanford Health—a non-profit, integrated health care delivery system, with headquarters in Sioux Falls, South Dakota—emerging from the shift as Union Hospital. According to Union's website, the new facility was "dedicated to assuring compassionate, quality healthcare for every individual. We continue to expand services, acquire state-of-the-art equipment to deliver quality care close to home, recruit an outstanding team of health professionals so you can feel confident in your care, and promote and introduce community programs that encourage healthy lifestyle choices." In February 2014, Sanford announced an $11 million upgrade at Union, demolishing the hospital first built in 1935 and replacing it with a new outpatient facility, the Sanford Vermillion Medical Center.

Thirteen months before that announcement, in January 2013, journalist Abby Rogers published results of a prison interview with Orville Majors in *Business Insider*. Her conclusion: "You'd never guess how much he hates people from talking to him."

And the same can be said for other healers turned killers, worldwide. A survey of convicted serial murderers, published in 1992, found 10 percent affiliated with the health care profession: doctors, nurses, orderlies, and even the occasional dentist. Deadly nurses caught and brought to book since Majors include the following:

Christine Malèvre, arrested in 1998 for killing an estimated 30 terminally ill patients at François Quesnay Hospital, on the outskirts of Paris. She admitted slaying four victims at trial, in January 2003, and then was convicted in six deaths, receiving a meager 10-year sentence.

Edson Isidoro Guimarães of Brazil, arrested in May 1999 for killing at least four patients with potassium chloride at Rio de Janeiro's Salgado Filho Hospital, suspected in 127 other deaths. In February 2000, he received a 76-year prison term.

Colin Norris, from Glasgow, killed four elderly patients with insulin injections during 2001 and 2002, at a hospital in Leeds, England. Convicted in March 2008, on four counts of murder and one of attempted murder, Norris was sentenced to life imprisonment.

Charles Edmund Cullen, ranked as the most prolific killer in New Jersey's history, was arrested in December 2003, confessing an estimated total of 40 patients' murders between June 1988 and his eventual capture. In April 2004, he admitted slaying 13 New Jersey patients and attempting to kill one other. Seven months later, he confessed to six murders and three attempted murders in Allentown, Pennsylvania. His prison sentences total 127 years.

Stephan Letter, linked to the deaths of at least 29 patients—probably more than 80—at a hospital in Sonthofen, Bavaria, between January 2003 and July 2004. Described as Germany's most prolific slayer since World War II, Letter faced trial in February 2006 on 16 counts of murder, 12 counts of manslaughter and one count of killing "on request." Convicted in November, he received a life sentence.

Abraão José Bueno, another Brazilian nurse, arrested in November 2005 for killing four infants with overdoses of sedatives, convicted in May 2008 and sentenced to 110 years in prison.

Petr Zelenka, a Czech nurse from Havlíčkův Brod, southeast of Prague, who killed seven patients and tried to slay 10 more with lethal injections of the blood thinner heparin, between May and December, 2006. Convicted on all counts in February 2008, he received a life sentence.

Daniela Poggiali allegedly used potassium chloride to kill at least 38 "annoying" patients, or those with "pushy" families—perhaps 96 in all—at a hospital near Ravenna in north-eastern Italy, afterward snapping ghoulish "selfie" photos with some of her victims, smiling and flashing a "thumbs-up" gesture or a "V" for "victory." Arrested in October 2014, she still awaits trial at the time of this writing, while jailers report her cell "flooded" with fan mail from admirers.

Why do medical practitioners violate their Hippocratic oath to "reject harm and mischief" by killing patients in their care? Motives identified so far, beyond raw arrogance and malice, include a twisted sense of "mercy" and the occasional "hero" complex, which compels some slayers to endanger patients, then seek praise for saving them at the last moment. When their efforts fail, murder charges ensue, as with pediatric nurse Genene Jones in San Antonio, Texas.

If any lesson for prospective victims and their kin may be gleaned from such cases, it is simply this: be wary and watchful in hospitals, clinics, rest homes, and even in physicians' offices. A white coat may disguise dark intentions and, while relatively rare, serial killers in the healing profession remain a clear and present danger worldwide.

Chapter 4
SARA ALDRETE
La Madrina Killer
By Sylvia Perrini

Sara Maria Aldrete was born on September 6, 1964, in Matamoros, Mexico, a city located on the southern bank of the Rio
Grande, an easy stroll or drive across the border
from Brownsville, Texas, in the United States. As a typical U.S.
border town, it suffered from prostitution and sex shows, plen-
tiful alcohol and drugs, extensive poverty and crime. Sara,
however, was born into a middle-class family; her father was a
respected electrician.

She was a bright child and crossed the border almost daily
to attend Porter High School in Brownsville. Here she is remembered by former teachers as having been a model student
and a well-behaved child. After school she attended a secretar-
ial school where she was considered a star pupil. Her teachers
encouraged her to enroll at the Texas Southmost College in
Brownsville, but before she did so, she married Miguel Zacha-
rias in 1983, a Brownsville resident and eleven years her senior. The marriage was not a success, and within five months
they had separated and were seeking a divorce. Following the
breakdown of her marriage, she moved back into a small top-
floor apartment at her parents' house on Calle Santos Degolla-
do, Matamoros, where she lived the majority of weekends and
during the vacations.

Towards the end of 1985, Sara successfully applied for resident alien status in the United States. Following this, she finally enrolled in January 1986 at Texas Southmost College as a
physical education major on a two-year "work-study" program. To help finance her education, she had two part-time
jobs: an assistant secretary in the college's athletic department
and an aerobics teacher.

Within a short space of time, Sara stood out at the college

both physically and academically. She was 6-foot-1, unusual for a Mexican woman, and achieved grades that earned her a place on the honor roll. In her spare time, she was an enthusiastic volleyball player and earned the college's outstanding Physical Education Award. Sara was attractive and, with her bright, gregarious personality, she was popular with the other students. She also attracted plenty of male attention.

To her college professors and fellow students, her future looked bright and full of promise.

However, there was a dark side to Sara, one that she kept hidden from her college mates. During an anthropology class, she learnt about the Santeria religion, which had its origins in the Yoruba peoples, a large tribal group from Nigeria and West Africa who practiced what was then called Orisha.

They believed in one all-powerful god called Oludumaré, who was served by lesser deities known as orixas, some of whom were able to control disease, the oceans, the weather, and other forces of nature; in many ways it was similar to the Greek and Roman mythologies. The religion made its way to the New World with the slaves brought over from Africa. Most of the slaves were banned from practicing their religion and forced to adopt Catholicism. But the slaves preserved their traditions by masking the ceremony in Catholic iconography, a process referred to as syncretism, which combines elements of competing religions resulting in a new religion in both name and practice. In Cuba, Puerto Rico, the Dominican Republic, Mexico, and Trinidad, the adapted religion was known as Santeria, which derives from the Spanish word for "saint." In Haiti it became known as Vodou, and in Brazil as Candomblé. Santeria, Candomblé and Voodoo developed differences over time, but the goal was the same—the placating of demons, gods, spirits and even the devil, to do the bidding of the worshipper.

Sara became obsessed with Santeria, and especially with the darker side of the religion. While at home in Mexico, she began dating drug smugglers, something else that was at odds with the persona of the clean, wholesome girl she presented at college.

Adolfo de Jesus Constanzo

Adolfo de Jesus Constanzo was born on November 1, 1962, All Saints Day, in Miami to Cuban immigrant Delia Aurora Gonzalez del Valle. Delia was just 15 years old and Adolfo was the first of her four children from three different fathers. At six months old, Delia took her son to be blessed by a Haitian priest, one who practiced *palo mayombe,* which is reputed to be the world's most powerful and feared form of black magic, a dark offspring religion to Santeria. The priest told Delia that Adolfo was "destined for great power." Delia, who had every faith in the priest, had her son from the age of nine apprenticed to a Haitian priest in Miami who instructed him in *palo mayombe.* This priest was not concerned with acts of goodwill or love spells, only in spilling blood, revenge and murder. Not only did the priest pass on his love for blood thirst to the young Adolfo, dispensing beatings, lessons, black magic and exposure to morbidity in equal measures, he also initiated him into homosexuality at a young age until virtually nothing had an effect on the boy. The priest who Adolfo referred to as his *Padrino* (godfather) had many drug dealers as his clients. He instilled in Adolfo the philosophy:

'Let the nonbelievers kill themselves with drugs. We will profit from their foolishness.'

Adolfo's mother, Delia, was a habitual criminal and was arrested numerous times on a variety of charges from shoplifting to check fraud and grand theft. She never did jail time and always got off with probation. She attributed this to the magic of her religion. Her neighbors in the various locales she lived in whispered that she was a witch. And anyone who enraged her was liable to find a headless chicken or goat on their doorstep. As a child growing up, Adolfo was used to the odor of death and rotting flesh, and his mother's reward to him for good behavior would be the gift of an animal to mutilate and kill. Around the time Adolfo turned ten, Delia and her children moved into a Spanish-style house on 94th Court in suburban Coral Park Estates, where Delia kept chickens and sheep in a filthy back yard. Also in the backyard Delia kept her *nganga* (cauldron). The family was shunned by neighbors out of fear and revulsion, and at school Adolfo was labeled a misfit and bullied. In 1984, the bank foreclosed on her house much to the neighbors' delight. The family then rented a series of homes, which were always filthy, vandalized and bloodstained from the remains of animals that she had sacrificed.

Adolfo took after his mother, indulging in petty crime, and was arrested twice for shoplifting. At school he was a poor student, not because of lack of intelligence but due to disinterest, and as a consequence graduated from his high school class nearly at the bottom. He only managed one semester in junior college before dropping out. He preferred instead to cruise Miami gay bars and to learn the secrets of witchcraft. He would rob graves to supply his priest's caldron and spill blood over voodoo dolls to curse his enemies. In 1983, during his ritual ceremony when he became a master in his religion and no longer an apprentice, Adolfo chose as his patron saint, *Kadiempembe*, his religion's version of the Devil. Adolfo had now become a padrino and sold his soul completely and totally to the Devil.

One of the things Adolfo did have in his favor as he turned into manhood was his looks and charisma. He was light-skinned, slim and close to six feet in height. He had long, dark hair that matched his dark eyes in his chiseled face. He moved with grace and self-assuredness; he had perfectly manicured hands and always dressed impeccably. Both men and women vied equally for his attention.

In 1983, he was offered a modeling job in Mexico City. In his spare time he set himself up reading tarot cards in the notorious Zona Rosa neighborhood, an area known for its nightlife, prostitutes and gay community. Here Adolfo soon realized that the Mexicans, unlike Americans, both feared and respected the power of the occult. It was here that he recruited the first of his disciples, Jorge Montes, a homosexual "psychic," and Omar Orea Ochoa, barely eighteen, who had been infatuated by the occult from an early age. Adolfo had seduced both of them and claimed Omar as his "woman" and Jorge as his "man." They were both besotted with Adolfo and fascinated by his psychic abilities and what they believed were his magical powers. In the middle of 1984, Adolfo relocated to Mexico City permanently. He set up home with his "woman" and his "man" and instructed them in his religion until they too had sold their souls to the Devil. Adolfo used sex as a means of controlling his followers and always assumed the dominant position in intercourse with men and used sex with other men as a means of humiliation and cementing control over them.

Despite the filth Adolfo was brought up in, he himself was meticulously clean and tidy, almost to the point of obsession. His house had to be clean and free of mess. His clothes had to be neatly folded and put away, and he would wash three or four times a day. If there were any messes in his house, he would fly into a rage at his "woman" and his "man."

He was soon in business reading the future for his clients and offering ritual "cleansings"—for those who believed their enemies had lain curses on them, with some paying up to $4,500. Adolfo would charge varying amounts, depending on which sacrificial beasts his clients wanted to be used, from roosters costing $6 a head to lion cubs costing $3,100 each. He soon attracted other followers as his "magic" reputation extended throughout the city.

Adolfo had arrived in Mexico City with just a couple of suitcases but soon had closets full of expensive fashionable clothes and drawers full of expensive gold jewelry. He would frequently send his mother in Miami expensive fur coats, totally inappropriate for the climate of Florida, and other expensive gifts.

He realized that, for top money, his clients would demand a show or ritual, thus in the summer of 1985, he and his most dedicated cult members began to raid Mexican graveyards for human bones for his own bloody cauldron. As his rituals became more elaborate, his fame and allure attracted a large cross-section of Mexican society. Soon his followers included doctors, businessmen, fashion models, politicians and high-ranking law enforcement officers. They seemed to worship Adolfo as if a minor god. They called him their padrino, their godfather. One law enforcement official that became particularly important to Adolfo was Florentino Ventura Gutierrez, a man who had many enemies on both sides of the law.

He had helped arrest the infamous Cuban national, Alberto Sicilia Falcon in 1976, whose highly sophisticated marijuana and cocaine network stretched from South and Central Mexico to the United States. Alberto Sicilia Falcon was a man who moved in elite circles on both sides of the border and was much wanted by the U.S. DEA.

Ventura was of mixed European and Indian blood, a mestizo. Before becoming an officer of the law, it was rumored that he had once studied to be a Catholic priest and was deeply superstitious. At the time he met Adolfo, Ventura was the director of the Mexican branch of Interpol, the International Criminal Police Organization. He had formerly been the *primer comandante* of the Mexican Federal Judicial Police—the U.S. equivalent of the director of the FBI. He was considered the most powerful police official in Latin America. The man was a legend and was immensely respected by many U.S. drug enforcement agencies. He was a tall, powerfully built man with thick black hair, a full face and a mustache. His eyes were hard and black, and he had a reputation for being efficiently brutal, cold and cruel. He had no qualms about using torture to extract confessions, which wasn't unusual in the Mexican judicial system. He was a man of whom several assassination attempts had been made, and whose home had been shot to bits. Every day that Ventura woke up, because of his numerable enemies, he was never sure if he would make it through the day, despite surrounding himself by police bodyguards.

Thus for a superstitious marked man, he was immensely

gullible to a man such as Adolfo who he befriended for help in cleansings and mystic protection from his enemies. During at least two years, Ventura paid Adolfo several thousand of dollars. It has also been speculated that apart from the money, Ventura would help Adolfo with his illegal enterprises and introduced Adolfo to other police officials such as Commander Salvador Garcia, who was in charge of drug investigations in Mexico City.

Adolfo quickly recognized that some of his best paying clients were drug smugglers, who wanted him to use his magic to protect their criminal enterprises. Many of these smugglers were from peasant families and had grown-up with a belief in witchcraft. Adolfo himself was anti-drug use and prohibited any of his followers from using drugs, but he had no qualms about profiting from their illegal business as had been instilled in him at a young age by his *padrino*.

Adolfo began to befriend and charm wealthy drug smugglers. He, for a price, would help them schedule their shipments based on his predictions and, many suspect, with information garnered from his law official friends. He also offered magic rituals that he claimed would make them and their bodyguards invisible to the police and other enemies. He claimed his rituals would prevent them from being caught when committing crimes, and to be protected from bullets and knives.

In 1986 Adolfo was introduced to the drug smuggling Calzada family by Ventura. At the time, the Calzada family was one of Mexico's biggest narcotics cartels. Adolfo won the head of the cartel over with his charisma, good looks and mumbo-jumbo and profited greatly from the cartel. By the beginning of 1987, he was able to buy a luxury apartment in Mexico City and a fleet of luxury cars. In his new luxury apartment he shared with his "woman" and his "man," he had set up a marble altar to the saints. In a separate room he called his *cuarto del los muertas*—the room of the dead—he performed his special evil ceremonies and was where he kept his bloody *nganga*, or cauldron. This room he kept locked.

Having been brought up in near poverty, Adolfo quickly became addicted to wealth, and he became obsessed with wanting more and would do anything to achieve that end. He began running drug scams of his own, one of which found him pretending to be a DEA agent to a cocaine dealer and confiscating his drugs and then selling them through his contacts for a profit of $100,000. As his wealth grew, he added greatly to his property portfolio.

In 1987, Adolfo began to believe that the Calzada family's continued success was down to him and not the cartel's smuggling skills. He asked for a larger cut of the cartel's profits and was curtly rebuffed. Adolfo was furious.

On April 30, 1987, on Walpurgis Night, known as "the night of the witches" in northern and central European paganism, Guillermo Calzada and six members of his household disappeared under mystifying circumstances from Calzada's office.

Bram Stoker, in his book, *Dracula's Guest*, wrote; "Walpurgis Night was when, according to the belief of millions of people, the devil was abroad—when the graves were opened and the dead came forth and walked. When all evil things of earth and air and water held revel."

***

They were reported as missing on May 1. When the police went to investigate at Guillermo Calzada's office, they noted evidence of some kind of religious ceremony. Six days later and over the following days of that week, various tied up and badly mutilated bodies were discovered in the rivers and canals around the city. In all, seven bodies, all badly mutilated, turned up in the murky waterways. They all showed signs of torture: ears, fingers, and toes had been cut off; hearts and genitals removed; part of the spine ripped from one body whilst two others had their brains missing.

Unknown to the police who were not yet aware of his existence, except for the ones who belonged to his cult, Adolfo had
crossed the line from offering animal sacrifices to human sacrifices to his patron saint, *Kadiempembe.* The police attributed
the carnage to drug wars. Columbian drug cartels were well
known for murdering entire families in revenge and to torture
and mutilate as a warning to others not to cross them. The
case remained for a while unsolved.

Adolfo had enjoyed the killings. It had given him a sense of
excitement and made him feel all powerful. The more his victims had screamed, the more powerful he felt. He told his followers as he added the severed organs to his bloody cauldron,
"Human sacrifice is not murder. Their spirits have not died.
They exist now to serve us."

Adolfo now needed another drug cartel to work with.
Commander Salvador Garcia, who had been moved to the
Mexican border town of Matamoros, told him about the once
powerful Hernandez family who lived in Matamoros. They
were primarily marijuana smugglers with the occasional kilo
of cocaine thrown in. However, since the second eldest brother, Saul Hernandez Riviera, manager of the family drug business, had been shot to death on a Matamoros street, an unintended death in one of the numerous gangland fights that occurred in the border town, the family business had suffered
and no longer had a clear leader, and was thus directionless.
Commander Salvador Garcia thought they could well do with
Adolfo's help. Salvador Garcia had told Adolfo that Elio Hernandez, who was now in charge of the family, was obsessed
with Sara Aldrete, a onetime girlfriend of Elio's who was now
dating drug-dealer Gilberto Sosa, who was connected to the
family. Adolfo asked Salvador to fill him in on everything he
knew about the family and Sara Aldrete.

Adolfo began to stalk both Gilberto and Sara Aldrete and
decided she would be the one to introduce him to the Hernandez family. He then set about getting to know her.

On July 30, 1987, as Sara was driving through Matamoros,

suddenly, out of the blue, a gleaming new Mercedes cut her off in traffic, barely avoiding a crash. The driver of the Mercedes leapt out of his car and apologized profusely to Sara, who felt annoyed by the incident. Sara felt herself immediately attracted to the debonair and handsome young man, dressed immaculately in a white suit. He introduced himself as Adolfo Constanzo and invited her for a drink. They went to a restaurant bar, Garcia's, a spacious white place with big open windows a block from the International Bridge. Her initial anger at the man for cutting her off vanished as he talked and she listened. Over the following days, Sara and Adolfo met regularly, and he read her tarot cards for her. The information he gave to her blew her mind, and she was in no doubt that he was a true psychic.

Two weeks after their first encounter, Adolfo purposefully ran into Sara and Gilberto in Brownsville. When Sara introduced the two men to each other, Adolfo pointedly refused to shake Gilberto's hand. Days later, Gilberto received an anonymous call telling him that Sara was seeing another man. When he confronted her about it and she vehemently denied the accusation, he refused to believe her and ended the relationship. Sara was upset and turned to Adolfo for comfort. He told Sara he had seen the break-up coming in his tarot cards. Sara was impressed.

Adolfo was bisexual and took Sara to bed in order to control her but made no secret after bedding her that he preferred men. In general, Adolfo seemed to only have sexual relations with women if there was some advantage to his cult to be gained. Their sexual relationship, much to Sara's disappointment, was short-lived, but she grudgingly accepted it as by that time she had become more and more mesmerized by Adolfo and his religious beliefs and more than impressed by his seemingly psychic abilities. Adolfo began to instruct her in his religion; she was an ardent student, and before long Adolfo had made her the godmother, "La Madrina," of his growing cult.

Ever since Sara had met Adolfo, she continued to cross the border almost daily to attend Texas Southmost, and despite playing her part in Adolfo's horrific religious human sacrifices as his "La Madrina," somehow managed to maintain her clean, wholesome personality to her fellow students and tutors. However, some wondered how she could afford a brand new Ford Taurus with a built-in cellular telephone.

One of Adolfo's favorite films at this time was *The Believers,* a 1987 horror film starring Martin Sheen. He, Sara, Jorge Montes, and Omar Ochoa and other cult members would watch it over and over. The film was about a New York cult with high society and police connections who were practitioners of *palo mayombe* and condoned the ritualistic sacrifice of children to achieve power and protection from the gods.

One prediction that Adolfo gave Sara was that Elio Hernandez would be in touch with her before the year was out to seek her advice about a problem. In fact, Adolfo had been told by Commander Salvador Garcia that Elio would look for any excuse to contact Sara. But Sara was unaware of that. When Elio contacted her in November 1987, Sara was yet more impressed than ever with Adolfo's psychic predictions and highly praised Adolfo's amazing powers to Elio.

The Hernandez family that had its roots in a small village near Matamoros had originally been dirt poor until they broke into the lucrative marijuana smuggling trade. Within ten years, the family owned villas and ranches all over Mexico, drove expensive cars, and were able to afford to educate their children. The extended family was large with members living on both sides of the border. When Saul Hernandez, the second eldest of four brothers, who ran the family business, was shot in a shoot out in Matamoros, the family business went into decline. Saul's eldest brother, Serafin Senior tried to take over the business but was arrested in the U.S. after a failed attempt to land a load of marijuana on an airstrip in Grimes County, Texas. Elio, the youngest of the brothers then seized power of the family business, which caused squabbles within the family.

Elio was ambitious, clever and ruthless. He realized that to build the family business up again, he needed help. When he heard from Sara about Adolfo's magical powers, he requested that she introduce them.

Elio traveled to Adolfo's luxury apartment in Mexico City. Adolfo used all his charisma and charm on Elio and offered his services to act as the Hernandez family's high priest and protect them from all enemies. He ensured Elio that, with his help, the family would have riches beyond their dreams. Adolfo said he would do all of this if they shared with him their drug profits. Elio, who rapidly fell under Adolfo's spell and was convinced that he was the answer to their problems, rapidly agreed.

Adolfo traveled to Matamoros and met the rest of the family and workers of the Hernandez family. He was taken to the family's Rancho Santa Elena, an isolated ranch near the Texas border west of Matamoros, which was the center of the family's drug operations. Here Adolfo commandeered a rundown shack sitting on a bed of cement as the new family temple. He furnished it with a new altar, statues of their saints, candles, various herbs and his pride and joy, a new large, black iron cauldron. Added to it were bloody sticks, scorpions, spiders, spices, a boiled alive black cat, tortoises and the head of a goat amongst other things. Soon more sinister offerings would be added.

The entire family and workers all became cult followers of Adolfo, who instructed them in his religion. He would frequently show them *The Believers* to brainwash them into believing that human sacrifice was okay. Adolfo set up a temple at the ranch along with a bloody cauldron. Soon regular human sacrifice ceremonies took place at the ranch in which the majority of the Hernandez clan took part. One of the first new clan members was Alvaro de Leon Valdez, nicknamed El Duby. He was known for his joy of hurting others, and he eagerly embraced Adolfo's violent and bloody rituals. Another early cult member of the Hernandez gang was Carlos de la Llata, yet another violent thug and coke dealer. The foreman of the ranch, Aurelio Chavez was another brutal man who also eagerly embraced the rituals, along with Malio Fabio Ponce Torres. Malio was from a wealthy family and was known to carry a stiletto knife that he had no hesitation in using if someone crossed him. Adolfo nicknamed him El Gato, The Cat. Adolfo also brought into the fold Elio's homosexual cousin, Sergio Martinez Salinas, nicknamed La Mariposa, The Butterfly. Adolfo told them all that, in his absence, they must obey Sara Aldrete as their *Madrina*, (Godmother) who was responsible for their continuing education of the religion. Alfonso also impressed upon them that they were a family, and his word was law. Any disobedience would be met with a long, slow death.

Adolfo was as good as his word. When he discovered a loyal cult member, Jorge Valente del Fierro, had snorted a few lines of coke, he was sacrificially killed and became another victim.

Adolfo's star was rising to such an extent he barely registered the death of his loyal follower Commander Florentino Ventura Gutierrez, even though he was in Mexico City at the time. On the night of September 16–17, 1988, Ventura Gutierrez was found dead. The official report filed by Mexico City's judicial police alleged that he had committed "suicide" late at night after murdering his wife and a female friend of them both following a drunken argument before killing himself. Several prominent Mexican newspapers declared that the official report was false as all three were bizarrely killed with the same burst of gunfire. The police remained resolutely silent on the media reports. Ventura's two children declared, "We don't believe all those lies." They also queried why the Mexican government closed the case just hours after the event. "Someday we will know the truth," said one.

The Hernandez family fortunes were restored. They put it all down to Adolfo's magic, and the numbers of human sacrifices were increased. The human sacrifices they used came from all walks of life: policemen, local farmers, rival drug dealers, local youths and American tourists.

Frequently the victims were first tortured and raped by Adolfo, who explained to his devoted followers that the more the victims screamed, the happier the gods were and the greater the family would be rewarded. It has been suggested by a few that the rituals of horror that Adolfo subjected his cohorts to were his chief means of breaking their will and binding them totally to his cult. During one of his visits to the ranch, Adolfo met Elio's nephew, twenty-year-old Serafin Hernandez Garcia Jr. Serafin was a U.S. citizen who spoke fluent English, unlike other members of the Hernandez family. He had been brought up in Houston before moving to Brownsville with his parents where, like Sara, he attended Texas Southmost College as a law enforcement student. Adolfo decided he would make a useful addition to the family because, as a U.S. citizen, he could cross the border with ease. Adolfo set about charming Serafin and initiating him into the ways of the cult. With plenty of money put in his pocket, he was easy to convert and became completely won over by Adolfo and believed him when he was told he was invincible and would be invisible to law enforcement officials. The violence of the cult and the bloody murders also unperturbed him; he didn't care if strangers died. Adolfo nicknamed him El Chaparro.

To many it is astounding that so many people could just disappear without a trace from a city like Matamoros with a population of around two hundred thousand. But people disappeared off the street nearly every night. It must be remembered that this was a border town where crime and drug trafficking was out of control and the police who were poorly paid, were easily corruptible; life was cheap and barroom shootings were common.

At the time that Salvador was transferred there from Mexico City, the comandante of the federal police in Matamoros was Guillermo Perez, a highly corrupt law official who was making fortunes from the drugs trade. He made millions by seizing drugs from small-time traffickers, jailing them and then reselling the drugs. The powerful drug lords who paid protection money to Perez would go untouched. He continued unabated until 1989 when he became a fugitive and left behind in his desk five million dollars of dirty money.

Unbeknown to the Hernandez family, Adolfo, through his friendship with Salvador, arranged for their drug smuggling to be ignored. The family firmly believed that it was Adolfo and his magic rituals that made them continue to thrive. They were moving successfully, on average, one thousand pounds of marijuana a week across the border. And they became so brainwashed by Adolfo that they truly believed that they were untouchable.

Adolfo's addiction to torture and murder intensified with each new killing ceremony. Sometimes he could barely wait a few days for a new sacrificial victim to be brought to him. His followers were only too happy to oblige him in his need.

In March 1989, Serafin and two others kidnapped a young cocaine dealer and took him to the ranch. Adolfo was waiting in anticipation of his victim. The young man was tough and refused to give Adolfo the pleasure of hearing him scream even when Adolfo began to skin him alive. Adolfo was furious, the ceremony was useless, he believed, unless the victim screamed and wailed with fear and pain from the depth of his being. He felt as if he had failed. Coupled with this was the worrying news that the corrupt federal police Commandente in Matamoros, Guillermo Perez, had fled town leaving behind, in his haste to leave before being arrested, $5 million of dirty money in his desk. He had been replaced by a young chief federal drug investigator in his mid-thirties, Juan Benitez Ayala, who had a reputation for being tough, educated, a workaholic and unable to be bought. He was short, around five-foot, good-looking and of native Indian descent; he had large innocent-looking brown eyes and shaggy black hair parted in the middle. Although short in stature, people were frightened of him. He was bringing some powerful people down. He would never eat in bars or restaurants, as he was fearful someone might slip something into his food or drink. He also, like many Mexicans of Indian descent, was highly superstitious and surrounded himself with strings of peppers, cloves of garlic and white candles to divert off evil.

Adolfo ordered Serafin to find him a young blonde male American university student. Adolfo decided the Hernandez cauldron needed some brains. Serafin said he would do it the following night. It was the time of spring break for American colleges, and hordes of students would routinely cross over the border to Mexico in search of cheap alcohol, drugs and sex. Mark Kilroy was such a student.

Mark was a 21-year-old University of Texas pre-med undergraduate who had decided, along with three fellow students, Bradley Moore, Bill Huddleston and Brent Martin, to visit the Mexican border town of Matamoros for an evening, a fashionable hangout for students since as early as the 1930s. All four boys were studious, athletic, tall, clean-cut, and didn't use drugs. They left their car in Brownsville and walked over the international bridge across the Rio Grande to Matamoros, Mexico. The narrow sidewalks and streets were packed with around 12,000 young college revelers weaving in and out of neon lit bars and mind-shattering loud music, lured by the 18-year-old drinking age (a dollar note seemed to be the only price of identity needed) and cheap prices. Marijuana and cocaine, heavily doctored with laxatives, baking soda, calcium, Tylenol and even talcum powder were widely available at a price.

The four boys hung around the bars until around two a.m. when they began heading back up Avenida Alvaro Obregon towards the bridge and the U.S. border. The Avenida was jam-packed and making progress was slow going. One way or another, on the walk back to the border, Mark Kilroy got separated from his friends. They presumed he would be following later, having perhaps bumped into an acquaintance. They waited at the border to no avail. They then made their way back down the Avenida searching for Mark among the now mostly closed bars and emptying streets. There was no sign of Mark. Thinking and hoping that they had somehow missed him, the young men returned to their car in Brownsville, hoping to find Mark there. The hope was in vain. They sat waiting in the parked car for the rest of the night and, in the morning, with still no sign of Mark, they contacted the police.

An extensive hunt for the missing student was launched by the Mexican and U.S. law enforcement on both sides of the Rio Grande. At first the investigation began as a regular missing-persons case. Students were frequently reported missing in the border town only to turn up the following day with a brutal hangover and little memory of the previous night. But when Mark failed to show up, the Mexican and U.S. law enforcement began to suspect foul play. The U.S. consul in Matamoros, Donald Wells, put out a description of Kilroy, which he circulated in hospitals and jails. Bradley Moore remembered that at some point, as they made their way back to the bridge, he had seen Mark speaking to a young Hispanic man with a scar on his face.

James and Helen Kilroy, Mark's parents, flew down from their home in Santa Fe to Brownsville to help with the search to locate their son. They printed out over 20,000 leaflets, which they distributed all over the Rio Grande valley, and offered a $15,000 reward for any information leading to his whereabouts. Many of the residents of Brownsville and Matamoros helped to hand the flyers out; one of those was Sara Aldrete.

Unlike many kids who get into trouble in Mexico, Mark Kilroy was different. His uncle was a U.S. Customs investigator in Los Angeles who wanted answers to his nephew's disappearance, thus triggering an informal group of various law officers with no jurisdiction in Mexico to investigate the disappearance. The streets of Matamoros were prowled by U.S. sheriff deputies, U.S. Customs personnel and the DEA all unofficially investigating. The Mexican state police claimed that Mark had crossed back into the U.S. and must have disappeared there. The only Mexican law enforcement officer seeming willing to help was the new federal drug investigator, Juan Benitez Ayala, and he had his plate full trying to clean up his department.

America's Most Wanted, the television crime program, featured Mark Kilroy's case on March 26th. Although the show generated numerous telephone calls and letters, there were no helpful clues. It was as if Mark had dropped off the face of the earth. But the media attention on the disappearance grew and threatened the tourism industry that Mexico so heavily relied upon.

Adolfo was surprised by the media attention that the disappearance of Mark Kilroy had generated but was at least relieved that no heat seemed to be on the ranch.

To young Serafin Hernandez Garcia, the fact that no one had seen him or Malio kidnap Mark on a busy street full of American kids made him truly believe he was invisible and totally protected. He so fully believed that he was invincible he unwittingly led the police straight to the ranch.

As part of the new Commandante Juan Benitez Ayala's fight against drug trafficking, he began to set up impromptu roadblocks to search passing cars and trucks for drugs, staffed by agents he trusted. Within a month of having taken up his new post, there had been more arrests and more drug seizures than in the previous few years in Matamoros.

On April 1, at the 13-kilometer checkpoint on the road to Matamoros, Benitez's federal drug agent, Raul Morales, set up such a roadblock. It was at a point on the road that smugglers would turn off to haul their illicit cargoes across the Rio Grande. Late in the afternoon, a shiny red pickup truck with Texas plates approached the checkpoint from Brownsville and, ignoring the warning signs and orange road cones, didn't even slow down but drove through the check spot as though oblivious to it. The agents on duty were so surprised by the audacity of the driver, they were left almost open-mouthed in disbelief. One of the agents thought he recognized the driver as Serafin

Hernandez. Raul and another federal agent jumped into an unmarked car and discreetly followed the red truck to a ranch just off the highway to Matamoros at a point known as the *curva de Texas* and kept watch. When Serafin left the ranch and drove towards Matamoros, they approached the ranch, which had a large, corrugated, well-bolted steel warehouse on its grounds. As their car pulled up outside the warehouse, there was the standard assortment of farm animals barking, bleating, crowing and screeching, plus the smell of manure and dust. A few parked cars and trucks were also in view. A short chubby man in work clothes appeared from a nearby shack and ambled over to them. Raul pretended to be a lost tourist and proceeded to engage the man in conversation. The man told him he was the caretaker of the ranch whose duties were to feed the animals and keep a general eye on the place. As Raul talked to the man, whose name he learnt was Domingo, the other agent wandered over to a sparkling new blue Chevy Suburban. The agent looked through the windows of the car and immediately noticed an expensive cellular phone inside. Glancing through the rear windows he, as an experienced narcotics officer, immediately noticed a fine green dust covering the rear seats and had no doubt in his mind that it had leaked from bales of marijuana. The agents, not wanting to alert the man to their true identities, apologized to the man for disturbing him and thanked him for his directions.

When Raul Morales reported the incident to Juan Benitez Ayala, the Commandante asked for the ranch to be kept under surveillance and for undercover police to find out all they could from informants about the Hernandez family. Meanwhile he said he would contact the U.S. DEA about the truck and see if they could get the phone number so that he could begin listening in on calls to and from the truck. Meanwhile, Domingo had told Aurelio Chavez, the ranch foreman, who had alerted Elio that two men had visited the ranch where, at the time, a ton of marijuana was stashed in the warehouse. Elio reported this news to Adolfo, who immediately ordered another ceremony to take place at the ranch for added protection before the load was moved across the border on April 8th.

Adolfo decided his sacrificial victim would be Gilberto Sosa, who had lately been annoying Sara. Sara arranged to meet Gilberto, and when he showed up, he was shoved into a truck and taken to the ranch. Here, police believe, she supervised his slow death, which included cutting off his nipples with scissors and boiling him alive.

The Mexican federal agents had meanwhile found out that the ranch belonged to Serafin Hernandez Rivera, young Serafin's Dad.

On Sunday, April 9, Juan Benitez Ayala finally got the information he had been waiting to receive from the U.S. DEA. The DEA gave Benitez information about ten cell phones registered to Hernandez Ranches, Incorporated. He immediately began to listen into the conversations taking place on the cell phones. One of the first calls he listened to was Serafin boasting to a friend about how they had smuggled a ton of dope over the border the previous night. Despite the surveillance on the ranch, the agents had missed that one. Serafin also told his friend that he was on his way over to his Uncle Elio's house on Avenida Lauro Villar.

Benitez decided to send his agents around to Elio's house and bring in Serafin and Elio for questioning.

Raul Morales, along with a couple of other agents, arrived at the house on Avenida Lauro Villar shortly before eleven in the morning just in time to see Serafin and a slightly effeminate-looking companion, both dressed in designer jeans and dripping with gold, enter Elio's house. The agents hung around outside until they saw Serafin begin to exit the house. They then made their move. They barged into the open doorway and pushed Serafin Jr. back in and handcuffed him, his friend, David Serna Valdez, and Elio before searching the house. The federal agents found no drugs, but an assortment of illegal firearm weapons, enough for the federal agents to arrest all three of them plus another man who was in the house,

Garcia Sergio Martinez.

After dropping the firearms off at police headquarters, the four prisoners were driven to Rancho Santa Elena. The agents were puzzled by the men's attitude. None of them seemed the least perturbed by their arrest and treated it almost jovially.

At the Rancho Santa Elena, the agents were joined by more back up. There was no sign of the caretaker, Domingo. Raul Morales dragged Serafin out of the police car and ordered him to open the bolted warehouse doors. Inside the warehouse, the narcotic agents immediately recognized the overwhelming smell of marijuana, but all they found was around sixty pounds (about twenty-seven kilos), which to the experienced agents meant there had been a lot more stored there very recently. Apart from the marijuana, they found more illegal firearms and a truck smeared with dried river mud with traces of marijuana inside. Morales assumed it was the truck that had completed the smuggling trip the night before.

Once the agents had finished searching the warehouse, they investigated a few other sheds, but nothing more of interest was found. All four prisoners were then taken back to Matamoros police headquarters for questioning. Still puzzling to the agents was their lack of concern as to the gravity of their situation.

They weren't the least bit concerned and boasted that the police would never be able to hold them. "We're protected," boasted Serafin. Back at the police station, they were thrown into squalid cells and left to stew overnight before the police began seriously questioning them. The following morning, the caretaker Domingo Reyes Bustamante turned up for work and was promptly arrested and hauled in front of Benitez. Unlike his bosses, Domingo was petrified, and without any hesitation answered Benitez's questions in a trembling voice. Yes, the Hernandez family smuggled narcotics. Yes, there was around a ton at the ranch a couple of nights previously. When he was asked to give names of who was involved, he named the four already arrested and several others.

When he was asked who visited the ranch, he replied that people came and went all the time. Looking at Benitez's desk, Domingo saw a photograph of Mark Kilroy. He pointed to it and said, "That kid was up there once."

Benitez and Raul Morales glanced at each other, and both men sat up straighter and stared intently at Domingo.

"What was he doing there?" Benitez asked.

"I fed him. I felt sorry for him; he was tied up in the back of a blue Suburban all night. I gave him some bread, eggs and water for breakfast. Then the bosses came and took him away. That's all I know."

What on earth Mark Kilroy thought was going to happen to him as he ate his bread and eggs was not, I imagine, as horrific as what actually happened.

***

Shortly after Domingo's startling news, Benitez realized he might be dealing with something far more than just drug smuggling. He decided it was time to have a word with Serafin. He went down to the interrogation cell and ordered Serafin to be brought to him. When Serafin was brought into the cell, Benitez held up a photograph of Mark Kilroy. "Do you know this guy?" he asked.

"Sure," said Serafin grinning. "That's the gringo everyone is looking for."

"How do you know him?"

"I kidnapped him," Serafin said with a touch of pride.

"Why?"

"Our Padrino wanted a blonde gringo student to sacrifice, to bring us more power and protection. He wanted his brain to add to the cauldron. Padrino has told us that killing makes us invincible. Even bullets can't kill us. That is why you will let us go."

Benitez ignored that comment. "Where is he now?" he asked.

"He's buried up at the ranch."

For the next several hours, Serafin told Benitez and the other agents about their religion and the other human sacrifices they had performed in their temple. He described how he had kidnapped Mark Kilroy. How the following day they had taken him to the shed they used as a temple and watched as Padrino beat, mutilated and tortured Mark before sodomizing him, and then split his skull open with a machete. Mark's brain was then removed and added to the Padrino's cauldron.

"Where is this temple?" Benitez asked.

"On the edge of the ranch," Serafin said.

Serafin spoke in awe of his Padrino, Adolfo de Jesus Constanzo, and his Madrina, Sara Aldrete. The agents listened in horror and some made the sign of the cross as Serafin continued proudly boasting of their sacrifices and the wonders of his religion.

When they had finished listening to Serafin, the other three prisoners were each interrogated separately, all of them repeating the same tale as Serafin, a tale of torture, human sacrifice, black magic and the power of their Padrino. None of them were worried at all to confessing. They all genuinely thought they were protected and would soon be released once Adolfo heard what was happening to them.

At the end of the questioning of the men, the Mexican agents felt thoroughly sickened and drained. In all their years of working as law officers, they had never heard anything so sickening and depraved as they'd heard that day. The tales of the four prisoners had sent shivers up and down their spines.

Following the confessions and with the men returned to their cells, Benitez telephoned Ernesto Flores, the detective in Brownsville in charge of the search for Mark Kilroy, and asked him to be at his office early the next morning on April 11. He didn't elaborate anymore.

Ernesto Flores arrived at Benitez's office at the police headquarters early in the morning. Also there were two U.S. customs officers who had been summoned. Shortly after arriving, without being given any explanation, the agents were told to be ready as they were going for a drive. While they were waiting in the station compound for a car to pick them up, Ernesto saw a young man with a Zapata mustache being led up from the cellblock. He was handcuffed and was being roughly handled by the officers escorting him. They shoved him into a waiting car followed by the heavily armed officers. It was Serafin. Shortly after, a car pulled up for Flores and the two U.S. customs agents. They climbed in and followed the car with the prisoner that was leading a convoy of unmarked police cars full of bulletproof-vested, heavily armed Mexican federal agents. Flores and the custom agents wondered what was going on and where they were going.

The convoy drove out of Matamoros town and west onto Highway 2. After about thirteen miles, they turned off the highway onto a rough, bumpy and dusty track and drove through flat, empty terrain sprinkled by farms, ranches and an occasional hovel. Emaciated sheep, goats and cows grazed on the parched fields and momentarily looked up as the large convoy passed them by. Eventually they passed a large warehouse and made a couple of more turnings before drawing up at a corral sitting in front of a 14-by-24-foot tin shack with boarded-up windows. It was Adolfo's temple.

As Flores and the U.S. custom officers wondered what they were doing there, they saw the armed officers and their lone prisoner exit from their car. Behind them, Benitez and other agents vacated their cars. Flores and the customs officers climbed out of their car, and they all stood in silence surveying the landscape. Just then, a breeze picked up and Flores caught the unmistakable smell of death.

At Benitez's command, several agents took the boards down on the shed's windows and then broke open the doors. Two agents began warily entering the red tarpaper-walled shed but then staggered backward, overcome by the stench emanating from within. A couple of other agents tried to enter by covering their mouths with handkerchiefs, but to no avail.

They exited the shed, retching from the appalling stench.

Benitez ordered the doors to be left wide open and the windows smashed to be able to hopefully enter later when perhaps the stench of death would have slightly abated. But with the doors open, the smell seemed to creep out into all the agents' pores and cling to their clothes.

"Where's the body?" Benitez yelled at Serafin.

"Which body?" Serafin asked.

"Are you trying to wind me up?" Benitez asked in a pissed-off voice.

"No, sir," Serafin said. "There's a bunch of bodies buried here. Which one do you want?"

Serafin began wandering around the corral and, pointing with his chin at various bits of ground, said, "There's one buried here and another buried there and another one over there."

"Where's Mark Kilroy?" Benitez asked.

"Over there in that corner," Serafin said, jutting his chin towards a corner of the corral. "I don't remember where exactly."

All this time, the proceedings were being videotaped by a police cameraman.

"Walk over there and see if you can remember," Benitez commanded.

Serafin walked over to the corner he had indicated and then said, "He's here by this coat hanger wire."

"Why is the wire sticking out?" Benitez asked.

"The other end of the wire is attached to Mark's spine because El Padrino wants to make a necklace out of it when his body has decomposed." He spoke as if he expected his 'El Padrino' to do this at some point.

Benitez told one of the agents to fetch him a shovel and a pickaxe. When the officer brought him the shovel and pickaxe, Benitez ordered Serafin to be un-handcuffed and, shoving the shovel into his hands, ordered him to start digging. Serafin did as he was told as machine guns were aimed at him. When Mark's body was uncovered, Benitez noted that his lower legs from just above the knees had been cut off. He asked Serafin if that was a part of the religious ritual.

"No, sir, it just made it easier to bury him," Serafin said totally remorseless.

Benitez had Serafin work for hours at gunpoint in the blazing sun digging up bodies. By around two-thirty in the afternoon, a dozen dead bodies had been recovered. Serafin said he didn't know where all the bodies were. At that point, Benitez ordered the other three prisoners to be brought out to the ranch to help locate the corpses. Mechanical diggers were also ordered in.

As the bodies began to be unearthed, Sara Aldrete telephoned Southmost College and said she wouldn't be coming in anymore, as she had to work out some personal problems. Then she, Adolfo, El Duby, and four or five others flew out of McAllen, Texas, to Mexico City.

In the days that followed, fifteen corpses in total were dug up from the ranch or nearby. A few of the bodies recovered had been beheaded; others had had their skulls smashed open by blows from a machete. Hearts, brains, lungs, genitals and other parts had been torn or cut from some of the victims. A few of these were later found to have been stewed in the stinking cauldron in the temple shed of the ranch. One victim was reportedly skinned alive, another boiled alive, and many had been sodomized before being murdered.

It was a grueling, chilling time for all the agents involved. And what chilled them the most was the remorseless attitude of the perpetrators of the crimes. Benitez and Flores realized they urgently needed to capture an extremely charismatic, psychotic madman named Adolfo de Jesus Constanzo and his Madrina, Sara Aldrete. A massive manhunt began in both Mexico and the United States for Adolfo, Sara Aldrete and other members of the cult. Agents visited Sara's apartment above her parents' house in Matamoros. There was no sign of Sara, but what they did find was her own altar, with black candles, beaded necklaces, and other accouterments of black magic in front of a blood-splattered wall. And most chilling of all were baby clothes in a bag near the altar.

When the media reports branded Sara Aldrete as a cult witch, the response among faculty members and students at Southmost College was one of absolute shock. It seemed unbelievable that the attractive, bright, intelligent, industrious girl they all knew could be mixed up with a wicked gang of murdering drug smugglers. "We never suspected anything," said one of her college friends.

Word of the mass black magic ritual slaughters soon had the world media flying into Brownsville and Matamoros before the last corpse had even been exhumed. Every hotel bed in Brownsville and Matamoros was occupied by journalists and all rental cars hired out. The television crews and journalists descended in droves to report on the excavations at the "Black Magic Ranch." Astonishingly, to the horror of the U.S. agents, Comandante Benitez did not seal off the crime scene to the media. Journalists and cameramen roamed around the ranch, prodding in haystacks and mounds of dirt, hoping to discover something that no one else had found.

Other journalists with handkerchiefs tied across their faces gingerly stepped inside the 'temple' where the air was still thick and foul. On the rough concrete floor stood an altar covered with the paraphernalia of black magic: black candles, strange statues, herbs, bottles of *aguardiente,* (cane liquor) and cigar butts.

By the altar were the instruments and vessels used in the sacrificial ceremonies: three small cauldrons and one large black cauldron and a blood stained machete. The small cauldrons contained goat and chicken heads, rooster's feet, turtles, bones, thousands of coins and some gold beads. The large iron cauldron held a cluster of wooden branches of varying sizes immersed in thick, foul-smelling evil goo of blood and body parts, both human and animal. Above the cauldron, drilled into the beams of the roof, were two wrist-sized hooks, where the victims' bodies were hung for their blood to be drained directly into the cauldron.

Sensational headlines were published around the world. This wasn't just a story about narcotic smuggling; it was a story about black magic and human sacrifice, a media headline heaven. Many of the newspapers described in gruesome detail how the cult had cut the hearts out of its victims like the Aztecs had done centuries before.

Meanwhile, a local Mexican radio station broadcast a report that members of the cult were still actively on the prowl and looking for more victims, adults and children, to kidnap and murder. This caused panic and made several parents take their children out of school and place them under house arrest.

When the work at the ranch was completed, Benitez held a news conference from the balcony overlooking the courtyard of the Federal Police building. In front of around two-hundred-and-fifty international journalists, Benitez paraded the four suspects and, much to the hungry media's delight, allowed them to fire questions at the prisoners. All four of them readily answered the journalists' questions about their various roles in the ritual killings.

Elio Hernandez proudly admitted that he'd been ordained as an executioner priest by Adolfo, the cult's high priest and leader. When asked who had murdered Mark Kilroy, Elio said it had been Adolfo personally. Elio and the others seemed to enjoy the limelight and, as television cameras zoomed in, Elio arrogantly displayed the satanic symbols branded on his back, arms, and chest. Even after three days in the harsh conditions of Matamoros jail, the prisoners remained undaunted and still seemed to think they were going to be magically freed. One reporter wrote that Elio had challenged Commandante Benitez to shoot him, saying with total conviction, "Your bullets will just bounce off."

It seemed to take a while to prove to them otherwise.

Benitez, at the close of the press conference, informed the mesmerized media that the investigation had now moved to Mexico City, where they believed there were more ritual murders linked to the cult's "Padrino," Adolfo.

Meanwhile in Mexico City, Adolfo, Sara, Duby, Martin and Omar watched the news on the television. They all individually went to the hairdresser's and cut and dyed their hair, which made them all look vastly different to the photographs of them displayed on the television. They visited Adolfo's various homes around the city and cleaned out any incriminating evidence and gathered any cash left in the properties. They then moved into a string of rented apartments, never staying too long in each one.

On April 17, in Houston, Texas, Serafin Hernandez Rivera, the owner of the Rancho Santa Elena, was arrested for possession and importing drugs.

Meanwhile, in Mexico City, the investigation into Adolfo and his cult proceeded. In Mexico City Adolfo had another group of followers totally unconnected to his followers in Brownsville and Matamoros, who may have been involved in the ritual killings of yet more victims. Mexico City journalists speculated that human babies had been ritually sacrificed by the cult.

On April 17, Mexican police armed with tear gas and machine guns raided Adolfo's luxury homes in Mexico City. Both his house on Calle Papagayos, 47, and his apartment in fashionable Colonia Roma, on Calle Pomona, 8, apartment 3, were deserted and had been emptied and cleared out of personal belongings. They remained full, however, of expensive televisions, stereo equipment and expensive furnishings.

In the house on Calle Papagayos, which was equipped with expensive security gear and had several luxury cars parked in the driveway, they found a great deal of gay pornography and some children's clothes. They also found two altars hidden behind some mirrors and various ritual paraphernalia but no signs of sacrifices. It looked as if the place had been scrubbed clean. But what they did find was Sarah Aldrete's passport, purse, and a used airline ticket in her name. This finding caused many to speculate that Sara had become Adolfo's latest victim, while others thought that this was a deliberate ruse by Adolfo and Sara to stop them from hunting for her.

The following day, on April 18, a U.S. grand jury issued a four-count indictment on Adolfo de Jesus Constanzo and ten of his cohorts on various narcotic trafficking charges. His mother and other members of his family claimed to journalists that Adolfo was just a good Catholic boy.

On April 21, the Mexican authorities formally charged the four captured cultists, Serafin Hernandez Garcia Jr., Sergio Martinez, David Serna Valdez and Elio Hernandez Rivera with multiple counts of kidnapping, murder, possession of illegal weapons and drug trafficking.

Meanwhile, Benitez, heavily superstitious and extremely disturbed by the findings at the ranch and the idea of Adolfo still at large consulted his own *curandero* (witch doctor) on how to disperse the demons at the ranch and capture Adolfo. The *curandero* recommended burning the temple to the ground and to burn his big black cauldron and televise it so Adolfo could witness it.

One quiet Sunday afternoon, when no one was looking, Benitez and a couple of his federal agents surreptitiously revisited the ranch with his *curandero* and a lone cameraman. The *curandero* entered the shed and began a purification ceremony. After about an hour, he asked a couple of the agents to drag the stinking cauldron to the entrance of the shed's door and into the daylight. He then instructed the agents to douse the shed and Adolfo's cauldron with gasoline and set it on fire. The burning shed and cauldron were all filmed by the cameraman until it all burned to the ground.

Adolfo watched the burning of his temple on the news from an apartment in Mexico City, where he and his cohorts were holed up. He felt enraged; he felt the Mexican federal police had invaded his privacy, violated his very being by destroying his magic in his sacred cauldron. He believed that by burning his cauldron that all the souls he had imprisoned in it had been freed, thus destroying his power. He began to lose it and ranted and raved for hours as he paced around the small, din-gy apartment they were holed up in like a caged animal. From that point on, Adolfo became overtly paranoid that his power was eroding and that he had been betrayed, and he kept an Uzi machine gun constantly by his side. Sara began to have doubts about his sanity and wondered if she had just been blind to it before.

The five fugitives eventually moved into a dingy fourth floor, two-bedroom apartment on 19, Rio Sena, Colonia Cuauhtemoc, a decaying downtown area of the city. It had been rented for them by one of Adolfo's Mexico City followers. By now all of their nerves were frazzled, and arguments be-tween them frequently erupted. Sara began to think that Adol-fo was going to kill her. By this time, he wouldn't even talk to or look at her. One day when no one was looking, out of her bedroom window, she tossed a note that read, *"Please call the judicial police and tell them that in this building are those that they are seeking. Tell them that a woman is being held hostage. I beg for this because what I want most is to talk—or they're going to kill the girl."*

A young man found the note but failed to pass it on to the authorities for a few days.

On May 6, Adolfo, looking out of the apartment window, noticed an unmarked police car outside the building on the opposite side of the street. He immediately thought they had been betrayed and that the police were there for them. He im-mediately began to go berserk. He began firing his machine gun out of the window and injured a police officer. Other po-lice who saw the gunman leaning out of the window thought he looked like the fugitive satanic cult leader Adolfo and radi-oed urgently for backup.

Almost instantaneously, two hundred armed police officers surrounded the building. A fierce forty-five minute gun battle began, with many hundreds of rounds of ammunition fired in exchange. At one point, Adolfo began throwing hundreds of fifty- and twenty-dollar notes out of the window, causing poverty-stricken Mexicans to risk their lives by trying to retrieve the notes, as they were yelled at by the police to stay back.

When El Duby warned Adolfo that he had only one lot of bullets left, Adolfo handed the machine gun to him and ordered him to shoot him and his lover Martin. When El Duby balked at the order, Adolfo hit him and cautioned him that if he refused to do the task, he would make his life in hell many times worse. El Duby, used to doing as El Padrino told him, agreed to do it. Adolfo positioned himself in a closet with Martin and, looking El Duby directly in the eyes, said, "now." El Duby raised the machine gun to his shoulder and sprayed Adolfo and Martin with bullets.

When armed police stormed the apartment, Sara Aldrete, Omar, and El Duby surrendered quietly and were taken to the basement of the Miguel Hildalgo District offices for interrogation.

Following Sara's arrest, she tried to proclaim that she had been kidnapped by Adolfo. She said the note she had thrown out of the window, which had now been handed in, proved it. The police weren't having any of it and claimed it was just an alibi in case of her inevitable arrest. She claimed she never knew about the murders until she saw them on television.

After a few days of interrogation, all three confessed to their part in the cult and the murders. They were then all taken to a maximum-security prison and placed in solitary confinement. They were only allowed out from their cells for two disorganized and massive media conferences.

Altogether, 14 members of Adolfo's cult were indicted on a variety of charges, including conspiracy, multiple murder, narcotics violations, obstruction of justice, and illegal weapons. Many of the cult members have never been found.

In August 1990, El Duby was convicted of killing Adolfo and Martin Quintana and sentenced to 35 years in prison.

In 1994, Sara was sentenced to 62 years while Elio Hernandez and Serafin Jr. each were sentenced to 67 years in prison. Omar Orea died of AIDS before he could be sentenced.

Before sentencing, all of them attempted to withdraw their confessions, claiming they had been obtained under torture and blamed everything on their padrino, Adolfo.

If any of them are released from prison, the American authorities will seek their extradition to prosecute them for the murder of Mark Kilroy.

Following her sentencing, Sara said during a media interview, *"I don't think that the religion will end with us, because it has a lot of people in it. They have found a temple in Monterrey that isn't even related to us. It will continue."*

Omar, before he died, spoke to a reporter about others who practiced black magic and sacrifice—sister groups of Adolfo Constanzo's.

Between 1987 and 1989, Mexico City police recorded 74 unsolved ritual murders, 14 of them involving infants. Adolfo's cult was suspected of 16 of these cases. But the authorities believe the others were carried out by a person or persons unknown.

If Serafin Hernandez had not run the police roadblock, which led them to the ranch, one wonders how long Adolfo's cult would have continued to murder unfettered. As it is, no one is really sure exactly how many people were murdered by the cult, or indeed how many active members were in it.

A low-budget slasher film loosely based on the Mark Kilroy and Adolfo Constanzo cult was in time made and entitled *Borderland.*

In an interview Sara gave in 2004, she still claimed all innocence of murder. She still claims that her confession was tortured out of her by the federal police. She claims she was blindfolded, stripped, had her toenails pulled out, hung upside down, and burned inside and out. She said a doctor has told her that because of the torture, even if she is released, she will never be able to have children. She also claimed that the Federal police took her to the morgue where Adolfo's body lay and ordered her to yank out his heart while they chanted, "There is your devil. There is your prince. Kiss him. Kiss him."

In a country where police torture to extract confessions is well known, it is difficult to confirm her claims. The police denied they tortured her.

She spends her time in prison teaching other inmates English, plays volleyball and runs a hamburger stall from her cell. In the prison yard, when she first arrived at the prison, she planted some seedlings. Those seedlings are now trees that offer shade to the yard. She lives in a dormitory with a dozen other women and realizes that might be her home until the day she dies.

Chapter 5
RODNEY ALCALA
The Dating Game Killer
By Peter Vronsky

There is one type of case that cops dread being assigned to: child abduction rape murders. On June 20, 1979, in California, Huntington Beach Police detective Art Droz and his wife Marylyn, a police sketch artist, were about to have such a case land on their desks. That afternoon, twelve-year-old Robin Samsoe vanished on her way to ballet lessons. Robin was the youngest of several children in the family. She was five feet tall, with golden California blond shoulder-length hair and bright blue eyes. A star gymnast and a dancer, she had just completed Grade 7 and was enjoying her summer holidays taking extra ballet classes. She was wearing a black one-piece dancing body suit, underneath white shorts and a red t-shirt.

Robin Samsoe

Robin spent the early afternoon at Huntington Beach with her best friend Bridget Wilvert, also twelve years old, who lived two blocks away from the beach. After returning to Wilvert's nearby apartment, the two girls hung out until it was time for Robin to go to her lessons. Robin borrowed Bridget's distinctive bright yellow Schwinn bike to ride to her ballet class in the Seacliff Shopping Center, about a ten-minute bike ride away. Several hours later, the ballet school called advising Robin's mother that she had not come in for her scheduled lesson.

Friends and family began a frenzied search for the girl along the route to the ballet studio from Bridget's house, and after they could find no trace of her or the bike, they reported Robin's disappearance to the Huntington Beach P.D. By 11:00 p.m. that night, police put out an urgent missing child alert.

According to Bridget, the two girls had spent the afternoon at the beach and afterwards at Bridget's house until it was time for Robin to leave for her ballet lessons. The only unusual thing that Bridget could recall was that, while at the beach, they were approached by a man with a camera wearing a plaid shirt, long pants and dress shoes. They thought it was funny to see him dressed that way on a beach. He was relatively young and good looking, with long frizzy dark hair, and in a very friendly and easy manner asked permission of the two girls if he could photograph them for "a class" he said he was taking. The girls immediately agreed. After taking a few shots of both girls, he closed in on Robin and putting his hand on her knee posed her, taking another photo of her.

This scene was being observed by Jackey Young, a neighbor of Bridget's who was sunning herself a short distance away. She too thought that the man was strangely dressed for the beach and began to wonder why a grown man approached these young girls and was photographing them. Growing a little suspicious, she approached the three as the man was taking a picture of Robin, crouched down with his back turned toward her. Young called out, "And what are you young ladies doing today?"

To Young's surprise, the man straightened up and walked away without turning toward her or saying anything. She chided the girls for talking with a stranger and allowing them to take their photograph. Young then escorted the two twelve-year-olds safely back to Bridget's house nearby and, after ensuring that the suspicious man was not lurking about, she continued to her own apartment in the neighborhood. At around

3:30 p.m. Robin left Bridget's house on the bike and was never seen alive again.

Police sketch artist Marilyn Droz was called in to meet with Bridget and develop a composite sketch of the man with the camera, the only lead police had at the time. The story of how Droz worked with the twelve-year-old girl to develop an effective portrait of the suspect is told in detail by Stella Sands in her book about the case.[1] The composite sketch produced by Droz of a curly, dark-haired stranger, along with a description of his approach to young females as a photographer, was broadcast on TV news and printed in newspapers and distributed and posted on fliers (there was no internet or social media in 1979). It immediately triggered a stream of calls to the detectives at the Huntington Beach PD.

Two parole officers phoned in to report that the sketch and M.O. resembled one of their past parolees, a sex offender who had been preying on young girls, approaching them as a photographer and then sexually assaulting them. He was currently out on bail, having been recently charged with forcibly raping a fifteen-year-old girl in Riverside. His name was Rodney Alcala.

Then two LAPD detectives called. The composite looked very similar to a suspect they were looking at in a series of sexual murders they were investigating in the Hollywood Hills. The suspect was an amateur photographer who worked as a typesetter at the *L.A. Times* newspaper and had a record of violent rapes of girls. His name was Rodney Alcala.

Next a real estate agent by the name of Donald Haines called. Eleven years ago, in 1968, he called police reporting what he thought was an abduction of an eight-year-old girl on her way to school. By the time the police arrived she had been taken to a nearby apartment, brutally raped and then beaten nearly to death across the face and head with an iron bar. The suspect escaped and was apprehended only several years later. The composite sketch, Haines said, looks exactly like him. His name was Rodney Alcala.

In those days before networked computer systems, before digital photography and before even readily available fax machines, somebody from the Huntington Beach PD had to drive to Riverside PD an hour away to get a copy of Rodney Alcala's mugshot. By now it was June 26, six days since Robin vanished. Detective Art Droz had already completed his long shift that day but decided to wait around until the mugshot arrived from Riverside. No doubt he wanted to see how his wife's composite sketch of the man on the beach compared to Rodney Alcala about whom *everybody* seemed to be calling. It was disconcerting how much this guy was getting around.

Rodney Alcala in the 1970s

When the mugshot arrived and was compared to the composite sketch of the suspect in the Samsoe disappearance, the resemblance was so compelling that Rodney Alcala instantly became a priority of the investigation. In the meantime, Art Droz went home to catch up on much-needed rest while the incoming shift began preparing to focus on Alcala. An hour later Droz called in to the squad room. Turn on the TV, he told them, their suspect Alcala is on *The Dating Game*. They laughed, but Droz wasn't joking.

When Droz had gotten home earlier that evening, he absent-mindedly turned on the television, which was tuned to ABC-TV's *The Dating Game*. As Droz sat down to read his newspaper, he left the TV audio droning on in the background, as three bachelors hidden behind a screen from a pretty bachelorette tried to charm their way into winning a date with her. Droz dropped his newspaper when he heard the host Jim Lange introducing the first contestant bachelor. He couldn't believe what he was hearing: "Bachelor Number One is a successful photographer who got his start when his father found him in the darkroom at the age of thirteen... fully developed. Between takes you might find him skydiving or motorcycling. Please welcome Rodney Alcala."[2]

There he was in a puppy-shit-brown colored polyester disco leisure suit, with matching huge bellbottom pants, shirt unbuttoned at the chest, big white collars winging out over the top of his jacket lapels, a head of long, curly dark hair and a slick bright smile. There was almost a sweetly effeminate edge to his boyish persona as he pitched in a soft voice, sleazy *Three's Company*-cheesy innuendo-laden lines competing with the other two bachelors for a date with the bachelorette.

Alcala appearance on *The Dating Game*

Bachelorette: "Bachelor Number One, I am serving you for dinner..."

Bachelor Number One: "Ohhhh..."

Bachelorette: "What are you called and what do you look like?"

Bachelor Number One: "I am called the banana and I look really good."

Bachelorette: "Can you be a little more descriptive?"

Bachelor Number One: "Peel me."

Here was their suspect in the Robin Samsoe disappearance, a convicted ultra-violent child rapist scheduled to stand trial in two months for a recent rape of a fifteen-year-old girl, and a serial killer suspect; a dating contestant on a network television show! As a cop Droz had seen a lot of weird things in his career, but this was the ultimate. This of course, would earn Rodney Alcala the moniker *"The Dating Game* Killer." Neither the police, nor Droz at the time, knew the worst of it: by the time Alcala appeared on *The Dating Game,* he had killed at least seven women and girls and would be eventually suspected of killing perhaps as many as 130 victims. "This guy is a killing machine," said later a LAPD detective who originally investigated the rape and attempted murder of the eight-year-old victim in 1968.[3]

As police began a surveillance of Alcala, on July 2 the body of Robin Samsoe was found in the San Gabriel foothill of Los Angeles, about a fifty-minute drive from Huntington Beach. In the twelve days that she had been missing, Samsoe's body had been picked apart by animals and began to decompose, mummify and skeletonize in the intense summer heat of the California hills. The corpse was in such a state that no cause of death could be determined, nor whether she had been sexually assaulted. Dental records confirmed that the body was that of Robin Samsoe. The distinctive yellow Schwinn bicycle Robin had been riding was never found, but a thrift shop owner in El Monte, on a direct route between where Alcala lived and where Samsoe's body had been found, later testified that on June 21, he had found a yellow Schwinn bicycle deposited in front of his store when coming to work in the morning and assumed it was a donation. It was quickly sold.[4]

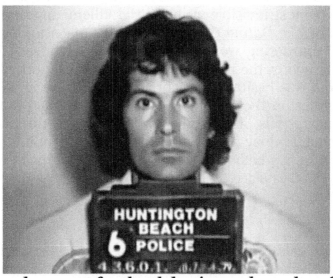

Alcala under arrest for the abduction and murder of Robin Samsoe. 1979.

    Rodney Alcala was arrested early in the morning of July 24, 1979. He would never be free again, but it would take nearly thirty years for the wily Alcala to be conclusively convicted in the murder of Robin Samsoe and a total of six other female victims. And as this is being written, a month ago in September 2016, Alcala was charged with an eighth murder among the over 130 he is suspected in having committed in the United States and Mexico. Possibly one of the most prolific serial killers in the United States, Rodney Alcala was mostly unknown until his story began to emerge in the late 2000s. While familiar to Californians in Orange County throughout his trials, mistrials, appeals and retrials from the 1980s and 1990s, he never entered into national notoriety until the 2000s when he was finally convicted once and for all, and brought to justice

on a number of previously unsolved homicides, primarily because of developments in DNA forensics between the time of
his crimes and arrest and the decades of his appeals in the
Samsoe murder. Strangely, Rodney Alcala is perhaps one of
America's most invisible visible serial killers, appearing in an
episode of *The Dating Game* on network television as he was
brutally murdering women across multiple states. His story
only emerged in the media in dribs and drabs, partly because
the media was hesitant to report fully on a case in which the
final verdict on the defendant was being dragged out in appeals and retrials. As a result, even today we still know very
little about Rodney Alcala or his background, childhood and
adolescence in which the development and making of most serial killers takes place.

***

Rodney Alcala was born on August 23, 1943, as Rodrigo
Jacques Alcala Buquor in San Antonio, Texas, to Raoul Alcala
Buquor, a Spanish language instructor, and Anna Maria
Gutierrez, immigrants from Mexico. He had an older brother,
Raoul, and older sister, Marie Therese, and a younger sister,
Marie Christine. In 1951, when Alcala was eight, his grandmother became ill and decided she wanted to spend her last
years in her home country of Mexico. The entire family up-
rooted from Texas and moved to Mexico to appease her. The
father was not happy with this move, and three years later he
abandoned his family in Mexico, returning to Texas. This suggests that perhaps Alcala was being raised in a powerfully ma-
triarchal household, without a strong father figure in his
childhood, often a factor in the early histories of serial killers,
along with abandonment, which Rodney must have felt when
his father left the family. Other than that, we have no accounts
of Alcala displaying any kind of typical nascent serial killer behavior like setting fires, animal cruelty, or wetting his bed.
There are no accounts of any kind of major trauma, malad-

justment, being subjected to bullying or rejection by his childhood peers, typical in other serial killer biographies. We know almost nothing about his childhood and adolescence other than that he was a good student and got excellent grades.

In that sense, Alcala's case is similar to that of Ted Bundy or Denis Rader "The BTK Killer" whose childhoods, although marginally dysfunctional, were not marked by any obvious instance of trauma, abuse and rejection that characterizes the childhoods of so many serial killers.

Soon after his father left, when Alcala was eleven years old, the family returned to the United States, taking up residence in East Los Angeles. Rodney was enrolled in a Catholic private school, but in 1960, at the age of seventeen, insisted on completing his final semester in a public high school. He was reportedly a popular student, participated in sports and editing the high school yearbook and graduated near the top of his class. (It is widely reported that Alcala has a genius level of 160 IQ.) Absolutely nothing extraordinarily unusual is reported in Alcala's adolescence years.

After graduating high school, Rodney Alcala joined the U.S. Army in 1960 where he was stationed at Fort Bragg, North Carolina, in an elite paratrooper program. His military record is vague and sketchy with the military releasing very little information to the public. He served as a clerk during his four years in the Army but suddenly in 1963 he went AWOL (Absent Without Leave) showing up at his mother's door in California where he apparently exposed himself to one of his sisters.[5] He ended up in a military medical facility in El Toro, California after a "nervous breakdown" and was eventually diagnosed by military doctors as having severe chronic anti-social personality disorder, a disorder known also as sociopathy, a disorder parallel to psychopathy. Unlike the military psychiatric record of serial killer Arthur Shawcross that was made public, we have no details of what exactly Alcala did to garner his diagnosis, which led to him receiving a medical discharge from the military in 1964. It remains a mystery.

Whatever was wrong with Alcala, it did not prevent him from returning to Los Angeles after his discharge and enrolling as a student at UCLA in its Fine Arts program, from which Alcala graduated in 1968 with a Bachelor in Fine Art (B.F.A.) degree, again near the top of his class. Again, there is nothing on the record about Alcala's behavior or any record of offenses in those years he was attending UCLA. Alcala worked part-time as a security guard and seemed to be focused on the art of photography.

That's all we know until Alcala suddenly perpetrated a dramatically brutal crime.

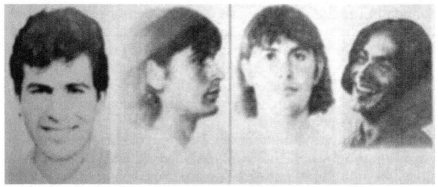

Alcala photos from the 1960s, which appeared in a 1971 FBI Wanted poster.

Most serial killers 'ramp up' to their first murder, escalating from minor offenses like window peeping, exposing themselves, fetish burglaries to rapes and assaults before they commit their first murder. It is rare for a serial killer to suddenly perpetrate a violent crime or murder without an extensive 'testing' period first. Serial killers are often obsessed since childhood with vague violent sexual fantasies and are unsure of exactly how they want to realize their fantasies or how to act upon them. Ted Bundy, for example, described how he would stalk women and disable their cars by letting the air out of the tires with no purpose in mind other than a vague need to see what the women would do. Necrophile serial killer Ed Kemper as an adolescent would peep through women's windows while holding a knife in his hand, but it would be years before he actually abducted and murdered his first victims. Often the first murder occurs as an unintended 'accident' during the commission of a lesser crime like a rape, assault or burglary, with the serial killer afterwards becoming addicted to killing. Serial killers who will go on to perpetrate bold and horrifically elaborate and violent murders, when killing for the first time often are hesitant, cautious, disorganized and restrained in the extent of the violence they unleash on their victims.

Aside from his undisclosed behavior that led to Alcala being medically discharged from the Army in 1964, there are no records of his being arrested by police for any offenses or accounts by witnesses of deviant or unusual behavior. Alcala was twenty-five years old, a UCLA arts grad, just two years short of the average age of twenty-seven that male serial killers commit

their first murder, when he suddenly committed his first crime in 1968, in Los Angeles. It was an unusually violent and bold crime to commit as a first offense. (It is possible of course, that Alcala, as smart as he was, committed multiple crimes prior without being detected or apprehended.)

Tali Shapiro, aged 8, Alacala's first known victim.

Eight-year-old Tali Shapiro was the daughter of a music industry executive. Their home had recently burned down and the family was temporarily residing in the legendary luxury Chateaux Marmont Hotel on Sunset Boulevard in West Hollywood. Tali was attending the Gardner Elementary School a mile to the east of the Marmont. Although there was a nearby bus stop, Tali did not like taking the bus. (Anybody who has ridden a bus in L.A. knows why...it's a zoo.) Instead Tali would leave early and walk east for approximately a half hour along Sunset Boulevard. The "Sunset Strip" of super-sized billboards, comedy clubs and music venues lay to the west of Chateaux Marmont, but to the east, along the route that Tali would walk, Sunset Boulevard was a grim and drab landscape of low rise businesses, thrift shops, liquor stores, small office and studio buildings and parking lots.

That an eight-year-old girl would be allowed to walk alone to school along this terrain of Sunset Boulevard is mind boggling to us today and strange even by the standards of 1968. By then the American urban landscapes had taken a dangerously violent direction. Child abductions and murders were not unheard of. Perhaps Tali's father, as Sixties-era music industry executive, who chose the rock'n'roll star's Chateau Marmont (where John Belushi would fatally overdose in 1982) as a temporary residence, was in a hippie 'take it as it comes everything is groovy' state of mind and thought it was okay for his eight-year-old daughter to walk to school on Sunset Boulevard alone. This was a year before Charlie Manson and his crazed cult of killer-hippies came howling down the Hollywood Hills leaving mutilated bodies of celebrities and wealthy Los Angelians in pools of their own blood on the floors of their upscale homes. We had vague notions of multiple killers, like the Boston Strangler and Harvey Glatman, but we hadn't named them "serial killers," let alone categorized and profiled them. Perhaps Tali's parents somehow felt that 8 o'clock in the morning was a safe time of day. Or perhaps, as Tali would later claim, her parents did not know she chose to walk to school.

On September 25, 1968, as Tali walked to school eastwards on the north side of Sunset Boulevard, Rodney Alcala pulled up in his car beside her. His vehicle would have been in the westbound lane, pointed in the opposite direction but conveniently in the direction of his apartment, about a five minutes' drive west of Chateau Marmont, on De Longpre Avenue, a pleasant palm and blossom lined street of low-rise apartment complexes, which arced downhill below the slopes of Sunset Boulevard, eventually turning in the direction of Santa Monica Boulevard below. It's possible, even likely, that Alcala had seen Tali walking to school on another day and, having fantasized about abducting and raping her, was this morning lying in wait for her, having stalked her.

Alcala offered to give the girl a lift to school. Typically, Tali knew not to get into a car with strangers and turned down Alcala's offer. Alcala simply told her he was friends with her parents and insisted she get in. Also typically, Tali was taught to be respectful and obedient of adults. She got in the car. Alcala then told her they were too early for school and he was going to stop off with her at his apartment and show her "a pretty picture." He then drove her to his apartment on De Longpre Avenue.

Unknown to Alcala, Donald Haines (who was going to contact the Huntington Beach PD eleven years later in the Robin Samsoe case) was driving to work that morning and saw Alcala luring the eight-year-old girl into his car. Haines on a hunch thought something was not right and followed Alcala and observed him leading the girl into his apartment. Haines immediately reported his suspicions to the police, and remarkably the police responded in a timely manner.

By the time LAPD Officer Chris Camacho arrived at the apartment, Alcala had already brutally raped the girl and bashed the back of her head in with an iron bar and then proceeded to crush her throat with it. When Camacho knocked on the door, Alcala popped his head out the window and told him he was taking a shower and would open the door in a couple of minutes. (Other accounts state Alcala calmly came to the door naked with a towel around him and politely asked police to wait for him to "dry off" and get dressed.) Camacho decided to kick the door open after waiting a few minutes. Upon entering the apartment, Camacho immediately saw a small girl lying naked in an enormous pool of blood, a metal bar crushing her throat. His first assumption was that the girl was surely dead, but he heard her moan and lifted the bar from her throat. Camacho had served two tours of duty in the Vietnam War and had seen his share of death and mutilation, but this scene would forever haunt him. He would later comment that he couldn't believe "so much blood could come out of a tiny little girl like that."[6] Tali Shapiro required twenty-seven stiches to close her head wounds and remained unconscious for days in the hospital. When she came to, she remembered being lured by Alcala and being shown a picture in his apartment but not her rape or beating. In 2010, some forty-two years later, she would testify against Alcala in his sentencing hearing after a third re-trial convicted him in the murder of Robin Samsoe and four other women.

Alcala, however, had escaped out the back door in the heat of the moment as the police waited out front for him to open his door. A search of the apartment quickly located Alcala's UCLA student ID card. LAPD homicide detective Steve Hodel (famous today as the author of *Black Dahlia Avenger,* in which he asserts that his father, Dr. George Hodel, is behind the notorious unsolved mutilation murder of Elizabeth Short in 1947) was assigned to the case.[7]

Hodel began a fruitless search for Alcala. His family, his mother, brother and sisters were not cooperating, claiming they had no idea where Rodney, or "Rod" as he was known to people close to him, was located. Former fellow students and professors at UCLA where Alcala had recently earned his Bachelor in Fine Arts, dismissed the idea that a sweet and nice guy like Rod, who "wouldn't hurt a fly" would commit such a violent crime. The case eventually ran out of leads with no trace of Alcala surfacing.

***

After escaping the scene of his rape and attempted murder of Tali Shapiro, Alcala made his way to New York City, arriving there in October 1968 under the assumed name of John Berger. Alcala probably chose the name of the famous art critic John Berger, best known for his bestseller collection of essays on art, published under the title *Ways of Seeing*. No doubt, as a student enrolled in the UCLA Fine Arts program, Alcala would have found Berger's essays on his required reading lists for some of his courses. (Although apparently, Alcala would later also use the alias "John Burger".) In the days before computerized databases and magnetic-stripped and chip-embedded identity cards, holographic marking, integrated photo identification, it was easy to assume and maintain a false identity.

Although the semester had already begun at NYU in New York City's Washington Square-Greenwich Village district, Alcala persuaded the admissions officer to admit him in the undergraduate fine arts and film program. Alcala did not reveal that he already held a BFA from UCLA and probably appeared to the admissions officer as a very talented, well read, perhaps even genius candidate for admission as an adult mature student.

Alcala settled into an East Village apartment funded in New York by part-time jobs and probably with help from his mother and other family members who, throughout his homicidal career, would insist that Rod had been unjustly accused. During the summers, Alcala worked at a girls' summer camp in New Hampshire as an art counselor. He was very popular among the adolescent girls attending camp. It is during this period that Alcala is widely reported as having attended filmmaking courses taught by Roman Polanski at NYU. While it is entirely possible that in between shooting *Rosemary's Baby* in 1967 (in New York), the murder of his wife Sharon Tate by the Manson clan in 1969 in Los Angeles and his making of *Macbeth* in 1971 in Britain, Polanski might have "taken time off" to give a seminar or appear as a special guest speaker/instructor at NYU film school, nothing appears on the record indicating Polanski did so in the years that Alcala was a fugitive in New York. Moreover, Polanski was spending most of his time in London 1968 to 1971. It's an unlikely story that probably originates in Alcala's own claims somewhere and has not been verified (at least to my satisfaction.)

While living in New York, Alcala approached hundreds of women, asking if they would agree to be photographed by him. Many of these photographs would later be found after Alcala's arrest in 1979 for the Robin Samsoe kidnapping-rape-murder. Alcala was handsome, well spoken, had a sense of humor and found it easy to break the ice with women he approached as a stranger using the photographer ruse.

On June 24, 1971, TWA airline hostess Cornelia "Michael" Crilley, aged twenty-three, was moving into a second floor apartment at 427 E. 83rd Street in what was then called Manhattan's "girl belt", a neighborhood where secretaries, airline hostesses and other single working women seemed to gravitate. Throughout the day she was in touch with her mother in Queens, but failed to call as promised later that evening. That evening, her boyfriend, an Assistant DA in New York, accompanied by a police officer, entered the apartment.

TWA hostess Cornelia Crilley's 1971 rape-murder in New York would remain a cold case until 2010.

Crilley was found in the bedroom, lying on her back partially clothed with a stocking tightly tied around her throat and her upper garments stuffed into her mouth. She had been raped and brutally beaten around her face and body and bitten on the breasts, which were covered in the killer's saliva. Despite an intense investigation, the NYPD was unable to develop any leads. It would be only forty years later, in 2011 that Alcala would be charged with Crilley's murder (and of another victim in New York) based on DNA evidence. In 2012 Alcala would plead guilty. But back in 1971, DNA forensics did not exist. It was only in 1987 that a U.S. court first convicted a defendant in Florida charged in a rape case using DNA evidence.

***

After three years of no progress in locating the fugitive in the Talia Shapiro rape, LAPD detective Hodel in July of 1971 asked the FBI to help by distributing a nation-wide wanted notice for Alcala. (Contrary to other sources, Alcala was never put on the FBI's "Ten Most Wanted" list, but merely listed as a fugitive wanted by the FBI for the federal offense of 'unlawful interstate flight' from a California kidnapping and rape charge.[8])

A month later, across the country in New Hampshire, two girls attending summer camp walked over to a nearby post office to mail some letters home. Drawn to the spectacle of ugly mugshots of FBI wanted fugitives displayed in the post office, their eyes were drawn to a picture of a fugitive that remarkably resembled their popular art instructor and counselor at the camp, the handsome and popular John Berger. At first, it was a joke. Everyone knew that Berger was a gentle NYU arts and film program student, living in New York who, for three summers now, had been reliably employed to teach adolescent and teenage girls at the summer camp. He was popular, polite, a great teacher and counselor, and there were no adverse reports of any improper or inappropriate behavior toward any of the girls in his charge.

Alcala worked as a girls' summer camp counselor until the FBI posted a wanted notice in the summer of 1971.

Word of the FBI poster spread, and campers, other counselors and staff rushed to the post office to view the wanted notice. Nobody could believe it, but eventually somebody finally called the FBI. Berger was taken into custody and fingerprinted. They matched the fingerprints the US Army had for Rodney Alcala and those taken from the scene of the Tali Shapiro rape. Detective Hodel flew to the East Coast to take Alcala back to Los Angeles to face charges in the 1968 rape and attempted murder of Tali Shapiro. Hodel would recall asking Alcala why he had raped and attempted to murder an eight-year-old girl, to which Alcala replied as if he really was John Berger, another person, "I don't want to talk about Rod Alcala and what he did."9

When Rodney Alcala was brought to Los Angeles, the Shapiro family were no longer living in California, nor were they understandably inclined to return and relive the attack on their daughter who by now was eleven years old. The prosecution concluded a plea-bargain deal with Alcala: in exchange for a guilty plea, charges of kidnapping, rape and attempted murder were reduced to simple child molestation, with Alcala being given in April 1972 an "indeterminate sentence" of one to ten years which would allow him to be paroled anytime a psychiatric board found that Alcala was "rehabilitated." After serving thirty-four months, prison psychiatrists concluded Alcala was "cured" and he was paroled at the age of 31 in August 1974.

Again, the word "serial killer" had not yet entered into popular usage, nor had the famous FBI serial killer study by Robert Ressler, John Douglas and Ann W. Burgess, which resulted in the categorization and profiling of serial killers as either organized, disorganized or mixed, been completed. The entire notion of repetitive sexual predators compulsively killing again and again was strangely elusive in the forensic psychiatric community, which by the 1960s and 1970s was in a Pollyanna state of mind that psychopaths can be cured with love and therapy and a "second chance" (and a third and fourth...) rather than being executed or incarcerated for life.

Police in California had just rearrested Edmund Kemper, who had been convicted of murdering his grandparents and was paroled as "cured" after a few years of prison therapy to then murder, decapitate and necrophile rape six college coeds, his own mother and her friend. Under psychiatric supervision during his parole in the murder of his grandparents, Kemper's psychiatrists declared him "cured" and recommended that Kemper's record be sealed in order that he could pursue a career in the California Highway Patrol. Unknown to the psychiatrists making this recommendation, Kemper had driven to his psychiatric interview and parked in the hospital lot with the head of one of his victims stowed away in the trunk. On that particular visit, Kemper's psychiatrists afterward wrote:

If I were seeing this patient without having any history available or without getting the history from him, I would think that we're dealing with a very well-adjusted young man who had initiative, intelligence and who was free of any psychiatric illness . . . In effect, we are dealing with two different people when we talk of the 15-year-old boy who committed the murder and of the 23-year-old man we see before us now . . . It is my opinion that he has made a very excellent response to the years of treatment and rehabilitation and I would see no psychiatric reason to consider him to be of any danger to himself or to any member of society.

The second psychiatrist in the Kemper case cheerfully added:

He appears to have made a good recovery from such a tragic and violent split within himself. He appears to be functioning in one piece now directing his feelings towards verbalization, work, sports and not allowing neurotic buildup with himself. Since it may allow him more freedom as an adult to develop his potential, I would consider it reasonable to have a permanent expunction of his juvenile records. I am glad he had recently "expunged" his motorcycle and I would hope that he would do that ("seal it") permanently since this seemed more a threat to his life and health than any threat he is presently to anyone else.[10]

One wonders what the psychiatrists' reports would read like had they looked into Kemper's car trunk instead of lapping up his bullshit.

Arthur Shawcross who was imprisoned for sexually assaulting and murdering two children was paroled on the recommendation of prison psychiatrists who blamed his actions on the horrible things Shawcross witnessed while in combat in Vietnam. He went on to kill twelve women while under psychiatric supervision on parole in Rochester, NY. Shawcross served as a clerk in Vietnam and saw no combat. Anybody with even slight experience in the "real world" would have recognized Shawcross's stories of mutilating Vietnamese women as absurd and physically impossible. Shawcross, for example, claimed he put a fire hose into a female Vietcong guerrilla's vagina, blowing her head off with the high-pressure stream of water. Not only is such a thing physically impossible, but no psychiatrist thought of asking where in the middle of a jungle in Vietnam Shawcross had a fire hose and fire hydrant hookup for a high pressure stream of water. His stories of splitting women between bowed trees, inserting hand grenades into their vaginas, etc., were idiotically cartoon-like juvenile stories—obviously fantasies coming out of a demented sadistically homicidal mind.

The problem is, psychiatrists spend almost their entire life in schools and libraries earning their degree with their head up their ass in theory and with very little exposure to real life, violence or the street. They are largely naïve savants, like sheltered super-intelligent children with psychiatric degrees in their pockets but easily manipulated by a street-smart psychopath like a Kemper, a Shawcross or a Rodney Alcala.

***

In August 1974 Alcala was paroled and moved into his mother's house on 1370 Abajo Drive in Monterey Park, where he set up his darkroom and was hired to shoot portraits in shopping malls in Los Angeles. Nobody bothered to do a background check in a pre-computer network era. Nine weeks after being paroled, on October 13, Alcala saw Julie Johnson in a Huntington Beach shopping mall. She looked like she was eight years old, although in fact she was thirteen. He convinced her to get into his car for a lift to school but then forcibly drove her to a remote bluff at Huntington Beach. There, Julie later testified, he forced her to smoke marijuana and began assaulting her. Before Alcala could get very far, a park ranger interrupted him and arrested Alcala.

The police discounted Julie's story, assuming she had made up the story about being "forced" to smoke marijuana and attacked. But a records check did show that Alcala was on probation for a child rape and attempted murder. Deciding that Julie would not make a believable witness for a rape charge, Alcala was instead charged with violating his terms of probation, and a new charge of providing a minor with narcotics was added. Alcala now served another two-and-a-half years before being again paroled on June 16, 1977. Upon his release, Alcala asked permission to go on a "holiday trip" to Chicago, Washington DC, and New York City. It was granted.

July 1977 was a hot and nasty month in New York. The city was in the grip of the last of the six Son of Sam serial killings. (David Berkowitz would be arrested in August.) Again, the term "serial killer" and the concepts related to it had not entered popular usage or public consciousness. Making matters worse for the embattled city, a blackout on July 13 had unleashed the worst in New Yorkers (unlike the blackout of 1965.) Some 1,616 stores were damaged in looting and rioting, and in the largest mass arrest in New York's history, 3,776 rampaging New Yorkers were arrested. Alcala was trolling for his next victim in the middle of this.

Ellen Jane Hover, age twenty-three, the daughter of Herman Hover, the owner of the legendary Ciro's nightclub in Hollywood where movie stars and celebrities used to gather in the 1950s, had recently moved into an apartment in New York at 686 Third Avenue, near E. 44th Street. Surrounded by glass towers near the United Nations and the Chrysler Building, Hover's apartment was one of those restored typical New York five-story walk-up tenement buildings with fire escapes over-hanging the street. One entered the building from Third Avenue through a door facing the sidewalk leading to a hallway with mailboxes and a staircase; there was no lobby or door-man. Her boyfriend would later state that on the day of the blackout, he saw Hover in the street in front of her apartment chatting with a thin young man with long hair tied into a pony-tail, who suddenly left when he approached. When he asked her who he was, she replied, "Oh, he's alright, he is a photographer."

On July 15, after electricity had been restored to New York, a neighbor recalled that around noon they saw a tall thin man with a ponytail knocking on Hover's door. That evening, Hover failed to appear at a scheduled dinner date and, contrary to her habit, did not call her mother who was living in New York. When Hover failed to surface the next day, the NYPD were called in. A search of her apartment revealed nothing unusual or out of place, but police did note that her diary was laying open on her table, with a notation for July 15: "John Berger, photographer."

Ellen Jane Hover vanished in New York in July 1977. Her body was found eleven months later on the outskirts. Alcala became a suspect early in the investigation but would not be charged until 2011 in her rape-murder.

The family hired a private investigator and offered a $100,000 reward for information on the whereabouts of Ellen Hover. Ads were placed in the *New York Times,* asking anybody with information on a photographer named John Berger to contact the family. Nothing and nobody surfaced. Ellen Hover became one of 17,000 people reported missing in New York City in 1977.

Again, in an era before electronic databases, the internet and electronic record keeping, there was no way for investigators to immediately connect "John Berger" with the alias used by the fugitive and sex offender extradited from New Hampshire in 1971: Rodney Alcala. Moreover, the NYPD was vastly overworked and under budgeted. That year they not only had to contend with the Son of Sam's six serial murders but with an additional extraordinary 1,919 murders (over five murders a day) and 5,272 reported rapes.[11]

It took police five months before "John Berger" was linked to Rodney Alcala. On December 14, 1977, at the request of the FBI and NYPD, Rodney Alcala was interviewed by LAPD about the Ellen Hover disappearance. Alcala was by now employed as a typesetter at the *Los Angeles Times.* He worked days and partied nights as a 'playboy' at singles bars and clubs during the pre-AIDS heyday of the hedonistic 'singles scene' of the 1970s. Well spoken, intelligent, and good looking, Alcala had no problem drawing women to him. He spent his weekends on the beach, photographing mostly young girls and women for his growing portfolio of thousands of photographs.

Surprisingly, Alcala readily admitted that he had met Ellen casually on the day of the blackout in front of her apartment and invited her to model for his photographs. On July 15, he said he took her out of New York to Westchester County and shot a series of photographs of her and afterwards dropped her off back at her apartment on Third Avenue. He stated he had no idea what happened to her after that.

Alcala was asked to take a lie detector test. He refused. With no body or other evidence of foul play, LAPD sent Alcala home. LAPD itself was overworked and was not anxious to pursue a case out of their own jurisdiction. At this point they had their share of serial killings and everyday murders. In fact, between October 1977 and February 1978, ten women were raped, strangled and dumped in the Hollywood Hills in what became known as the Hillside Strangler Murders, perpetrated by the duo serial killer cousins Kenneth Bianchi and Angelo Buono. The term "serial killer" or DNA forensics had still not entered into popular use.

Detective Donald Tasik of the NYPD Missing Persons Squad was obsessed with solving the disappearance of Ellen Hover. After interviewing people in New York who were familiar with Rodney Alcala's preferred photo locations, he repeatedly searched a tract of woodland in Westchester County on the old Rockefeller estate overlooking the Hudson River. On his twenty-fifth search, using a garden hoe in June 1978, he uncovered the body of Ellen Hover buried in a shallow grave. Her body had been well preserved, enough for police to lift a distinct dental impression from a bite mark on her breast. For inexplicable reasons, it wasn't until 2003 that NYPD got a warrant to take a dental impression from Rodney Alcala, already convicted for five subsequent serial murders. When police came to his cell to take a dental impression, Alcala reportedly said, "What took you so long?"

Rodney Alcala would be indicted in 2011 for the two New York murders of Ellen Hover in 1977 and Cornelia "Michael" Crilley in 1971. He pled guilty. But this had only been the tip of the iceberg. We now know that by the time Alcala had been brought in for an interview in December 1977 regarding the disappearance of Ellen Hover in July, he had committed an additional three murders.

***

Having murdered Ellen Hover in New York on July 15, 1977, Alcala then returned to Los Angeles and asked permission from his parole officer in August to visit his family in El Paso, Texas, and in Mexico. On that trip he committed a murder we only learned about in September 2016, a month ago at the time of this writing. When police arrested Alcala in 1979 in the murder of Robin Samsoe, they seized hundreds of photographs of women and children he had kept hidden in a storage locker he rented in Seattle. The subjects in the photos were women and children, in various states of undress and consciousness. Some of the photographs (edited by police) were explicit; others were banal candid and posed photographs. After the third and final retrial of Alcala for Samsoe murder in 2010, Huntington Beach PD and NYPD released to the national media approximately one hundred photographs from Alcala's stash in March 2010, in the hope that other victims might be identified. The photos made a big splash on the internet with headlines like "Eye of a Serial Killer." Since 2010, several dozen women recognized themselves in the photos and came forward reporting that happily they survived their encounter with the serial killer photographer and were unharmed. It was only in 2016 that finally a murder victim was identified from one of the photos.

Christine Ruth Thornton, age twenty-eight, was pregnant and living in San Antonio when Alcala came to visit his family. The two somehow met. A motorcycle enthusiast like Alcala, Thornton ended up going on a road trip with him and never returned. When her mother in San Antonio tried reporting her as missing, police refused to take a missing persons report on the grounds that she was an adult.

In 2013, her sister Kathy Thornton saw the Alcala photos on the internet. One of the photographs was of a pretty twenty-something woman, wearing a yellow top and flip-flops and looking to be about six months pregnant, sitting astride a Kawasaki 500 motorcycle in desert-like scrubland. Recognizing her missing sister, Kathy immediately contacted Huntington Beach PD, but in a bureaucratic snafu was told that her sister had contacted them to report herself as alive and well.[12]

(Left) Christine Ruth Thornton went missing in August 1979 in San Antonio after joining Alcala on a road trip. (Right) This photo of Thornton taken by Alcala perhaps hours before he murdered her was the first photo from thousands that police found in Alcala's possession positively identified as a murder victim. Huntington Beach Police had posted over a hundred photos on the internet in 2010 and Thornton's sister recognized her. Alcala was charged with her murder in September 2016.

Refusing to accept the notion that Christine was alive all these years without contacting her family, the Thorntons now submitted their DNA samples to NAMUS, the National Missing and Unidentified Persons System. In 2015, NAMUS came back with a DNA match to an unidentified murder victim found by ranchers in April 1982 near a dirt track road known as Lombard Road, about six miles north of Interstate 80 and 1.5 miles east of US Highway 30. The corpse was out in the open and wearing the same faded yellow smock and flip flops that the subject in Alcala's photo is wearing. Investigators matched the terrain visible in Alcala's photo to the terrain near the site where Christine Thornton's body was discovered. The back end of a car visible in the photo matched the description of the car Alcala owned at the time, and the same motorcycle that appeared in other photographs Alcala had taken was found disassembled in his storage locker. Alcala had apparently murdered Thornton shortly after taking the photo. In September 2016, Sweetwater County, Wyoming, filed first-degree murder charges against Alcala, but announced in October 2016 that they will not be proceeding with a trial because Alcala is in a prison hospital too ill to travel for trial.[13]

The internet is currently awash with photographs of missing women from the late 1970s, who appear to resemble some of the still unidentified women in the Alcala photos posted by the police, and Alcala is suspected in as many as 130 murders in California, Washington State, Texas, New York, New Hampshire and Mexico. As LAPD detective Steve Hodel later commented, "This guy is a killing machine. I personally believe he has to be good for a lot of crimes between anytime he was out [of prison] and back East."[14]

But much of his killing was still in the future.

That summer, having killed Ellen Hover in New York in July and Christine Thornton in Wyoming in August 1979, Alcala was now on a blood-lust roll. Upon returning to his mother's home in Monterey from his trip, he began escalating in Los Angeles in a frenzy of rape murders in a series that would remain invisible to police for decades.

***

In September 1977, Alcala had been hired as a typesetter at the *Los Angeles Times*. True crime authors and journalists writing about this case comment indignantly how Alcala as a convicted sex-offender could have been hired by the *LA Times* as if somehow the manual work of a typesetter required a sophisticated background check. And again, in the pre-digital network age, background checks were very haphazard if the *LA Times* even decided to run one.

Witnesses who worked with Alcala at the newspaper, later remarked that he was good looking, popular, friendly and a reliable employee who liked to date and party and who would often show them 'art' photographs he took of young women and children, and that some of the pictures, even of the children, had erotic elements to them. That too shocks people that nobody seemed disturbed by Alcala's erotic photos of children. But in 1977, child pornography was a vague notion. It was only in 1977 that the Federal Government focused on the notion of child pornography with the passage of *Protection of Children Against Sexual Exploitation Act*, and it was not until the 1980s that precise definitions of what exactly constituted child pornography were introduced after the 1982 Supreme Court case of *New York vs. Faber* when it was held that child pornography is not protected under the First Amendment right to free speech.[15] As one fellow worker, a woman to whom Alcala proudly showed his photos of young girls and children, later explained, "I was young then. If I had more sophistication, I might have questioned some of the photographs he so proudly displayed in his portfolio. Especially those of young girls. They were naked... I was neither smart enough nor mature enough to realize that I was actually viewing child porn."[16]

Even Alcala's parole officer, Olivia Gomez, would testify later that when Alcala, a convicted violent child rapist, returned from his trip to New York in 1979 and showed her photographs he had taken of children in sexually suggestive poses, she did not take any action, not recognizing the images for what they were.[17]

***

On the weekend of October 8, 1977, in San Francisco, nineteen-year-old Pamela Jean Lambson, an aspiring actress and singer, was seen by store clerks being approached by a ponytailed photographer on Fisherman's Wharf. Her nude, bruised and battered body was found the next day by a jogger in nearby Marin County on a trail on Mount Tamalpais. In 2011, Marin County Sheriff's Department Detective Ryan Petersen would declare, "We're absolutely certain Rodney Alcala is responsible for the murder of Pam Lambson."[18] The Sheriff's Department released a composite sketch from 1977, which hauntingly resembled Alcala, but when no sufficiently intact DNA samples could be taken from the old 1977 evidence, Alcala was not charged in this case.

San Francisco PD composite of the suspect in the 1977 disappearance of Pamela Jean Lambson.

On November 10, 1977, police found eighteen-year-old Jill Barcomb's nude body curled up in the fetal position on a service road between Mulholland Drive and Beverly Ranch Road in the Hollywood Hills. Jill had arrived in Los Angles the previous month in search of opportunity and a new life after a troubled adolescence in the small town of Oneida in upstate New York. She survived the Hollywood streets for five weeks.

Police thought Jill Barcomb had been raped and murdered by the Hillside Strangler in 1977. Alcala was charged in her murder only in 2005.

The crime scene report described her as being found on all fours low to the ground, her knees bent with the tips of her toes on the ground and her inner thighs and knees pointed outward and nude from the waist down. A blood-smeared sweater had been pulled up exposing her breasts and back. Her face was forced so tightly against her chest with the top of her head touching the ground that it appeared to the investigators at the scene as if her neck had been broken. Her buttocks were spread wide with her hand directly under her lacerated anus covered in blood dripping from her vaginal and anal area. There were three separate ligatures tightly knotted around her neck: One of her pant legs, a woman's belt, and two knee-high nylons knotted together. Her face and head were severely battered and covered in blood. Several rocks were found nearby with blood on their points. The area around her body was splattered with blood. She was barefoot but the soles of her feet were clean.

The autopsy report indicated that she was beaten around the face and head so severely that fragments of her skull had been driven into her brain. A bite mark on her right breast was so deep that it nearly severed her nipple, and four blood smears on the breast were left by the killer's hand as he twisted and bit her breast. Her body was covered in similar smears where the killer had, according to the coroner, pinched, squeezed and twisted her flesh. Her body was covered in deep scratches, and as she was being sodomized, the killer clawed with his fingernails in a sadistic frenzy the area between her anus and vagina. Her pubic area was singed from some kind of flaming device being placed between her legs. Virtually all the wounds on her body, the coroner concluded, had been inflicted while she was still alive. As most serial killers who mutilate their victims usually inflict the wounds on the victim *post-mortem* (after death) when they are satisfied that they have complete control of their victim, mutilation like this while the victim was still alive indicated a particularly rare, vicious and highly sadistic offender who needed to experience their victim in terror and pain before killing her. It appeared that the killer would strangle Barcomb until she would lose consciousness and then revive her to begin the process anew until she finally died. This style of controlling a victim and taking them to the edge of death and then bringing them back as a form of torture again indicated an ultra-sadistic offender.

Cause of death was attributed jointly to blunt trauma to the head and strangulation. Blood smears from the killer's hands on her hip and leg indicated that she was carefully posed in that position that she had been found in. Jill Barcomb was subsequently identified through fingerprints taken in a previous juvenile arrest, and her body was returned to Oneida and buried in a closed casket.

That October and November, LAPD were deep in an investigation of a series of murdered women who were raped, battered and strangled and then dumped in the Hollywood Hills. The unknown perpetrator had been dubbed as the "Hillside Strangler," actually two offenders, cousins Kenneth Bianchi and Angelo Buono. One of the Hillside victims was fifteen-year-old Judith Miller of Hollywood who police discovered was acquainted with the recently arrived Jill Barcomb. It was not a far stretch for LAPD to assume that Barcomb's murder was somehow connected to the Hillside Stranglings and Judith Miller's murder. After their arrest, Buono and Bianchi denied that Barcomb was one of their victims, but nobody really paid much attention to their denials. Serial killers for various reasons, only known to them, sometimes deny killing some victims while admitting to having murdered others. Again, in 1977, there was no DNA technology, the word "serial killer" had not entered our popular vocabulary, and the art and science of categorizing and profiling the "signatures" of serial killers had not been developed. It was only in 2005, after LAPD ran DNA tests on the fluids swabbed from Barcomb's rectum back in 1977, that a match to Alcala was returned. Alcala was already in prison and successfully appealing for the third time his conviction in the kidnapping murder of Robin Samsoe when the charge of murdering Jill Barcomb was added.

***

On December 14, 1977, LAPD had questioned Rodney Alcala as a suspect in the disappearance of Ellen Hover in New York City. Two days later, on December 16, LA County Sheriff's Department received a call that twenty-seven-year-old cardiac-case nurse Georgina Wixted had not shown up for work and was not answering her phone.

**Georgina Wixted was found raped and murdered in her
apartment in Malibu in 1977.**

When police entered Apartment 4 on the ground floor of
the Malibu Surf Apartments at 22648 Pacific Coast Highway in
Malibu, they discovered Wixted's nude body covered in bruis-
es, lacerations and blood on the floor of her bedroom. She had
been posed with her legs spread open outward toward the door
with a pair of pantyhose tightly knotted around her throat. A
bloodied claw hammer lay near the body. Bloody bedding,
blood-soaked pillows, and a bloody nightgown were tossed
near her on the floor, and the mattress was soaked in blood.
The toilet, the bathroom sink, the soap and towels were all
covered in blood. The autopsy documented a similar pattern of
injuries similar to Lambson a month earlier. There were massive facial and skull fractures from hammer blows, lacerations
to the genitals. Injuries to her vagina also indicated that an object had been forced into her. Her arm had been dislocated and

fractured. Almost all the wounds had been inflicted while she was still alive. Seminal fluids were found in the mouth, anus and vagina, which is also infrequent in these types of cases. Many sexual serial killers are unable to ejaculate at the scene of their rape-murder until they leave the scene, often taking either pictures or video or totem souvenirs to which they later repeatedly masturbate to ejaculation as they recall what they had done. Only a particularly vicious, confident and experienced serial killer can be comfortable enough to ejaculate while raping and murdering his victim at a crime scene. The kind of serial killer who a day earlier had been questioned by police in the murder of another woman and had the arrogance to tell them that indeed he had been in the company of that woman on the day of her disappearance but had nothing to do with her death.

The night before, Georgina had been at Brennan's Pub in Marina Del Rey with a female friend, who Georgina dropped off afterwards in Santa Monica before heading presumably toward her apartment in Malibu. It is conceivable that she had been seen by her killer in the pub and followed home. Twenty-six years later, on June 5, 2003, after a DNA match, Rodney Alcala would be charged in her rape-murder.

On March 22, 1978, the Hillside Strangler Task Force called on Alcala at his mother's house in Monterey Park to question him as a possible suspect in the series of slayings. Alcala was able to provide satisfactory alibis for his whereabouts during the murders, but the investigators saw some marijuana in the house and Alcala was charged and jailed for about a month on a minor possession charge.

***

In the early hours of June 24, 1978, one of the residents of an apartment complex on 617 Illinois Court in El Segundo went down to the laundry room with several loads to do. He found a naked woman on the concrete floor lying dead face up covered in blood and posed with her legs open facing the entrance. A leather shoelace attached to a sandal was tightly wound around her throat, and her face and head were battered by a piece of wood found on the floor nearby. Her neck was covered in bite marks, there were abrasions and contusions on her breasts and genitals, and she had been viciously raped vaginally and anally. Seminal fluid was recovered from her vagina. Cause of death was attributed to strangulation, and it was determined that her wounds had been inflicted while she had been alive. The blood smearing on the floor indicated that after death she had been dragged face down and turned over and posed face up with her legs open in front of the entry in a way that would "greet" first responders to the scene.

Charlotte Lamb, stalked and murdered by Alcala in 1978.

The victim was identified several days later as thirty-two-year-old Charlotte Lamb, a legal secretary who lived at 2434 Fifth Avenue, Apartment 203 in Santa Monica, five blocks from the beach. As in the murder of Georgina Wixted, a night club/bar was involved in her movements the night of her murder. Her friends told police that they had talked with her last in the evening of June 23 and that she had plans to go to Moody's, a nightclub in Santa Monica. Police would later locate her car parked less than a block away from Moody's. It's likely she was lured from Moody's by Alcala, leaving her car behind and taken by him to the location where she was murdered. Nor is it clear how and why Alcala picked that particular location to take her to, nearly eight miles away in an anonymous cul-de-sac in the middle of El Segundo, if not at random. In 2005, a DNA match led to Alcala being charged in her murder.

***

In September 1978, with at least seven murders in New York, California and Wyoming behind him, Rodney Alcala made an appearance on ABC-TV's *The Dating Game*. (The episode that Huntington Beach PD detective Art Droz saw in June 1979, during the Robin Samsoe disappearance investigation was a rerun.)

Alcala was Bachelor No. 1. One of the other two contestants vying to win a date with the Bachelorette was an aspiring actor Jed Mills, Bachelor No 2. He would later play bit parts on *Laverne & Shirley* and *Baretta*. He is best known for his role as the fat-free yogurt shop owner on *Seinfeld*. Decades later, after he found out whom his opponent on the show was, Mills recalled, "He was quiet, but at the same time he would interrupt and impose when he felt like it. And he was very obnoxious and creepy—he became very unlikable and rude and imposing as though he was trying to intimidate. I wound up not only not liking this guy ... not wanting to be near him ... he got creepier and more negative. He was a standout creepy guy in my life...[He] was kind of good-looking but kind of creepy. He was always looking down and not making eye contact. Every once in awhile he would spit out things then go back to his aloofness. He was a kind of a creepy guy."[19]

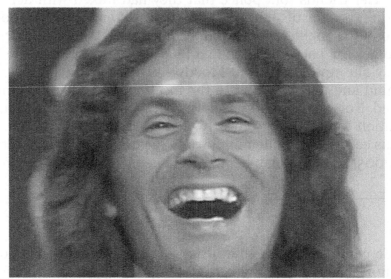

Alcala was Bachelor No. 1 on an episode of *The Dating Game* taped in September 1978. He had murdered at least seven women by the time he made his appearance as a contestant on the nationally broadcast game show.

Armand Cerami, Bachelor No. 3, later recalled, "The people [in the audience] were actually snickering, even low-murmuring boos as to his answers."[20]

"I didn't get he was a killer, but I certainly got that he wasn't one of the boys," Jed Mills concluded.

Cheryl Bradshaw, a drama teacher who was the Bachelorette contestant, initially picked Alcala as the winner. The two of them had won a date for golf lessons and admission to a theme park. Bradshaw later recalled that after the show, as she talked to Alcala backstage, "I started to feel ill. He was acting really creepy. I turned down his offer. I didn't want to see him again."[21]

'Bachelorette' Cheryl Bradshaw on *The Dating Game* picked Alcala as the winner for a date with her.

There was a lot of speculation in the media that perhaps Alcala was "triggered" by Bradshaw's rejection to commit his murders. Obviously he was not, considering the sadistic rage with which he perpetrated the crimes before his appearance on *The Dating Game.* There was a lot of speculation on how Bradshaw perhaps escaped with her life when she refused to go on a date with Alcala. It is unlikely that an offender as intelligent as Alcala would have harmed Bradshaw having been introduced to her on national television. Moreover, as we shall see, Alcala had a tremendous capacity to compartmentalize his sadistic homicidal persona and maintain relationships with women and have girlfriends who to this day, based on their relationships with him, find it hard to reconcile the man they knew with the one accused of committing the series of horrific serial murders. But that is what some serial killers are like, dividing the world between women they may adore and cherish, like their mothers, sisters, wives and daughters, and those they choose to torture, rape, mutilate and kill.

The end of the 1970s, a few years before the AIDS epidemic broke out, were a particularly sexually hedonistic period for Americans, especially for women riding on the crest of the feminist "women's liberation movement." Sexual freedom began to take hold in the counter-culture 'drop out' hippie movement of the 1960s, but by the 1970s middle-class,

139

gainfully employed women embraced it. Thousands of 'singles bars' mushroomed in American cities offering a place for people to meet for anonymous one-night stands. It became a new thing to try after centuries of American puritan culture, and many otherwise "respectable" and conformist women tested with gusto the fruits of this new sexual freedom, not because they necessarily desperately needed to, but because they could. With his psychopath's charisma, Latino dark and handsome classical good looks, and glib sense of humor, Alcala was the perfect one-night-stand. For some women, he would become their last one-night-stand.

The charming and handsome 'singles scene' playboy Rodney Alcala would alternate between courting and dating women and killing and raping them, by a logic only known to him.

Alcala's sexual obsession for girls was overlooked in the 1970s when the notion of child molestation and child pornography had not yet entered public consciousness. Police are still hoping to identify some of the children appearing in photos found in his stash, including this one held in Alcala's arms.

In March 1979, Rodney Alcala met twenty-two-year-old Beth Kelleher at a disco. Instead of raping and killing her, he chose to date her. During his future trials, she would end up testifying for the defence, and thirty years later in an interview, although admitting that she became convinced that he had actually committed the rape-murders he was accused of, she still had feelings for him. She told CBC News, "When you are with Rodney you are totally with Rodney and he focuses on you. You are the one that his attention is on... he is not going to talk about anybody else. He makes you feel like you're the only person he wants to be with... the only person he wants to be with then and there. He treats you really, really well. He treated me well..."

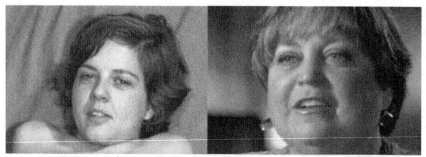

**"It's always nice to be loved." Alcala's girlfriend, Beth
Kelleher, then and today. She dated Alcala in 1979 shortly
before his arrest and appears in one of the photos from
Alcala's stash posted by police on the internet.**

She described how she felt when Alcala phoned her from
prison in 2010: "It was as if thirty years had fallen away. The
voice over the phone was the same voice from thirty years ago
that I had loved... And it was... interesting to have all those
weird feeling coming back... Oh My God, this is fun. He was
still [the] same intelligent smart aleck person that he was to
me over the phone... getting all the trial stuff out of the way it
was as if we were just the same friends we were thirty years
ago..."

When asked in an interview by CBS News *48 Hours* host
Harold Dow how she could have such warm feelings toward
somebody convicted for the rape and murder of children and
women, Kelleher replied, "It's always nice to be loved."22

***

A month before Alcala met Kelleher, on February 13, 1979, he
picked up a fifteen-year-old runaway who was hitchhiking,
Monique Hoyt. She would later state that he appeared to be a
"charming, nice, mild man" and she not only readily got into
his car but spent the night with him in his apartment at his
mother's house. Alcala told her she was pretty enough for a
photo contest, and the next day she agreed to drive out into a

deserted area in the mountains to pose nude for him. At one point, Alcala told her he wanted to shoot some "silly" photos and asked her to pull her t-shirt over her face. As soon as Hoyt complied, Alcala hit her on the head with a tree branch, knocking her semi-unconscious.

Hoyt was a street-smart kid and pretended to remain unconscious as Alcala now raped her vaginally. But when he began sodomizing her, she cried out, at which point Alcala stuffed her t-shirt into her mouth and choked her into unconsciousness. When she came to she realized that her wrists and ankles were now tied. Cleverly, Hoyt began to manipulate Alcala, pretending to beg him, "Don't tell anyone what just happened. Please don't say a word... could I stay at your house? Could we go there together?"

It worked. Instead of killing her, Alcala untied her and they returned to his car. As they drove back into the city, they stopped at a roadside service station to buy a soda. Alcala went to use the restroom while Hoyt told him she'd go wait in the car. The moment Alcala left for the toilet, Hoyt ran across the road to a motel screaming that she had been kidnapped and raped, asking for the police to be called.

Alcala was arrested later that evening at his mother's home. Alcala claimed to the police that Hoyt had agreed to be photographed in "simulated" sex acts and agreed to be tied up as part of the photo session. (Reminiscent of the Harvey Glatman "Glamor Girl Serial Killings" in the 1950s.) Alcala stated that Hoyt inexplicably began to struggle and yell and that he had then choked her into unconsciousness and stuffed her t-shirt in her mouth. Alcala explained, "You're in an unreasoning situation. Your brain and you just don't know what to do... you're not reasoning... you're not thinking... I raped her."

When Alcala was arraigned before a judge, the prosecution asked for a $50,000 bail for the convicted child rapist and sex offender, an inconsequential amount considering his record and the charges laid before him and the fact that he was a suspect at the time in the Hillside serial slayings. The judge incredibly reduced the bail to a mere $10,000 which his mother immediately posted and took her son home to kill at least twice more. His trial was scheduled for September, 1979.

In March, Alcala began dating Beth Kelleher. In April 1979, Alcala gave notice to the *Los Angeles Times* that he'd be leaving to open his own photography business.

***

In June 1979, twenty-one-year-old Jill Parenteau was a supervisor in a data entry company taking business school courses at night. She lived on the second floor, Apartment M at 1921 Peyton Avenue in Burbank. She was close to her family and stayed in almost daily contact with her best friend, Kathy Bowman. On June 14, she did not call Bowman and failed to appear at work. Eventually, one of her co-workers, Janet Jordan, was asked to stop off on her way home and look in on Jill at her apartment. Inside, she caught a glimpse of Jill's body on the floor next to her bed and immediately fled the apartment and called Burbank Police.

Alcala apparently stalked Jill Parenteau before raping and killing her in her Burbank apartment after she returned from a Dodgers game in June 1979.

144

Jill Parenteau was found nude, face up with her legs spread facing the doorway. Her upper torso was propped up by pillows and her head and face were severely battered. Ligature marks were visible around her neck, and torn knotted nylon stockings lay by the side of the bed. A cord from a lamp ran under her body and was wrapped around her throat. Blood-soaked blankets, sheets, a robe, shoes and socks were tossed around the bed. Her jewelry box lay open on the dresser. Police noted that a louvered window with seven glass slats had been removed and the screen cut in an L-pattern, opening an area large enough for the killer to crawl through into the apartment. The lightbulb in the stairwell outside the apartment had been unscrewed. It is likely that the killer had targeted Jill, stalked her and was waiting for her that evening to come home from a Dodgers baseball game she had attended. Police found the torn used ticket, along with the program and her purse on the kitchen table.

The autopsy reported the usual severe blunt trauma to her face and head and strangulation, scratches and bites on her breasts, genitals and body, and deep wounds to the vaginal and rectal areas. Sperm was recovered from her mouth and vagina, but anal smears were inconclusive. The wounds had been all inflicted while the victim was still alive, and the final cause of death was strangulation.

Alcala was now on a killing frenzy, trolling for victims. In those few days before Robin Samsoe was abducted and murdered on June 20, Alcala approached several girls on beaches in the Huntington Beach area, inviting them to be photographed for a "bikini" contest. He asked several for their phone numbers and addresses. Some would rebuff Alcala, others would agree to be photographed. Alcala was trolling like a shark every day along the beaches, no longer encumbered by having to put in a day's work at the *Los Angeles Times* which he had quit in April.

Throughout this, he continued dating Beth Kelleher, who would later recall how, when the trial concluded and the prosecution presented the timeline of Alcala's killings, she looked into her journal where she kept a daily record of what she did, including her dates with Alcala. Kelleher told CBS in 2010, "I'd look and go, 'Ok...saw him on a Monday, killed a girl on a Tuesday, saw me on a Wednesday...' There was no difference in personality... no difference in the things we did, the things we talked about..."

On the morning of June 20, fifteen-year-old Lorraine Werts and her friend Patty Elmendorf were roller-skating on Sunset Beach, near Huntington Beach. When Patty stepped away to use a restroom, Alcala suddenly came up on Lorraine and asked her to pose for a "bikini photo contest." Interested in modeling, she agreed, and Alcala snapped some photos of her. But when he began asking her if she was dating, where she lived and for her phone number, she hesitated. At that point, her friend Patty emerged from the restroom, and the two girls abruptly skated away. A few hours later, Rodney Alcala came upon twelve-year-olds Robin Samsoe and her friend Bridget Wilvert at nearby Huntington Beach.

He obviously had either stalked Robin after she left the beach or had lingered in the vicinity and accidentally encountered Robin on her bike on the way to her ballet classes, lured her into his car and drove her to the San Gabriel mountains where he presumably raped her and then murdered her. When her body was found on July 2, it had been so disfigured by animals and exposed to California July heat, that the coroner could not determine cause of death or whether Samsoe had been sexually assaulted.

On July 24, 1979, Rodney Alcala was arrested. He would never get out again, although he would spend the next thirty years desperately trying to do so.

***

Alcala was tried, convicted, and on June 20, 1980, he was sentenced to death in the abduction and murder of Robin

Samsoe, exactly one year to the day of Robin Samsoe's abduction: a remarkably speedy trial. Aside from witness statements, entered into evidence were Robin's earrings that Alcala put into his Seattle storage locker, along with thousands of photos of women and children he had taken by the time he had become a suspect in her murder. Alcala appealed the sentence.

In the meantime, no sooner had Alcala been sentenced in the Samsoe murder, a month later in July, Burbank Police charged Alcala in the June 14 murder of Jill Parenteau. Police had determined that Alcala had met Parenteau in a bar a few months before her murder and she had rebuffed him. She then began receiving obscene phone calls which would stop whenever Alcala was out of town and resume when he would return. Although DNA testing was still not sufficiently advanced, blood testing had developed by then to the extent that the police claimed that fluids taken at the scene through blood testing matched Alcala with a ten percent certainty. But a year later, prosecution announced that they would not bring Alcala to trial, citing insufficient evidence for a conviction.

In September 1980, Alcala stood trial in the rape of fifteen-year-old Monique Hoyt in Riverside. He was quickly found guilty and sentenced to nine years for the rape.

In 1986, Alcala's appeal of the death sentence in the Robin Samsoe murder was overturned by the California Supreme Court. It held that there were some serious issues with the use of jailhouse informants who claimed Alcala had described to them how he had murdered Samsoe and with the erratic and contradictory witness testimony of a forest service worker, Dana Crappa, who worked in the area where Samsoe's body had been found and claimed she saw Alcala leading Samsoe from his car down the slope where her body was later found. Moreover, Alcala's prior record as a sex offender, according to the decision, had been improperly introduced into the case. Alcala was going to get a new trial in the murder of Robin Samsoe.[23]

Alcala's second trial began on April 23, 1986. On June 20, 1986, coincidentally on the seventh anniversary of Robin Samsoe's murder, a jury sentenced Alcala to death again. Alcala, of course, again appealed his sentence, a process which dragged on until December 31, 1992, when the California Supreme Court rejected his appeal. Everyone now assumed, barring an appeal to the U.S. Supreme Court (should they accept to hear it) that it was 'game over' for Alcala.

Alcala had built himself a comfortable little nest in prison in the fifteen years he had been fighting his conviction. He was outfitted with a color TV and a typewriter to write his appeals. Highly intelligent, he counseled other inmates on their appeals. He became a formidable "jailhouse lawyer." He filed a stream of legal motions against the prison for the right to have dental floss, baby oil, and toothpicks. He enjoyed watching movies on TV, telling a journalist who interviewed him that *When Harry Met Sally* was his favorite recent Hollywood film and that he did not like violent movies.

On December 31, 1992, the California Supreme Court rendered a decision on Alcala's appeal of his second conviction in 1986. His appeal was refused. The Supreme Court ruled that while there were irregularities and errors in the second trial, they were of insufficient significance to impede a fair trial. Alcala's conviction and death sentence were affirmed.

Alcala now wrote a three-hundred-page book, *You, the Jury,* in which he made his case for innocence. The book was published by his older sister Marie Buquor in Fremont, who supported her brother throughout his trials, along with his mother, and retailed for $24.50. Alcala's younger sister, Krissy, also vehemently insisted her brother was innocent, stating, "There's just no evidence that ties [my brother] to this. You think the system of law protects the innocent, but it doesn't work that way."

For the next nine years, Alcala pursued his appeal beyond the California court system into the federal courts. And on March 30, 2001, after twenty-two years of jailhouse lawyering, he finally got a breakthrough. A higher federal court overturned the verdict in the second trial!

Federal Court judge Stephen V. Wilson ruled that Alcala did not receive a fair trial in 1986 because by then the forestry worker witness Dana Crappa had refused to testify, stating she could no longer remember anything. Instead her recorded testimony from the first 1980 trial was entered into evidence. Moreover, the judge ruled that Alcala's attorneys had failed to call witnesses in support of an alibi Alcala was claiming for the time that Robin Samsoe vanished. (Alcala claimed he was applying for a job at Knott's Berry Farm, far from Huntington Beach, on the afternoon of June 20.) Now the prosecution began dragging out the process by appealing the ruling in favor of Alcala. Appeal and counter-appeal would drag on for the next nine years, with Alcala not coming to trial for a third time until January 11, 2010.

The problem for the prosecution was that in a third retrial of Alcala on the Robin Samsoe murder, with problems with witnesses, some dying, some discredited in the appeals, the chance of getting a conviction again was significantly reduced. The possibility that Alcala could go free, and then sue the State of California for wrongful conviction looked very tangible.

But since 1987, a year after Alcala's second trial, DNA forensic evidence became admissible in U.S. courts, and by the 2000s, its sensitivity and accuracy had been highly developed. In 2002 California passed a law allowing for DNA samples to be taken from convicted inmates and submitted into a database of DNA samples from other crime scenes and cold cases. This would be the downfall of Rodney Alcala.

In 2003, the DNA from the Georgia Wixted murder in Malibu matched the DNA taken from Alcala. Then, in 2004, the DNA from Jill Barcomb, originally thought to be a victim of the Hillside Strangler also came back positive to a match with Alcala. In 2005, the murders of Charlotte Lamb found in the laundry room and Jill Parenteau in Burbank returned DNA matches to Alcala.

In order to ensure a conviction in the murder of Robin Samsoe, the District Attorney decided to join all five cases together into one trial. Even if a third jury could not be persuaded on the evidence available in the Samsoe case, the evidence for the other four murders would be presented in the same trial. Now five years of appeals as to whether the cases could be merged into a single trial would drag on until 2010. Alcala also dragged the process by arguing for the right to act as his own attorney and appealed the judge's refusal until finally a higher court affirmed his right to act as his own attorney. Alcala was sixty-five years old, with scraggily shoulder-length grey hair when his trial began on January 5, 2010.

On February 25, 2010, Alcala was convicted in all five murders, including the Robin Samsoe murder, and on March 9, 2010, in the penalty phase, the jury again sentenced him to death.

In 2011, based on DNA matches, the State of New York indicted Alcala in the 1971 murder of Cornelia Crilley and the 1979 murder of Ellen Hover. Alcala pleaded guilty on December 14, 2012, and in January 2013, New York Supreme Court Judge Bonnie Wittner handed down a sentence of 25 years to life in prison for the two murders.

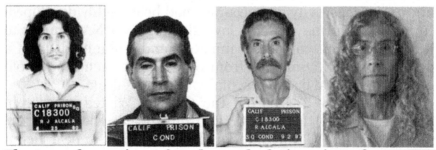

The transformation of Rodney Alcala in prison from 1979 to 2016.

In the meantime, the internet, awash in the photos from Rodney Alcala's locker released by police after his conviction in California in 2010, was trigging numerous calls from women either reporting themselves alive or from family members of women missing from the 1960s and 1970s whom they believed were depicted in the photos. Alcala was also named as a suspect in several murders in Washington State to which he travelled and where he kept his locker and in New Hampshire where he worked summers as a camp counselor. Alcala is a suspect in a total of 130 unsolved homicides in the United States and Mexico between 1968 and 1979, potentially making him America's most prolific serial killer.

But none of the photos published by the police in 2010 had been conclusively linked to any homicide victim until September 2016, when Alcala was charged in Wyoming for the murder of Christine Thornton, seen posing on his motorcycle in one of the photos. On October 28, 2016, as this account was being written, the District Attorney's Office in Wyoming announced that they would not be proceeding with an extradition or trial of the now seventy-three-year-old Alcala because he was too ill to stand trial and was hospitalized in a California prison hospital.

Whether the State of Wyoming is merely using this as an excuse to avoid a costly trial of a defendant already sentenced to death and convicted in seven murders remains to be seen. But unless Alcala expires in the near future in the prison hospital, or even if he remains alive behind bars, I fear and suspect we have not heard the last of The Dating Game Killing Machine.

Chapter 6
CHRISTOPHER WILDER
The Beauty Queen Killer
By JJ Slate

Serial killers take many shapes and forms. Some lie dormant for years, only killing when the desire becomes too great to bear. Others, like Christopher Wilder, go on crazed killing sprees, losing their grip on reality as they attack as many victims as they can in a short period of time. This is a story of a man who completely lost control.

Christopher Bernard Wilder was born in March of 1945 in Sydney, Australia. His father was an U.S. Navy Officer who met his wife in Sydney during World War II. Chris was the first child for the couple, who would eventually go on to have three more sons. He nearly died on the day he was born and was even read his last rites by a priest, but was able to recover. Just two years later, he was pulled out of the family swimming pool as he floated facedown in the water and was revived by a family member. A year after that, he suddenly fell into a coma during a long cross-country trip in his parents' car, but ended up recovering from that brush with death as well.

After the war, the Wilders briefly moved to the United States but soon returned to Australia in the 1960s. When Chris was seventeen years old, he and a few other teens cornered a pretty girl on the beach after school one day. Chris told the girl he'd protect her from the others if she agreed to have sex with him. She agreed and he promptly turned her over to the teens, who gang raped her in the dunes while Chris watched. The other teens were arrested for gang rape and Chris was mandated to undergo psychiatric treatment, which included the use of electric-shock treatment.

After Chris graduated high school, he decided to return to the United States for good in 1969. Working in construction allowed him to pick up odd jobs here and there in the Palm

Beach and Miami, Florida areas. It also afforded him with the beach-bum lifestyle he longed for. He spent nearly all his free time swimming and surfing. In 1979, he teamed up with an entrepreneur and they started their own electrical and construction companies. The investment paid off. In just a few short years, business was booming and Chris found himself raking in millions of dollars. He invested his money back into real estate and spent most of his spare time surfing and taking up a new hobby: racing sports cars. He was friendly and well liked among his community, especially among the ladies. Few people had anything bad to say about Chris Wilder. To outsiders, the thirty-something bachelor seemed to have it all.

Christopher Wilder

But things had already started to spiral out of control for Wilder by the time the money started rolling in. In 1977, he lured the sixteen-year-old daughter of one of his clients into his car and sexually assaulted her. As he clawed at her clothes, the terrified teen lied and screamed she had venereal disease, hoping he'd let her go. Wilder forced her to perform oral sex anyway and then offered to take her home to her parents, who called the police when they heard what happened.

Forced to undergo psychiatric therapy before his trial, a tearful Wilder confessed to a psychologist, "I saw her and something came over me. I knew it was wrong, but I did it anyway."

The psychologist labeled Wilder "psychotic" and wrote in his report that he "is not safe in a structured environment and should be in a resident program geared to his needs."

Wilder wanted to plead guilty and undergo treatment for his "illness," but a judge ordered him to stand trial instead. Unfortunately, a jury acquitted him of all charges soon after, and he walked out of the courtroom a free man.

A few years later, Wilder approached two teenage girls, posing as a world-renowned photographer named David Pierce. He told them he was looking for fresh new faces for a photo shoot he was conducting and offered to make them famous if they would agree to pose for him. Eventually one of the girls went home, leaving her friend alone with the sexual predator. Wilder took her to get pizza for lunch, but she immediately started to feel drowsy after eating and later told police she suspected she'd been drugged. After lunch, she found herself in the cab of his pickup truck where the man she'd just met raped her. The girl managed to escape, but she wrote down the license plate of the truck and police picked up Wilder the next day.

This time, Wilder was allowed to plead guilty to attempted sexual battery and was given five years probation and remanded to undergo psychological counseling with a sex therapist. He accepted his punishment and kept up with his parole officer and visited his therapist regularly, who believed he was making good progress. During his therapy sessions, he confessed he had fantasies of enslaving women and administering electric shocks to them while he used them as his own personal sex slaves, but he insisted the therapy helped him feel better. He also admitted to experiencing "black outs" where he would disappear for a few days and claim not to know where he'd gone or what he had done. Still, he insisted these gaps in his memory were becoming less and less frequent and his therapy was working.

What neither the parole officer or his sex therapist knew was that Wilder was still out prowling for young victims. He kept up his ruse as a photographer, even carrying a camera with him at all times and passing out fake business cards whenever he encountered a pretty face.

In December of 1982, Wilder flew to Australia for a visit with his family. While there, he kidnapped two fifteen-year-old girls and drove them to a park where he forced them to strip naked and pose for his camera. He then tied them up and drove them to a hotel room where the girls managed to escape. Police were able to trace the vehicle back to Wilder and arrested him the next day.

Charged with indecent assault and kidnapping, police revoked Wilder's passport and told him he'd need to remain in the country until his court date, which was scheduled for May, five months later. His parents bailed him out of jail and police returned his passport after hearing his claims he'd lose hundreds of thousands of dollars in contracts if he wasn't allowed to return to the U.S. to conduct his business. He was free to go.

Chris Wilder would never again return to Australia, and he never stood trial for his crimes there.

He's Come Undone

Just over a year passed before Wilder struck again, but the police wouldn't be able to fit the puzzle pieces together until it was too late.

On February 26, 1986, an aspiring young model and past Miss Florida contestant named Rosario Gonzalez disappeared from her place of employment at the Miami Grand Prix. It wasn't until weeks later that police realized Wilder had been at the track that same day—he'd been racing a Porsche 911 in the IMSA-GTU series.

Rosario Gonzalez (left) and Beth Kenyon (right).

A week later, Wilder's ex-girlfriend, a Miss Florida finalist and crowned Orange Bowl Princess, Beth Kenyon, also went missing. According to her phone records, one of the last people she spoke to was none other than Chris Wilder. When police approached him, he claimed he hadn't seen Beth in nearly a month. Even after a man at a gas station identified Wilder as the man he saw Beth with the day she disappeared, he stuck to his guns. Soon after, police would find Beth's Chrysler parked at the Miami International Airport.

Beth's family hired a private investigator to dig into Wilder's past. While they knew him from when he and Beth dated, and even though they'd liked him, they strongly felt he was connected to their daughter's disappearance. Once Beth's family learned of Wilder's violent history and his connection to Rosario Gonzalez, who was still missing, they were able to persuade the FBI to get involved. On March 16, the *Miami Herald* ran a story referencing how police wanted to speak to a local racecar driver about the disappearances of Rosario Gonzalez and Beth Kenyon. While he wasn't named specifically, Wilder knew his time had run out. Two days later, he boarded his three dogs in a kennel, packed a suitcase, withdrew approximately $50,000 from his bank account, and locked up his home for good. He backed his newly purchased '73 Chrysler New Yorker out of his driveway with an interesting choice of tools inside: a loaded .357 revolver, handcuffs, duct tape, rope, a sleeping bag, and a modified electrical cord that had been slit down the middle with a special switch attached to it. Then, Wilder disappeared into the night.

The Killing Spree Begins

On Sunday, March 18, 1984, twenty-one-year-old Terry Ferguson drove to the Merritt Square Mall in Merritt Island, Florida, to do some shopping. Ten hours later, when she still hadn't returned, her father drove out to the mall to look for her. He found her locked car parked in the J.C. Penney's parking lot. Inside were the clothes she'd been wearing when she left home that day. Police couldn't find any witnesses who'd seen Terry leave the mall, but they did find one woman who'd seen her talking to a man with sandy brown hair and a beard with a camera slung around his shoulder. She later picked Chris Wilder's photo out of an FBI line up as the man she'd seen.

Less than a week later, Terry's body was discovered facedown in a Polk County creek, over an hour's drive west from where her car was found. She was dressed in a pink blouse and Calvin Klein jeans, and the diamond promise ring her boyfriend had given her was still around her left ring finger. The coroner estimated she'd been dead for at least three or four days.

On Tuesday, March 20, nineteen-year-old Linda Grover was kidnapped at the Governor's Square Mall in Tallahassee, Florida. Unlike the others, Linda lived to tell her story.

She later told police she'd been approached by a bearded man in a blue pinstriped suit with a camera around his shoulder. He had an Australian accent and told her he was a photographer looking for a new "fresh face" for a magazine shoot he was doing. Flattered, but uneasy, Linda told the man she was not interested, but he convinced her to walk over to his car to look at his work. Standing outside his older model Chrysler sedan, he showed her various magazine and photo layouts. When Linda politely declined his offer again, the man punched her so hard in the stomach it nearly made her tumble to the ground. Before she could regain her footing, he hit her again in the face and pushed her into his car.

The man drove her to a wooded area where he put duct tape over her mouth and tied her up before putting her in the trunk of his car. She later told police they drove for what seemed like hours while she lay terrified in the trunk, wondering what would happen to her. At some point, he stopped the car and pulled her out of the trunk, at which point she noticed it was nighttime. He pulled a sleeping bag over her head, zipped it shut and threw her into the backseat of his car.

The next time they stopped, the man dragged her (still in the sleeping bag) out of the car and carried her into a motel room. For the next several hours, she was sexually abused and tortured. He attached an electrical cord to her legs and administered painful electrical shocks to her while he subjected her to various sex acts. At one point, with her hands and legs restrained, the man had taken out a tube of superglue and dripped gobs of the adhesive onto her eyelids, even using a hair dryer to harden the glue. With her eyes caked with dried superglue, she could barely see through the slits.

At some point, she managed to break free from her restraints and the two struggled. The man picked up the hair dryer again and crashed it down on her forehead, splitting open her scalp but failing to knock her unconscious. She made it to the bathroom, where she locked the door behind her and began screaming bloody murder and banging on the walls.

Panicked, the man gathered up all of his and her belongings, including her clothes, and fled into the night. Linda stopped screaming and peeked her head out of the bathroom to see she was now alone in the motel room. She wrapped herself in a sheet and made her way down to the hotel lobby, where she told the night manager to call the police.

Linda was able to pick Chris Wilder out of another FBI line-up and the case was pushed to the top of the list. The hunt was on.

At some point the next morning, Wilder returned to the same mall parking lot in Tallahassee where he'd abducted Linda. Using the keys he'd taken from the motel room, he drove her car to a bar a few blocks away, where he sat for a while after ordering himself a drink. He later moved the car to the parking lot of a bank and ditched it before leaving town in his white Chrysler.

Later that day, Wednesday, March 21, Wilder approached twenty-three-year-old Terry Walden while she was walking across campus at Lamar University in Beaumont, Texas, where she was a nursing student. He asked her if she'd be interested in modeling. Terry turned him down, but he kept following her, asking her to come over to his car where he could show her some samples of his work. She again told him no, calling him a pervert, and the man only left her alone when her friend approached them in the parking lot. Terry told her husband about the creepy man when she came home that evening.

Two days later, Terry failed to pick her daughter up from day care after her classes ended, and her husband immediately reported her missing to the police. The family and the police searched for Terry and her missing 1981 orange Mercury Cougar all weekend, but it wouldn't be until Monday when her body was found floating facedown in a canal.

Terry had been stabbed three times in the chest with a fillet-type knife that had to have been at least eight to ten inches long. She'd been stabbed with such force that the knife had even poked through her back and fractured two of her ribs. Her heart, lungs, and pulmonary artery had all been punctured during the stabbing. The coroner also found adhesive marks around her mouth, indicating her killer had put duct tape over her mouth, but had removed it at some point. Investigators also found rope nearby, confirming their theory she'd been tied up at some point. The killer had removed the rope and duct tape before throwing her into the canal.

Terry's orange Cougar was still missing, and police put out an all-points bulletin (APB) to find the missing vehicle and, hopefully, the suspect in her killing. One day later, the FBI would connect the dots and add Chris Wilder's cream-colored Chrysler to that same bulletin.

On Friday, April 6, the Chrysler was located in downtown Beaumont with its license plates removed. After securing the vehicle, police found bloodstains inside but no murder weapons. They believed Wilder had likely ditched the car on the same day of Terry's murder and left town in her orange Cougar. But that had been fourteen days ago. Where had he headed next?

On Sunday, March 25, just two days after killing Terry Walden, twenty-one-year-old Suzanne Logan disappeared from the parking lot of Penn Square Mall in Oklahoma City. When she failed to pick up her husband later that day after his shift at the Save-A-Stop, he reported her missing to police. Without any witnesses or evidence, police deemed Suzanne a probable runaway and did not register her in the missing persons database.

Unbeknownst to her husband and family, Suzanne had been kidnapped in broad daylight by Chris Wilder. He drove straight from Oklahoma City to Newton, Kansas, about 180 miles away, where he checked into a room in the I-35 Inn. He was gone before the sun came up the next morning. When the maid entered the room to change the sheets and tidy up, she found clippings of blonde hair in the trashcan, but nothing else out of the ordinary.

Later that day, a fisherman discovered the dead body of a woman near the shore of Milford Reservoir. A coroner determined she'd been killed less than an hour before her body was found. She'd been raped and tortured. Her killer had used a knife to kill her, plunging it deep into her chest. Her blonde hair had been crudely cut from her head and her pubic hair was shaved.

Sadly, because she had never been entered into the missing person's database, and her body had been discovered so far away from where she'd last been seen, Suzanne remained a Jane Doe for ten days until police were able to make the connection. And by then, of course, Chris Wilder was long gone.

On Thursday, March 29, Wilder abducted eighteen-year-old Sheryl Bonaventura at the Mesa Mall in Grand Junction, Colorado. Her parents found her yellow Mazda RX-7 parked in the parking lot later that day and filed a missing persons report. Local police took the report seriously and immediately began an investigation because they had seen an alert go out to be on the look out for Christopher Wilder. Witnesses from the mall told police they had seen a man matching the suspect's description that day, and he'd even approached several young girls with his ruse of being a photographer.

The FBI continued to track Wilder's whereabouts by following the missing persons reports and using credit card transactions, but they could never seem to be in the same location at the same time. They were always one or two steps behind, and the bodies were stacking up.

Sheryl and Wilder were spotted with another unidentified woman at a diner in Silverton, Colorado, about 100 miles south of Grand Junction. Sheryl struck up a conversation with one of the waitresses there and told her that she and her friend were traveling to Durango to visit some relatives before heading to Las Vegas, where they were going to work as models.

Somewhere in the next day or so, Wilder shot and stabbed Sheryl to death and disposed of her nude body on the side of the road near the Kanab River in Utah. She was not found until May 3.

On Sunday, April Fool's Day, Wilder stalked and abducted seventeen-year-old Michelle Korfman after she'd participated in a *Seventeen* cover modeling competition at the Meadows Mall in Las Vegas.

By the next day, police were hot on their trail. They had

several witnesses from the competition who'd claimed a man had approached them asking them to model for a presentation he was working on. All of them had turned him down except Michelle. One witness watched them walk toward the parking lot together. She was able to point him out in a photo line-up.

Michelle's chocolate-brown Camaro was missing from the parking lot and police added the vehicle to their APB still out for Terry Walden's orange Mercury. Michelle's Camaro was soon located in a rear parking lot of Caesar's Palace by a guest who recognized it from a news report. The doors were locked and the trunk was empty. Michelle was nowhere to be found.

On April 3, Wilder made it to Lomita, California, a town forty miles south of Los Angeles. The next day, the *Grand Junction Daily Sentinel* ran a story about the disappearance of still-missing Sheryl Bonaventura. The article named Chris Wilder as a suspect in her disappearance, as well as in six other murder-abductions.

April 4 was also the day Wilder met sixteen-year-old Tina Risico. He watched as she filled out an application for a job at a local delicatessen in Torrance, California. When she was finished, he asked her if she'd be interested in making money as a model and offered to pay her $100 if she'd accompany him to a photo shoot that day. Tina agreed and the two hopped into the stolen orange Cougar. Wilder drove Tina to a secluded beach near Santa Monica, where he shot a roll of film while she posed for him in the sand.

When Tina told him she really needed to head back home, Wilder pulled a gun on her and tied her up. He drove her to Prescott, Arizona, where he checked into a Motel 6. That night, he sexually abused and tortured Tina.

Tina's parents knew she'd gone to the deli to apply for a job, and when she hadn't come home that night, they went straight to the police. The manager at the deli told investigators he'd seen a man approach her as she was leaving. He described the man as having light brown hair and a beard, with a camera slung around his neck. A few days later, when police

showed him a photograph of Chris Wilder, he positively identified him as the man who'd left with Tina.

At this point, it seemed everyone was looking for the
"Beauty Queen Killer," as the media had now dubbed him.
Tips were coming in from everywhere and police could hardly
keep up. They worried he might flee to Mexico. They knew
they had a dangerous serial killer on the loose, and he wasn't
going to stop killing until they caught him. On April 7, papers
announced the Beauty Queen Killer had made it to the FBI's
ten most wanted fugitives list.

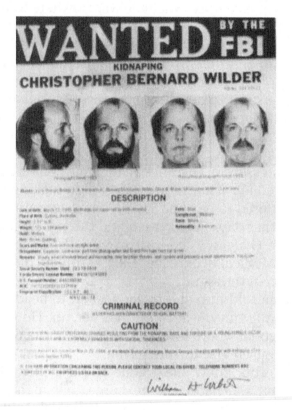

Days later, the owner of a dating service called the FBI. He
told them he recognized Chris Wilder as one of the men who'd
used his service and created his own video dating profile,

which he turned over to authorities.

The recording was made just three years earlier and showed a calm, attractive man talking about what he was looking for in a mate. "My objective is hopefully meeting the right person," he said to the camera. "Somebody with depth. Somebody that might have some background. Somebody that I can feel comfortable with. Quite frankly, I am seeking a long-term relationship that might one day become permanent. Right at this moment, I am not seeking marriage, but someday I will." The FBI immediately released the tape to the media and warned the public to stay away from this man.

"We are doing this so young girls can know what he looks like and what he sounds like," FBI agent Dennis Wrich explained to the media. "And God forbid, if he approaches you, don't go near the guy."

Meanwhile, Wilder had been driving across the country with his latest captive, Tina Risico. He'd apparently decided he liked her and thought she might be useful to him in some way. On April 10, in Merrillville, Indiana, sixteen-year-old Dawnette Wilt stopped in at a store in the mall to fill out a job application. A girl walked up to her as she finished filling it out and introduced herself as Tina, an employee. She asked Dawnette to wait for a moment while she went to get the manager.

Tina disappeared and then reappeared with Chris Wilder, who introduced himself as the manager. He told the teen he was looking for someone to model clothes in the shop and asked her if she'd be willing to accompany him to his car to fill out some additional paperwork.

As they stood outside the stolen Cougar, Wilder pulled a gun on Dawnette and pushed her into the backseat of the vehicle. Tina drove while Wilder tied Dawnette up, covered her eyes and mouth with duct tape, and molested her.

They spent the night in a motel room in Wauseon, Ohio, where Dawnette was subjected to more sexual torture, including electric shock torture. He warned both girls if either of them tried to escape, he'd kill them both.

The next day, the trio arrived in Niagara Falls, where Tina and Wilder took in the sights together, with Dawnette bound and blindfolded with duct tape in the backseat of the vehicle. They checked into another hotel that same night, where the sexual sadism and electric shock torture continued on Dawnette.

The next morning, Wilder drove the two girls to a small town just south of Rochester, New York, where he pulled over near a wooded area. He forced Dawnette out of the car and into the woods, where he removed the binds from her hands and legs, but left the duct tape covering her eyes. He forced her down to her knees and tied her arms again before attempting to suffocate her.

Dawnette pulled her head free and Wilder retaliated by plunging the knife he'd used on Terry Walden and Suzanne Logan deep into her chest and twice into her back. He then turned to walk back toward the car, callously leaving Dawnette to die.

But, miraculously, Dawnette did not die. She played dead until she knew Wilder had driven off and then struggled out of her binds and removed the duct tape from her eyes. Bleeding profusely, she stumbled back to the road and flagged down a motorist who was shocked to see a young girl covered in so much blood walking out of the forest. Once Dawnette was stable enough, she told police all about the last few days she'd spent with the serial killer and the teen who'd helped him kidnap her. She also told them how she'd heard them talk about possibly crossing the border into Canada.

Meanwhile, Wilder and Tina had made their way back to Rochester and were on the hunt for a new vehicle. He knew he'd never make it into Canada in the orange Mercury Cougar he'd stolen from Terry Walden. At a mall near Victor, New York, he pointed out a pretty woman stepping out of her gold Pontiac Trans-Am. Tina quickly approached the woman and asked her to come look at something near her car. When thirty-three-year-old Beth Dodge approached the orange Cougar, Wilder pulled a gun on her and forced her into the vehicle. He grabbed the keys from the woman's hand and handed them to Tina, telling her to follow behind them.

Wilder drove toward a secluded area near a gravel pit and stopped the car suddenly. He pulled Beth from the car and shot her in the back, between her shoulder blades. She died instantly. The Cougar was left abandoned near her body, and Wilder and Tina took off in the new Trans-Am.

Even though Beth's body was discovered just hours later and police quickly made the connection with Chris Wilder and the abandoned Cougar, he still somehow managed to elude police as he drove the stolen Trans-Am from New York to Logan International Airport in Boston. Wilder told Tina he didn't want her to be with him when he died.

Though she'd complied with his wishes for the past week, Tina was truly terrified of Wilder. She believed he could and would kill her at any moment if she disobeyed him. When he told her he was buying her a one-way plane ticket back to Los Angeles and handed her a wad of cash, she didn't really believe him. Even right up until the moment she stepped on the plane, she didn't believe she was going to escape him. When the door to the plane sealed shut, she finally realized she was out from under his grasp. She couldn't believe it.

The End of the Road
Wilder was spotted leaving Boston on Friday, April 13, driving north toward Beverly, Massachusetts. He pulled over after seeing a stranded motorist along the side of the road that morning. He offered nineteen-year-old Carol Hilbert a ride to the nearest gas station, which she graciously accepted. But when they passed a gas station without slowing and she asked him to stop, Wilder pulled a gun on her and told her to keep her mouth shut. At the next exit, Carol opened her door and rolled out of the vehicle to safety while her captor stepped on the gas and sped away.

By noon, he'd made it to New Hampshire and was closing in on the Canadian border. Twelve miles from the border, in a town called Colebrook, Wilder stopped for gas. As he filled up, two state troopers pulled into the station after recognizing the stolen Trans-Am.

They approached him and Wilder immediately seemed to know they were police, even though they were driving an unmarked car and dressed in street clothes. Wilder dove inside his driver's side door, grabbing his gun from the glove compartment.

Without thinking, one of the troopers threw himself on top of the suspect's back in an attempt to squeeze his arms down in a bear hug and keep the gun from going off. They struggled a bit, but Wilder was able to maneuver the gun to point inward and the gun went off. The bullet went straight through his chest, out his back, and into the trooper's chest. Another shot rang out and Wilder went limp in the trooper's arms. The second bullet went straight through Wilder's heart, killing him instantly.

The Aftermath

After Chris Wilder took his own life, the families of the victims struggled with what might happen next. Many of them were angry the killer was able to escape this life without punishment. They'd anticipated a lengthy trial, and many of those affected by his heinous crimes had longed to be there when he was given a lethal injection. Some of the families were still looking for their missing loved ones.

On May 3, a family driving through Utah discovered the nude body of Sheryl Bonaventura. Just a week later, two bicyclists discovered a badly decomposed body in Los Angeles County. A month went by before it was identified as Michelle Korfman's body.

Unfortunately, the families of Rosario Gonzalez and Beth Kenyon have not been able to find closure. The bodies of their daughters have never been found, despite numerous searches of Wilder's properties.

In addition to the eight known victims killed during his killing spree in the 1980s, Chris Wilder is suspected of the murders of at least eight other women. One of those cases, the murder of two fifteen-year-old girls, Marianne Schmidt and Christine Sharrock, remains one of the most infamous unsolved cases in the history of Australia. Wilder would have been twenty years old at the time of the murders, known as the Wanda Beach Murders, in Sydney, Australia. The two girls disappeared on a deserted beach one afternoon in January of 1965. Their bodies were discovered the next day by a man walking through the dunes. Marianne's throat had been slit and she was stabbed several times. It appeared to investigators on the scene that her friend, Christine, had probably fled after watching her friend's attack, but the killer had caught up to her, dragged her back, and murdered her next to her friend. Christine died from a hard blow to the back of her head. Her skull had been fractured, and the killer had then stabbed her several times. Neither girl appeared to have been raped, but police did find semen on both girls. Unfortunately, that DNA sample has since gone missing from the laboratory, where it had been stored for decades. In 2012, trace DNA testing from the shorts of one of the victims was identified as a male profile, but nothing else could be determined at that time.

Chris Wilder is also the suspect in several other murders in Florida, including that of Mary Opitz, a seventeen-year-old last seen walking towards a parking lot in January of 1981, and Mary Hare, another seventeen-year-old who disappeared a month later from the same parking lot. Mary Hare's body was found in June of that year, dead from stab wounds, but Mary Opitz was never found.

Several other aspiring models disappeared in Florida in the early 1980s and were later found dead, and though police suspect Chris Wilder may have played a role in their killings, they have failed to connect him to these crimes. It is likely their families will never receive closure.

For those women who survived the brutal nature of Chris Wilder's attacks, one thing is for certain. They looked straight into the piercing blue eyes of a monster that day. And they are beyond lucky to be alive today.

Chapter 7
HENRY LUCAS AND OTTIS TOOLE
"Hands of Death"
By Michael Newton

Henry Lee Lucas was always unlucky in love. His second fling at marriage—albeit without any formal vows or license—paired him with the 15-year-old niece of an acquaintance, Frieda Lorraine Powell, known for some reason never clarified as "Becky." In the early months of 1982, when he was thrice her age, the mismatched couple roamed from Florida to California, dodging child protection workers who sought Powell for escaping from an orphans' home. Henry facilitated that escape, moon-eyed with lust, but got more than he'd bargained for.

By May, surviving like a pair of human limpets, they latched onto Jack and O'Bere Smart in Hemet, California, freeloading until the Smarts proposed a plan: Henry and Becky would depart for Ringgold, Texas, and take care of O'Bere's 82-year-old mother, Kate Rich. They moved in with Rich on May 14, but local kin ousted the couple four days later, after Becky cashed two forged $50 checks on Rich's bank account. Next, they joined a small religious sect in Stoneburg, led by Rueben Moore—the All People's House of Prayer—but left on August 23, hitchhiking eastward. Lucas returned the next day, despondent, telling Moore Becky had "run off" with some nameless trucker.

Kate Rich vanished from Ringgold on September 16, and police feared the worst when Lucas left Stoneburg the following day. Officers found his abandoned car in Needles, California, on September 21. He drifted back to Texas, where someone torched Kate Rich's modest home on October 17, and deputies jailed Lucas on a fugitive warrant from Maryland, then released him when authorities there dropped a pending auto-theft charge. Lucas endured surveillance until June 4, 1983, when he told Moore that he was leaving town to find Becky and Rich, wherever they might be, to "clear his name." He left a pistol with Moore for safekeeping and rolled out of town in a rusty old junker, which died in San Juan, New Mexico. Moore made the round-trip to bring him back, and officers were waiting on June 15 to jail Henry for possession of a firearm, banned in Texas for ex-convicts.

Lucas sat in jail for four days, resisting every ploy of Montague County Sheriff Bill "Hound Dog" Conway until the night of June 18. That evening, he called jailer Joe Don Weaver, first complaining of a bright light in his cell, then clinging to the bars and almost whispering, "Joe Don, I done some bad things."

His first confession was a note scrawled with pencil and paper provided by Weaver. It read: "To Whom It May Concern, I, Henry Lee Lucas, to try to clear this matter up, I killed Kate Rich on September [*sic*] last year. I have tried to get help so long and no one will help. I have killed for the past 10 years and no one will believe it." Elaborating for the record, he described inviting Rich to church, then killing her, raping her corpse, dissecting it and burning it in a stove at the All People's House of Prayer. Police found bone fragments inside the stove and plucked eyeglasses from the yard nearby, identified by Rich's daughters as belonging to their mother.

Next, Lucas briefed interrogators on the final hours of Becky Powell. While camping on the night of August 23, she'd quarreled with Lucas over "finding Jesus" and had slapped him. Henry stabbed her, then dismembered her, and scattered her remains over the desert, coming back some two weeks later to conceal the parts in several shallow graves. He led investigators to the site, and they retrieved the skeletal remains of a Caucasian female matching Powell's height and age. Since DNA profiling was unknown in U.S. courts, no positive I.D. was possible, but Henry faced a second murder charge in any case.

It should have been enough to earn Lucas a seat in the electric chair at Huntsville Prison, but he wasn't finished talking yet.

***

In fact, as it turned out, there had been many "bad things."

America's most controversial murderer was born August 23, 1936, at Blacksburg, Virginia. The Lucas family home was a two-room, dirt-floor cabin in the woods outside town, where Henry's alcoholic parents brewed bootleg whiskey, his mother doing occasional turns as the neighborhood prostitute. Viola Lucas ran her family with a rod of iron, while husband Anderson Lucas—dubbed "No Legs" after his drunken encounter with a freight train—dragged himself around the house and tried to drown his personal humiliation in a nonstop flow of liquor.

The Lucas brood consisted of nine children, several farmed out to relatives, institutions, and foster homes over the years. Henry was one of those "lucky" enough to remain with his parents, and mother Viola seems to have hated him from birth, seizing every opportunity to make his life a living hell on Earth.

Both Anderson and Henry were the targets of her violent outbursts, man and boy alike enduring wicked beatings, forced to witness the parade of strangers who dropped by to share Viola's bed. When she shot one of them, post-coitus, blood sprayed Henry's face. Sickened by one such episode, Anderson Lucas dragged himself outside to spend a night in the snow, contracting a fatal case of pneumonia. Henry survived, after a fashion, but his mother's cruelty seemed to know no bounds.

When Lucas entered school, in 1943, she curled his stringy hair in ringlets, dressed him as a girl, and sent him off to class that way. Barefoot until a kindly teacher bought him shoes, Henry was beaten at home for accepting the gift. If Henry found a pet, his mother killed it, and he came to understand that life—like sex—was cheap. When Henry gashed his left eye, reportedly while "playing with a knife," Viola let him suffer until doctors had to surgically remove the withered orb, replacing it with glass. On another occasion, after Viola beat him with a piece of lumber, Henry lay semi-conscious for three days before "uncle" Bernie Dowdie—Viola's live-in lover—took him to a local hospital for treatment. Bernie also introduced the boy to bestiality, teaching Henry to kill various animals after raping and torturing them. Already doomed, Henry quit school in fifth grade and never returned.

At age 15, anxious to try sex with a human being, Lucas picked up a girl near Lynchburg, strangled her when she resisted his clumsy advances, and buried her corpse in the woods near Harrisburg. The March 1951 disappearance of 17-year-old Laura Burnley remained unsolved for three decades, until Lucas confessed to the murder in 1983.

In 1952, police nabbed Henry and two of his half-brothers for burglary. Sentenced to the Beaumont Training School for Boys, Lucas escaped from the Christiansburg County jail and then surrendered to serve his time. Beaumont authorities recorded his IQ as 76 ("borderline deficiency") and logged his relationship "of a sexual nature" with a black inmate, further noting erratic behavior that shifted suddenly from friendly to violent. Released in 1953, he settled briefly with half-sister Nora Crawford, who accused him of raping her 12-year-old daughter.

In June 1954, a series of burglaries around Richmond earned Lucas a six-year prison term. He walked away from a road gang on September 14, 1957, stole a car, and drove to see half-sister Opal Jennings in Ohio, where he met a girl named Stella before police jailed him on a federal charge of driving the hot car across state lines. He served 18 months on that count, and then returned to Virginia's state pen and a series of homosexual affairs noted by his jailers. A second escape attempt, in December 1957, saw Lucas recaptured the same day, but he was still discharged from prison on September 2, 1959.

Henry returned to Opal, now residing in Tecumseh, Michigan, and asked girlfriend Stella to marry him. He was furious when aged Viola turned up on the doorstep, nagging him incessantly to break off the engagement and return to Blacksburg. Both of them were drinking on the night of January 11, 1960, when she hit him with a broom and Henry struck back with a knife, leaving her dead on the floor. Arrested five days later, in Toledo, Ohio, Lucas confessed to the murder and boasted of raping his mother's corpse, a detail he later retracted as "something I made up."

Convicted of second-degree murder in March 1960, Lucas drew a sentence of 20 to 40 years. Two months later, jailers transferred him to Ionia's state hospital for the criminally insane, where he remained on a regimen of drugs and electroconvulsive therapy until April 1966. Paroled due to overcrowding on June 3, 1970, Lucas promised his keepers, "I'll leave a present on your doorstep." He later claimed to have murdered two women mere blocks from the prison, but police deny having any such cases on file.

From prison, Henry returned to Tecumseh and moved in with relatives. In December 1971, police booked him on a charge of molesting two teenage girls, reduced to simple kidnapping at trial, and Lucas went back to the Jackson state pen. Paroled in August 1975, again over his own objections, Henry worked briefly at a Pennsylvania mushroom farm, and then married Betty Crawford, a cousin's widow, in December 1975.

Three months later, they moved to Port Deposit, Maryland. Betty divorced him in the summer of 1977, claiming that Lucas molested her daughters from a previous marriage. Meanwhile, according to Henry's confessions, he had already committed a series of random murders, traveling and killing as the spirit moved him, claiming victims in Maryland and farther afield, ranging from Delaware to Texas. Sister Almeda offered him work at her husband's wrecking yard, then accused Henry of molesting her granddaughter. Feigning contrition, Henry "borrowed" Almeda's pickup and fled Maryland, dumping the totaled truck in Jacksonville, Florida.

He was moving on a swift collision course toward Ottis Toole.

***

Once Henry started talking, he went on for nearly two years, boosting his confessed body count from 75 to 150, then to 360, finally adding murders committed by friends and accomplices to reach a total "way over 500." Early on, he fingered frequent traveling companion Ottis Toole as a collaborator, piquing interest of police from coast to coast and into Canada. Detectives from around the country gathered in Monroe, Louisiana, in October 1983, comparing notes and going home convinced that Toole and Lucas were responsible for at least 69 murders. A second conference at Monroe, in January 1984, raised the total to 81. By March 1985, police in 20 states had "cleared" 90 murders for Lucas alone, plus another 108 committed with Toole as an accomplice.

Texas Rangers seemed to have a tiger by the tail. In late November 1983, they moved Henry to a lockup in Williamson County, base of a newly established "Lucas Task Force." Scores of officers lined up with files, sketches and photographs to question Henry about this or that cold case. Before long, he was also on the road. A California tour, in August 1984, reportedly "cleared" 14 open cases. Five months later, in New Orleans, Lucas "solved" five more. In the first week of April 1985, he led a caravan across the state of Georgia, closing the books on 10 murders. In West Virginia, Lucas confessed to killing a man whose death had been ruled suicide, thereby netting the widow a hefty life insurance settlement, while Rangers allegedly hosted a $3,000 celebration, spending most of the cash on whiskey and hookers. By then, Ranger critic Phil Ryan claimed Henry was "dictating orders" to his keepers, geared toward improving his living conditions.

But Henry closed cases, and for all the later accusations of a massive fraud, he seemed sincere. Sporting a "Jesus Saves" t-shirt, he spoke about redemption and the need for answers sought by grieving families. He didn't seem to feel remorse, exactly, but explained his crimes as a compulsion. Hitchhikers were favored prey. "Just about everyone I pick up, I kill 'em," he said. "That's the way it always turn out." From Florida, Toole chimed in, "We picked up lots of hitchhikers, you know, and Lucas killed most of the women hisself, and some of them would be shot in the head and the chest, and some of them would be choked to death, and some of them would be beat in the head with a tire tool." For Henry, at least, the motive was frequently necrophilia. "To me a live woman ain't nothing," he said. "I enjoy dead sex more than I do live sex." In some cases, like one from Kennewick, Washington, corroborating evidence appeared: a match to Henry's blood found on a towel, which he'd used to wipe the hand he gashed while wielding the murder knife.

The more Henry talked—and the more Toole added to the grim saga of slaughter—the greater curiosity became about the backup man already jailed in Florida.

***

A Jacksonville native, Ottis Elwood Toole was born on March 5, 1947. His alcoholic father soon took off for parts unknown—but not before, in Toole's account, forcing five-year-old Ottis to service one of the father's male friends. Ottis remained in the care of a religious fanatic mother and a sister who dressed him in girl's clothes "to play," a trauma shared with Lucas and at least five other notorious serial killers.

Toole's early confusion was exacerbated by his grandmother, an alleged Satanist who called Ottis "the devil's child" and sometimes took him on the graveyard runs that yielded human body parts for use in "magic" charms. Toole ran away from home repeatedly but always drifted back again. He suffered from seizures and found release by torching vacant houses in his neighborhood. Questioned later about his choice of targets, Toole replied, "I just hated to see them standing there."

By his own admission, Toole committed his first murder at age 14. The victim, a traveling salesman, picked him up outside town and drove him to the woods for sex. Afterward, Toole "got nervous" and ran the man down with his own car. Classified as retarded with an IQ of 75, Toole quit school in the eighth grade and logged his first arrest, for loitering, in August 1964. Others followed, building a rap sheet filled with counts of petty theft and lewd behavior. He married briefly, but his bride departed after three days' time, repulsed by Toole's overt homosexuality. By 1974, Toole was touring the western states in an old pickup truck. Acquaintances thought nothing of it, but later evidence suggests he may have claimed at least four victims in a six-month period.

Police suspect Toole in the death of 24-year-old Patricia Webb, shot in Lincoln, Nebraska, on April 18, 1974. Five months later, on September 19, a lone gunman invaded a massage parlor in Colorado Springs; employee Yon Lee was stabbed, her throat slashed, before the attacker moved on to rape, shoot, and stab coworker Sun Ok Cousin, and then set both women on fire. Lee survived to describe her assailant as clean-shaven, six feet two, and 195 pounds, driving a white pickup truck. Authorities arrested and ultimately convicted Park Estep, a mustachioed soldier who stood five feet ten, tipped the scales at a mere 150 pounds, and owned a red pickup. Meanwhile, on October 10, someone snatched 31-year-old Ellen Holman from Pueblo, Colorado, shot her three times in the head, and dumped her near the Oklahoma border. Detectives now believe Toole pulled the trigger in that crime.

No one living today can say with certainty when Toole first met Henry Lucas. Estimated dates for their fateful encounter range from 1976 to 1979, with some established facts weighing against the latter year. Most accounts agree that Henry met Ottis in a Jacksonville soup kitchen, sometime in 1976 or '77, then traveled on without him, but returned to live with Toole's family in 1978. Aside from sex with Toole, Lucas was drawn to Toole's young niece, Becky Powell, another mentally defective child. It seems that Powell shared Lucas with Uncle Ottis, though Henry maintained that he only had sex with Toole as "a favor" but never enjoyed it.

Between romantic interludes, Lucas and Toole worked together for Southeast Color Coat, but "came and went" as they pleased, according to the owner. Each time they made it back to Jacksonville, they were rehired. It was what they did, or claimed to do, *away* from Jacksonville that would become the stuff of legend and enduring controversy in the early 1980s, lasting to the present day.

Toole's mother died following surgery in May 1981, prompting Ottis and Henry to hit the road with Becky and her brother, Frank Powell Jr. The kids got homesick in Arizona, so Lucas and Toole reversed directions to Jacksonville, living with Toole's sister Drucilla—mother of Becky and Frank—until they stole a truck and drove the kids to Delaware. The happy travelers broke up when Ottis landed in a hospital and Maryland police detained Henry for car theft, holding him until October 6. Two months later, Drucilla killed herself with a drug overdose, landing Becky and Frank at a children's shelter in Bartow, Florida. Henry sprang Becky from custody in January 1982 and they headed west again—the last time Toole would ever see his niece. He learned her fate only when Lucas finally confessed her murder to police in Texas.

***

The strangest aspect of the tales spun by Lucas and Toole was their mutual insistence that many of their murders were performed at the behest of a satanic cult called "The Hand of Death." Together, they agreed that they had been recruited for the cult by "Don Meteric"—a pseudonym supplied by author Max Call for a Florida resident who directed some of their crimes, including child kidnappings and sex-slave trafficking, along with contract killings and human sacrifices incorporating cannibalism. Evidence remains elusive—but did anyone really investigate after Lucas and Toole spilled the beans?

Ex-G-man Kenneth Lanning, once renowned as the FBI's child molestation "expert" and persistent debunker of "Satanic panic" worldwide, heard the stories told by Henry and Ottis. Author Max Call claimed that Bureau helicopters scoured the Everglades, searching in vain for the cult camp described by Lucas and Toole, but Lanning's take on the matter was more revealing. "There's nothing to it," he told interviewer Sondra London in the 1990s, "so why investigate?"

Why, indeed? The story sounds absurd on its face—and after all, it's not as if any other serial killers ever professed a devotion to Satanism. At least, not if we rule out Charles Manson's "family"; Chicago's "Ripper Crew"; "Night Stalker" Richard Ramirez; "Death Angel" Donald Harvey; "Son of Sam" David Berkowitz; the cult led by Adolfo de Jesús Constanzo in Matamoros, Mexico; or Russia's, seven-member sect, revealed after its second set of double murders in June 2008—the list goes on and on.

Take it back in time, to Gilles de Rais, the richest man in 15th-century France, who tortured, sodomized, and disemboweled at least 140 young boys in occult rituals aimed at transmuting lead into gold. Between 1585 and 1610, Hungarian countess Erzsébet Báthory topped Gilles by some 510 victims, dispatched through torturous rituals mingling black magic and sexual sadism. Spanish witch Enriqueta Martí i Ripollés killed at least 12 children in 1912, using parts of their bodies in "potions" for sale to gullible clients. "High Priestess of Blood" Magdalena Solis led her Mexican cult in the vampiric ritual murders of eight victims during the 1960s. Thirty years later, Indonesian sorcerer Ahmad Suradji sacrificed the first of his 42 female victims, continuing until his arrest in 1998.

Still, even in these more enlightened, post-J. Edgar Hoover times, it is considered rash in some quarters to contradict assertions from the FBI. Critics of that view cite Hoover's 40-

year refusal to admit the existence of organized crime (while taking regular, free vacations at mob-owned resorts), his 1953 creation of a task force to "prove the nonexistence" of a national crime syndicate, and his belated "discovery" of *La Cosa Nostra* only when prodded to the point of forced retirement by the Kennedy brothers. Hoover also panned the Ku Klux Klan as "pretty much defunct" in 1956, when membership was rising toward a 30-year peak of 50,000 in Dixie. Pressed on a similar denial—that of any known "snuff" films—the Bureau hedges now, insisting that it only meant "commercial" films produced for sale to wealthy connoisseurs. Too many films, videotapes, and DVDs have now been seized for bland denials to survive.

Sondra London—deemed highly controversial for her romantic attachment to Florida serial killers Gerard Schaefer and Danny Rolling in the 1990s—corresponded with Toole for seven months before their first meeting in July 1991. Eight years after Toole's death, she wrote:

> *Ottis Toole's background in a generational form of "devil-worship" that involved the ritual use of human remains and the drinking of blood has been well documented. Years later, he volunteered information about his lifelong cult involvement in debriefings with law enforcement and attorneys as well as interviews with journalists. He named the real "Don Meteric" as a man who had known his grandmother and provided cars for Henry to drive on their journeys, as well as plenty of drugs and booze to use along the way.*
>
> *He identified the location of the Process Church headquarters in New Orleans [linked to Manson and company by prosecutor Vincent Bugliosi] and accurately described their occult philosophies. He mentioned the cult name "Dagon Abraxas," which is not the sort of name you hear on every street corner, as being in charge of a ranch south of the border where they*

181

took guns and minor children. He explained how their Florida employers and/or associates would sign them in and out of work to provide alibis, when they were really off doing jobs for what he called "the cult."

From private conversations with Toole, London claimed she had identified the real "Meteric," but she never shared his name—perhaps because Toole's jailhouse friend, Gerard Schaefer, had begun to threaten London's daughter with a visit from The Hand of Death to further her "sex education."

Against those affirmations, we have earnest statements from the FBI that no such cult ever existed, it was all part of a "hoax"—except, of course, that they investigated nothing, since they showed up for the game convinced that "there was nothing to it."

At what point do we simply shake our heads and flip a coin?

***

Enter Hugh Aynesworth, 54-year-old reporter for the *Dallas Times-Herald*. At 22, he claimed he had been present during JFK's assassination, at Lee Harvey Oswald's arrest, and at Oswald's murder by gangster Jack Ruby, though critics dispute all three assertions. From that time till he interviewed Ted Bundy with coauthor Stephen Michaud for *The Only Living Witness* (1999), some said Aynesworth's chief pursuit in life had been debunking JFK conspiracy theories, discrediting alleged witnesses, and lampooning New Orleans District Attorney Jim Garrison's trial of Clay Shaw on conspiracy charges in 1969. As critic Jim DiEugenio observes online, "refusing a conspiracy is his life's work."

Between Oswald and Bundy, Aynesworth stumbled onto Henry Lucas, first supporting Lucas's confessions and then refuting them with a blizzard of sometimes inaccurate "facts." Viewed in hindsight, Aynesworth's role in the drama was nearly as strange as Henry's itself.

In a series of *Times-Herald* stories, beginning on April 15, 1985, Aynesworth attacked Henry's "hoax" on the public, allegedly perpetrated with connivance of sundry police departments, all anxious to feed Lucas cold-case details and clear their books. Aynesworth claimed to have learned of the fraud from Henry's own lips, in October 1983, and yet, one month later, he signed a contract to write Henry's biography. That deal fell through when Aynesworth learned of Henry's prior literary contract with a Waco used car dealer, but still he pressed on, supporting the "hoax."

In September 1984, Aynesworth appeared on CBS-TV's *Nightwatch* program, raising no objection as the show aired Henry's confessions to hundreds of slayings. As late as February 1985, Aynesworth published a Lucas interview in *Penthouse* magazine, prompting Henry with leading questions, accepting Henry's responses as fact. In one choice passage, Aynesworth said, "According to the numbers, you started killing furiously after [1970]. What triggered this? Would you just feel like you had to kill somebody?" And later: "So after killing all over the country for four years, you met Ottis Toole in 1979 [*sic*], and for two or three years you often traveled with him."

Aynesworth's trouble with dates was not his sole deficiency with presentation of the facts. While listing other authors who tried to "cash in" on the Lucas story, he failed to mention his own contract with the killer. His timeline of Henry's movements, spanning two full pages in the *Times-Herald*, was replete with errors. Hugh pegged Henry's "first meeting" with Toole in 1979, though Lucas had moved in with Toole's family by 1978. He cited payroll records from Southeast Color Coat to prove the killers seldom left Jacksonville, though office manager Eileen Knight confirmed that they would often "come and go." He claimed that Lucas spent "all the time" between January and March 1978 with girlfriend Rhonda Knuckles, never leaving her side, but ignored the testimony of a surviving witness, tailed by Lucas across 200 miles of Colorado and New

Mexico in February of that year. (The woman recalled Henry's face and recorded his license number for police.) At one point, Hugh was so anxious to clear Henry's name that he listed one victim twice, killed on two occasions four days apart, in July 1981.

Still, despite Aynesworth's frequent sins of omission and fabrication, there *was* much to criticize in Henry's rambling tales. Police found one alleged victim, a Virginia schoolteacher, still alive and well. Some of Henry's claims were clearly absurd, including confessions to murders in Spain and Japan, plus delivery of poison to the People's Temple cultists in Guyana. On the other hand, there were also problems with Henry's retraction. Soon after the Aynesworth story broke, Lucas smuggled a letter to authors Jerry Potter and Joel Norris, claiming that he had been drugged and forced to recant his original confessions.

Another lie?

We may never know the full extent of Aynesworth's meddling or his final motives, but this much is known. By the time his series finished, Lucas claimed to have killed only three victims: his mother, Kate Rich, and Becky Powell. By April 23, he had denied the Rich and Powell slayings, despite directing officers to their remains. And his mother's death, of course, had been "an accident."

This time, instead of contradicting a conspiracy, Aynesworth created one, blaming it all on Henry and innumerable crooked cops, oddly omitting Toole—and of course, one-time cheerleader Aynesworth himself. In the process, he muddied the waters, and soon had some authorities singing his tune.

***

Authorities reacted in various ways to Aynesworth's "exposé." Arkansas filed new murder charges against Lucas on April 23, eight days after his change of heart, and other jurisdictions remain unimpressed by his belated pleas of innocence. In

Marrero, Louisiana, relatives of victim Ruth Kaiser point out that Lucas confessed to stealing a stereo after he killed the 79-year-old woman, a theft that was never reported and therefore could not have been "leaked" by police. As they recalled, "He described things we had forgotten about, details that never appeared in the paper and that we never put in a police report."

Investigator Jim Lawson, of Nebraska's Scotts Bluff County sheriff's office, questioned Lucas in September 1984 regarding the February 1978 murder of schoolteacher Stella McLean. "I purposely tried to trick him several times during the interview," Lawson said, "but to no avail. We even tried to 'feed' him another homicide from our area to see if he was confessing to anything and everything in an effort to build a name for himself, but he denied any participation in the crime." Commander J. T. Duff, intelligence chief for the Georgia Bureau of Investigation, describes Henry's April 1985 tour thus: "Lucas was not provided with any information or directions to any of the crime scenes, but gave the information to law enforcement. When a crime scene was encountered, Lucas voluntarily and freely gave details that only the perpetrator would have known."

Ottis also recanted some of his confessions, though he spun no tale of trying to embarrass the authorities. Instead, he took offense primarily when lawmen branded him a liar—or when they withheld the cigarettes and coffee he demanded as an opener for any interview.

A case in point is the aforementioned Colorado Springs massage parlor massacre from 1974. Toole confessed to the crime in September 1984, providing details, but embarrassed prosecutors mounted a furious counterattack. After hours of hostile grilling, Toole threw in the towel. "Okay," he said, "if you say I didn't kill her, maybe I didn't." In a strange, unsatisfying compromise, imprisoned suspect Park Estep was later released on his first parole bid, though his name was not formally cleared. The curious display of mercy by Colorado's parole board convinced some observers that the state accepted Toole's guilt but refused to publicly acknowledge an error at trial.

By November 1985, police in 18 states had reopened 90 "Lucas cases," but what of the other 108? And what of the telephone conversation between Lucas, in Texas, and Toole, in Florida, monitored by police in November 1983? At the time, Henry and Ottis had not seen or spoken to each other in at least seven months, deprived of any chance to work up a script, but their dialogue lends chilling support to the later confessions.

Lucas: Ottis, I don't want you to think I'm doing this as a revenge.

Toole: No. I don't want you to hold anything back about me.

Lucas: See, we got so many of them, Ottis. We got to turn up the bodies. Now, this boy and girl, I don't know anything about.

Toole: Well, maybe that's the two I killed my own self. Just like that Mexican that wasn't going to let me out of the house. I took an ax and chopped him all up. What made me—I been meaning to ask you. That time when I cooked some of those people. Why'd I do that?

Lucas: I think it was just the hands doing it. I know a lot of the things we done, in human sight, are impossible to believe.

Indeed.

Beyond a doubt, the most confusing, convoluted case on record for the killer pair is that of six-year-old Adam Walsh, snatched from a Hollywood, Florida, shopping mall on July 27, 1981. His severed head surfaced in a canal near Vero Beach 10 days later, but no other trace of him was ever found. Toole first confessed to Adam's murder on October 21, 1983, startling Assistant Police Chief Leroy Hessler with claims that were "grisly beyond belief." Hessler told the media, "There are certain details only he could know. He did it. I've got details that no one else would know. He's got me convinced." Despite that endorsement, officers reversed their stance a few weeks later, issuing statements that Toole was "no longer a suspect" in the crime.

Adam's father, John Walsh—later host of TV's *America's Most Wanted*—clung to belief in Toole's guilt, buttressed in 1988 by a ghoulish letter from Toole (actually penned by cellblock buddy Gerard Schaefer), detailing Adam's torture and death, demanding $50,000 for return of his remains. Twelve years after Toole's death, in December 2008, police again reversed themselves and pronounced Toole Adam's killer, officially closing the case. By that time, of course, all DNA samples pertaining to Adam's murder had vanished from law enforcement files.

One author who disagrees on Toole's guilt in the Walsh case is Arthur Jay Harris, who blamed the slaying on Milwaukee headhunter Jeffrey Dahmer, allegedly vacationing in Florida in 1981. By the time a second volume of his work appeared, Harris went further, claiming Adam Walsh was still alive somewhere, somehow, the head recovered in his name never photographed, autopsied, or compared to Adam's pediatric dental records. While his alleged survival joins the pantheon of American urban legends, stretching back across more than a century from Billy the Kid and Butch Cassidy to Elvis Presley, Adam's parents remain unconvinced.

Whatever one believes, this much is clear: no shortage of enigmas lingers in the wake of ramblers Lucas and Toole.

***

The justice system took its time with Henry and Ottis, dealing first with Toole. Two houses burned in his Jacksonville neighborhood on May 23 and 31, 1983, followed by teenage accomplices denouncing Ottis to police on June 6. In jail, he confessed to 40-odd fires spanning two decades and was convicted of second-degree arson on August 5, drawing a 20-year sentence.

Meanwhile, in Texas on June 21, prosecutors arraigned Lucas on charges of murdering Kate Rich and Becky Powell. Henry waived his right to counsel and admitted stabbing Rich, indulging in necrophilia with her corpse, then dismembering it and incinerating it in his wood stove. "I killed Kate Rich," he told the court, "and at least a hundred more. I know it ain't normal for a person to go out and kill girls just to have sex with them." Almost plaintively, he asked the judge, "Will I still be able to go on helping find bodies?"

Overnight, Lucas rocketed to international infamy, dragging Toole along for the ride. Ottis supported Henry's claims and added more of his own, "clearing" 25 murders in 11 states while claiming he assisted Lucas in at least 108 more. On August 2, 1983, authorities arraigned Lucas for the October 1979 rape-slaying of a still-unidentified woman known only as "Orange Socks," the sole piece of clothing she wore when found along Interstate 135 in Texas. Ten days later, while awaiting trial on that charge, Henry recanted his confessions to Becky Powell's murder, and then waived trial on Kate Rich's death in September, pleading guilty and accepting a 75-year sentence.

In November 1983, after a judge rejected pleas from Henry's attorney to rule his taped confessions on Powell inadmissible, Lucas faced trial in that case and testified on his own behalf, weeping in remorse as he denied any memory of Becky's death. Against that claim, the state played videotapes of his calm confession to stabbing Becky and raping her corpse before he scattered her truncated remains in the desert. Convicted and sentenced to life, Henry congratulated his prosecutor, saying, "You did a good job."

Next, in March 1984, came Henry's trial for killing Orange Socks. Once again, confessions weighed against him, including taped admissions that he picked the victim up while she was hitchhiking, raped and killed her, then had sex with her again before dumping her corpse in a culvert to which he later led police. Defense counsel countered with an insanity plea, professed memory lapses during Henry's confession, and allegations that deputies "refreshed" his memory during interrogation. Convicted on April 2, Lucas received a death sentence.

Back in Florida that same month, Ottis Toole faced trial for the arson-murder of 64-year-old George Sonnenberg, burned to death at his Jacksonville home in January 1982. That conviction earned Toole a death sentence, followed before year's end by another for the February 1983 slaying of 19-year-old Ada Johnson in Tallahassee. At the same time, he confessed to the Pensacola murder of 19-year-old David Schallart, a hitchhiker found dead along Interstate 10 in northern Florida, on February 6, 1980. Both death sentences were later commuted to life on appeal, though *not* by Governor Jeb Bush, as some sources claim, since Bush did not take office until 28 months after Toole's demise.

April 1985 brought exposure of the so-called "Lucas hoax," but it had little impact on Toole. In 1991, Ottis pled guilty to four more Florida slayings, committed during 1980 and 1981, receiving a quartet of fresh life sentences. Prosecutors charged alleged accomplice Henry Lucas in the same four cases, but declined to extradite him for trial.

A sideshow to the main events occurred in October 1992 when Lucas's pen pal Phyllis Wilcox—a 40-year-old mother and grandmother from Missouri—briefly posed as Becky Powell, claiming that since she existed, Lucas was obviously innocent of her slaying. Investigators soon saw through the ruse, and Wilcox admitted hatching the lame-brained plot after 11 months of soulful correspondence with Henry, claiming that a four-hour prison visit had convinced her Lucas was "the most wonderful man that I had ever met." As she told an Internet blogger in 2000, "After our first meeting, my feelings for Henry were stronger than ever before. I had really fallen in love with him and I had to fight to keep Texas from taking him away from me." Stranger still, her husband had first suggested correspondence with Lucas and accompanied Wilcox on one prison visit, along with their youngest daughter. The strange tribe escaped prosecution and soon vanished from headlines after procuring their 15 minutes of fame.

Meanwhile, advocates ranging from Amnesty International to Sister Helen Prejean of *Dead Man Walking* fame rallied to Henry's defense, with Amnesty citing "the belief of two former state Attorneys General that Lucas was in all likelihood innocent of the crime for which he was sentenced to death." On March 31, 1998, Judge Dan Carter scheduled Henry's execution for June 30.

Governor George W. Bush—a staunch advocate of capital punishment, who presided over the (sometimes dubious) executions of 152 other inmates during his six years in office—commuted Henry's sentence to life imprisonment on June 26, 1998, marking Lucas as the only condemned prisoner spared from death during Bush's tenure. Addressing reporters, Bush said, "Henry Lee Lucas is unquestionably guilty of other despicable crimes [for] which he has been sentenced to spend the rest of his life in prison. However, I believe there is enough doubt about this particular crime that the state of Texas should not impose its ultimate penalty by executing him." In fact, commutation left Lucas facing five life terms plus 210 additional years for nine other slayings (or 11, claimed in certain conflicting reports).

Helen Prejean panned Bush's decision as being motivated "more by expediency than conscience" with an eye toward his presidential bid in 2000. She further branded the Texas Board of Pardons and Appeals a "farce," claiming that Bush made his decision *before* the panel's recommendation of mercy, rendered after the fact by a stacked vote of 17 to one in the governor's favor. In short, she opined, "Bush showed where the real power lay," making a safe cosmetic move since Lucas would never leave prison alive.

Finally, at least so far as relatives of murdered victims were concerned, only Fate would properly adjudicate the cases lodged against Lucas and Toole.

***

Death comes to us all, and serial killers—or serial liars—are no exception. Decades of chronic intoxication caught up with Ottis Toole on September 15, 1996, when he died from cirrhosis of the liver at Florida's state prison in Raiford. (Hate mail collaborator Gerard Schaefer had been hacked to death in his Raiford cell nine months earlier, his mother blaming Toole for the assassination, while authorities charged two-time killer Vincent Rivera.) Toole's medical records fail to support the pervasive rumors that he also suffered from AIDS. John Walsh chastised police for failing to seek a deathbed confession from Toole, confirming his guilt in son Adam's murder.

Henry Lucas outlived his old partner by four-and-a-half years. On March 13, 2001, guards found him dead in his cell at the O. B. Ellis Unit in Huntsville, Texas. They logged the official cause of death, at age 64, as heart failure.

And what should we now, at long last, believe about Lucas and Toole? Amidst the contradictory confessions, recantations, and renewed confessions, the analyses and outright lies by fringe observers, is there any hope of finally divining "Truth"?

Texas Ranger Phil Ryan, an outspoken critic of his own department's Lucas Task Force, suggested to the *Houston Chronicle* that Henry was "at most responsible for 15 murders." Dr. Eric W. Hickey, author of *Serial Killers and Their Victims,* professor emeritus at California State University, Fresno, and dean of the California School of Forensic Studies at San Diego's Alliant International University, cites an unnamed "investigator" who interviewed Lucas multiple times as placing the final body count closer to 40. Even skeptic Sara Knox, writing from halfway around the world at Australia's University of Western Sydney, says that Lucas maintains a "reputation as one of the world's worst serial killers—even after the debunking of the majority of his confessions by the Attorney General of Texas." As for Toole, no one today disputes the six Florida murders for which he was sentenced to life in a cage.

The final tally? No one living knows. But was there something in the blood or in their twisted, gothic backgrounds that compelled Lucas and Toole to kill and kill again?

Perhaps we might ask Robert Joseph "Bobby Joe" Long, a distant cousin of Lucas, born at Kenova, West Virginia, 17 years after Henry, in October 1953. Afflicted with an extra "x" chromosome at birth, Long developed prominent breasts during puberty, suffering untold humiliation before surgery relieved the problem. He also sustained multiple head injuries, purportedly causing hypersexual behavior, and endured a strange relationship with his mother, sharing her bed until he was a teenager, all the while despising her many boyfriends. Married in 1974 and divorced after siring two children, Long subsequently became a serial rapist, claiming an estimated 50 victims contacted through classified ads throughout Florida between 1981 and 1984. In March 1984, he graduated to murder, strangling at least 10 women over the next eight months. His downfall came in mid-November, when victim Lisa McVey spun a tale of her own abusive childhood to Long, and he released her alive. She instantly described her rapist and his car to police, landing Bobby Joe in jail by November 16. Today, Long faces one death sentence, 28 life prison terms, four 99-year sentences, and one paltry five-year term (for aggravated assault with a weapon, lacking intent to kill).

A product of nature, nurture, or an unsavory mixture of both? It seems unfair to draw from Dave Matthews's lyrics of "Blood in the Water," but *something* reached across a generation to bind Lucas and Long, blood relatives who never met, just as coincidence or circumstance brought Lucas and Toole together in the 1970s, while Bobby Joe was enduring his ghastly formative years nearby.

The final verdict, as with so many cold cases still unsolved across the continent, remains unknown.

Chapter 8
DAVID ALAN GORE & FRED WATERFIELD
The Killing Cousins
By RJ Parker

Vero Beach, Florida, was a quiet town until six horrifying murders occurred, and nothing was the same ever again. The murders that took place in Florida from 1981 to 1983 shook the entire state.

David Alan Gore and Fred Waterfield, who came to be known as the "Killing Cousins," were responsible for these murders and also charged for numerous rape and assault cases in the same area. These two serial killers were sick and remorseless, and derived twisted pleasure out of raping, assaulting and torturing helpless women, at their mercy.

Gore was born in Florida in August of 1953. From an early age, he exhibited signs of mental delusion and an affinity to violence. Fred Waterfield, born in New Jersey in 1952, was his maternal cousin who also seemed to share his contorted interests. During their teens, the boys discovered that they had a common curiosity: they each had devious sexual fantasies that would later turn them into the most wanted killers in the country. Growing up in a rural area near Vero Beach, David Alan Gore seemingly lived a fairly normal life. His only friend was his cousin, Waterfield.

At first sight, Gore appeared like any other southerner and gave no sign of his actual violent nature. It was later discovered that he had been obsessed with firearms as a teenager and even studied gunsmithing. Waterfield, on the other hand, was a high school football star and was known to have violent outbursts and temper problems. When Gore and Waterfield discovered that they had the same aggressive streak, they decided to team up together, carrying out several heinous crimes.

When their case was investigated and analyzed by experts, it was revealed that Waterfield could have possibly been the one who masterminded the killing spree. His persuasive skills and dominance might have been responsible for Gore's actions. Many analysts and psychologists were of the opinion that Waterfield could have infiltrated Gore's thoughts and influenced the way he handled his victims. Their initial rape attempts were instigated by Fred Waterfield when he followed a female motorist and flattened her vehicle's tire with a rifle he possessed. However, she escaped on foot, and both the cousins were unsuccessful in their attempts to catch her. Soon after that, they targeted another woman going from Vero Beach to Miami but had to abandon their pursuit midway when she stopped at a busy street.

In one of Gore's letters that he wrote from prison, he stated that Waterfield had already started out early during his teen years. He had witnessed his cousin raping a girl on their school bus on afternoon. Waterfield was a football star and quite popular in school. In contrast, Gore was a lonely child who had no friends. According to some experts, it was Gore's shy and docile nature that made him susceptible to Waterfield's charms and popularity. Despite his occasional outbursts, Waterfield seemed like a regular high school football star with fairly good looks. Gore wrote in his letter that his cousin had no problems in getting a date but had no respect for women whatsoever. In fact, he regarded them as scum and good for only one purpose: fulfilling a man's sexual desires.

When the cousins entered adulthood, they started to display alarmingly suspicious behaviors that began to garner attention. Gore was fired from his first job as a gas attendant when his supervisor discovered that he'd drilled a hole into the women's bathroom, allowing him to spy on occupants. Waterfield also could not hold on to a job and frequently had to move around due to his unstable nature and penchant for violence. Together, they formed a morbid alliance and hunted women along the beach and surrounding areas. Their first reported victim was a girl they'd raped near Vero Beach. She notified the police, but later dropped the charges due to embarrassment and her fear of testifying in court. However, in some reports, it had been said that their actual first victim was one of their sisters. Gore was involved in the incident and even helped hold her down while his cousin carried out the abuse and rape.

In early 1981, Gore took a job working with his father as caretaker of a citrus grove, while at night he patrolled the streets as an auxiliary police officer. His badge, as the sheriff's deputy, put him in a position of power, and he knowingly took advantage of it by luring innocent victims. Waterfield had taken up a managerial position at an automotive shop in Orlando, but he frequently visited Vero Beach with his cousin. He realized that his cousin's badge could help their situation and actually play a part in procuring victims.

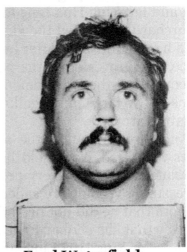

David Alan Gore   **Fred Waterfield**

There are various accounts describing their first murder. Some of them highlight Waterfield as the instigator while others say it was Gore's idea. Nevertheless, all of them report the same horrific scenario of a mother and daughter being held captive, brutally raped and killed.

In February of 1981, Gore spotted seventeen-year-old

award-winning math student Ying Hua Ling. She went to Vero Beach High School and was disembarking her school bus when she was cornered by Gore. The Ling family had emigrated from Taiwan and was settled in Florida. Ying's father was an inspector at a fruit packing plant in the area. Her mother, Hsiang Huang Ling, had been waiting for her daughter when the incident occurred.

Gore saw the opportunity to take both of his victims together. He used his badge to get Ying Hua Ling into his truck. Then he 'arrested' her mother, Hsiang Huang Ling, and handcuffed her. In a sworn statement that he later gave to the police, Gore said that he drove them to an orange grove. He then called his cousin, Fred Waterfield, and while he waited for him to get there, he raped both mother and daughter. In his statement he said that he gunned down the mother, Hsiang Huang Ling and left Ying Hua Ling for his cousin. Waterfield reached the orchard and raped the girl, asking Gore to "get rid of her" when he was finished. After he was caught and detained by the police, Gore revealed to the police where and how he had left the corpses of the two women. The police discovered their remains in two large thirty-gallon pesticide drums located within the citrus grove.

Another account of the situation is a little different. It states that Fred Waterfield had offered to pay David Gore a thousand dollars for every pretty woman that he could target successfully. When Gore called him to the orchard, Waterfield told him that he did not need the older woman and tied her up in a way that she choked to death. He then proceeded to abuse and murder Ying Hua Ling, after which he told Gore to get rid of the corpses. Waterfield slipped him around four hundred dollars to cover their tracks at the crime scene.

During his earlier statements, Gore had pointed towards Waterfield as the actual perpetrator of the killings and abuse, but he later changed his testimony and took responsibility of the murders. He had apparently experienced a sudden religious awakening and found his Savior, Jesus Christ. In a sworn statement, Gore admitted that he had killed Hsiang Huang Ling and her daughter Ying Hua Ling after his cousin had raped her.

Experts who have analyzed the killings and both statements of Gore and Waterfield have preferred to base their conclusions on the evidence discovered and the known events leading up to the situation.

Both the cousins, Gore and Waterfield, were deranged and mentally disturbed men with psychopathic tendencies. Their statements are a reflection of their state of minds. Hence, the police and experts only picked up the hardcore, relevant facts that led them to uncovering the remains of the victims and determining the possible scenarios leading to the crimes.

Hsiang Huang Ling   **Ying Hua Ling**

The killing cousins' serial rape and murder spree started right after the Ling incident. Both Gore and Waterfield had been roaming around free when they found their third victim. Five months after the vanishing of Ying Hua Ling and her mother, another woman, Judy Kay Daley, was reported missing. The thirty-five-year old, former resident of Fort Pierce was visiting from California when she disappeared from Round Island Park, situated in Indian River County. Following that, several reports were filed of missing women and girls. Gore eventually confessed that he had killed six and targeted several more for rape and abduction.

More Victims
Gore had been stalking Judy Daley for quite some time. She was on a short visit from California when she became the cousins' next unfortunate victim. On July 15, 1981, Gore spotted her alone in Round Island Park and saw it as an opportunity to kidnap her.

Judy Kay Daley

In his later statement to police, he said that he disabled her car so he could pretend to come to her assistance later on. Daley, upon discovering that her car was having trouble, indicated to Gore that she needed help. The unsuspecting woman saw his police badge and actually thought that he was going to come to her aid. Gore lured her into his truck, offering to take her to the nearest station for help. However, once inside his truck, he handcuffed her and drove to a trailer in the citrus grove. There, he raped her and strangled her to death.

Daley's remains were discovered three years later, in June of 1984, when the police followed a tip from Gore, which led to them uncovering a garbage bag buried in the citrus grove near Vero Beach. There they discovered body parts, which DNA proved belonged to Judy Kay Daley.

Angelica LaVallee   **Barbara Ann Byer**

Angelica LaVallee and Barbara Ann Byer were the cousins' fourth and fifth victims. Gore had been arrested for suspicious behavior some time back and had just been released on parole. Both LaVallee and Byer were runaways from Orlando and were hitchhiking along Interstate 95. The killing cousins spotted the girls and lured them into their truck.

The incident occurred on May 20, 1983, just along I-95 in Brevard County. Gore and Waterfield picked up the hitchhiking teenagers and tied them up in their truck. They headed in the direction of Vero Beach with the abducted girls captive and at gunpoint. Gore later said in his statement that Waterfield made him drive while he raped both the girls. Once near Vero Beach, Gore killed both LaVallee and Byer by shooting them in the head. After his arrest, he led authorities to Byer's body, which was found dismembered and buried in a shallow grave in a citrus grove located west of the beach. LaVallee's body was never found; he claimed to have dumped it in a canal nearby. Authorities tried to recover her body, which had allegedly been disposed in the canal off I-95, also west of Vero Beach, but were not able to find anything.

Seventeen-year-old Lynn Elliot and her fourteen-year-old friend, Regan Martin, attended Vero Beach High School. The girls were spotted by Gore and Waterfield when they were on one of their hunting cruises around the beach. Regan Martin, who was found alive by the police officers, later recounted the incident and revealed that she had been hitchhiking with Lynn Elliot when the cousins had picked them up. She stated that the men had abducted them at gunpoint and took them to a house, where they were separated and repeatedly raped.

Lynn Elliot

Gore later said that their plan was just to "pick up a girl

and take them to my parents' house, which was empty." His parents were allegedly out of town on a holiday. Gore admitted to having a pair of handcuffs and a nine-shot, .22 caliber revolver that he had managed to steal from his father.

They were driving in Waterfield's truck and had just picked up Elliot and Martin. According to Gore, just a few minutes after the girls got in the truck, the glove compartment somehow opened and revealed the gun. He realized that it was too late to do anything about it, so he took a hold of it and pointed it at Regan Martin's head. Gore stated that the girls initially thought that he was joking around with the gun. He told them that it was not a joke and that he was deadly serious. They then turned to Waterfield (whom he referred to as "Freddie") and silently pleaded with him. He also reiterated the fact that this was no joke.

Gore handcuffed the girls while Waterfield was driving. The girls were terrified by the time they reached the house. Once there, Gore tossed the keys to his cousin, who brought the girls in and led them to the bedroom. They were locked up in the room while both the cousins stepped out to talk. In his statement to police later, Gore said that Waterfield was concerned about his sister whom they had passed on the way to his parents' house. She had seen the girls in the truck and, to avoid suspicion, Waterfield felt the need to make an appearance at his repair shop.

He left orders for Gore to keep the back door open for him so he could slip in again when he returned. When he was gone, his cousin separated the girls and tied them up. He also told them that if they "cooperated," he would release them soon.

Gore sexually assaulted Lynn Elliot first and left her alone in the room as he went on to rape Regan Martin. Seizing the opportunity, Lynn attempted to escape. However, the noise drew out her rapist, who saw that she was gone and ran after her. Lynn Elliot could only get to the driveway, as her hands were tied, and there she lost her footing. Gore panicked upon realizing that the situation was spiraling out of control. He kept running after her and finally caught her when she fell. But Lynn didn't give up. She kept on fighting even after he told her to stop and screamed at her. She was desperate to get away. Gore pulled out the gun and shot her. Lynn continued to fight and resist him when he tried to drag her back, so, he threw her to the ground and shot her twice in the head.

Gore panicked even more upon seeing the dead girl lying outside on his driveway. Afraid that someone had witnessed the entire incident, he ran back into the house.

Capture and Conviction

David Alan Gore was already panicking as he bolted nude after Lynn Elliot. He'd shot her twice as she fought him so that she would "shut up." He knew that someone had witnessed the entire shooting scene outside his house. It turned out to be his neighbor's boy who was cycling nearby. When Gore went back inside, he turned on the police scanner and came to the conclusion that the boy had seen everything.

Quickly, he hid the body in the trunk of his parents' white Mercury Monarch. According to his statement, a "frenzied panic" had taken hold of him and he couldn't think of anything else to do. He ran back into his house and realized that the only thing he could do at that point was to stay there and wait.

Meanwhile, the neighbors had called the police and officers began arriving on scene shortly. They surrounded the house and soon discovered Elliot's body through the trail of fresh blood that led to the trunk of the car. After a ninety-minute standoff and a struggle that ensued between the police and Gore, they were able to capture him.

In an effort to get him to surrender, the police officers called up his family. They captured him in less than two hours and found Regan Martin tied up in the attic. Soon enough, they also discovered that Waterfield was his accomplice in the kidnappings and arrested him within hours.

Gore cracked in police custody, confessing to the crimes that he had committed alongside his cousin, Fred Waterfield.

In the beginning of August of 1983, a grand jury examined the case and charged David Alan Gore with first-degree murder, along with two counts of kidnapping and sexual assault. By January of 1984, Gore's trial had been moved from Vero Beach to St. Petersburg, Florida.

The St. Petersburg jury convicted Gore on first-degree murder, two kidnappings, and three sexual assaults against Regan Martin and Lynn Elliot. On March 16, 1984, the same jury returned an 11-1 vote in favor of the death sentence.

Waterfield was convicted separately. He was charged with two first-degree murders of LaVallee and Byer, along with manslaughter charges for his part in Elliot's death. He was sentenced to two life-imprisonment terms to be served consecutively.

Gore's sentence was confirmed in August of 1985, when the Supreme Court affirmed his first-degree murder conviction issued punishment in the form of the death penalty. In March of 1988, his death warrant was signed by Governor Bob Martinez. The Florida Supreme Court confirmed his death sentence on July 5, 2007. Finally, after being on death row for almost twenty-eight years, David Alan Gore was executed by lethal injection on April 12, 2012. He was fifty-eight years old at the time and had tried to appeal to the United States Supreme Court against his death penalty. The appeal was rejected and his sentence went through as decided.

Sentencing

David Alan Gore was convicted in 1984 but his execution sentence was carried out in 2012. He constantly appealed his punishment and managed to delay it time and again for a long period. Gore had been convicted of killing six women after brutally assaulting them and subjecting them to torture. He is said to have accounted for his killings in an interview and within various prison letters. According to those who knew him, his actions were triggered by the uncontrollable urge he had for killing and he felt no remorse whatsoever.

The only apologetic tone he took on was during his last statement before the execution. He dedicated the statement to Lynn Elliot's family and admitted that what he had done was very wrong. In his own words, the statement said, "I would like to say to Mr. and Mrs. Elliot that I am truly sorry for my part in the death of your daughter. I wish above all else my death could bring her back. I am not the same man today that I was 28 years ago."

After that he proceeded to talk about how he'd found God and that he was not afraid of death anymore. He actually said that he was looking forward to spending the rest of eternity with Jesus Christ. Gore admitted to having a "tremendous amount of remorse" for his actions and even asked for forgiveness from the Elliot family.

Gore had tried for many years to delay or overturn his execution sentence. His attorneys used the legal system as a cover to get his death penalty rescinded. Five consecutive life terms were also negotiated as part of his punishment.

In 1989, a judge of Florida's Supreme Court managed to put his death penalty on hold when Gore's attorney argued that he was drunk at the time of Elliot's murder. The federal judge allowed for a sentencing do-over after the claim and stated that Gore should be given time to substantiate it. The judge's stance was that Gore should be able to present evidence in court backing his claim that he was actually drunk at that time and not in control of what he was doing.

However, in 1992, another jury took over and negated the claim. There was a resentencing hearing, after which a judge reinstated the death penalty.

There were almost four hundred inmates on death row in Florida since the state had reinstated the death penalty. David Gore was the seventy-third person to be executed, despite forty other inmates being on death row longer than he. Governor Rick Scott had been updated with all the heinous crimes and past history of the serial killer. He signed Gore's death warrant in a short span of time, even rejecting Florida's bishops' appeals to spare his life. The bishops do not believe in death penalties and firmly oppose execution.

Gore made one last final appeal to the United States Supreme Court, citing his attorney problems and the lengthy time period on death row. His appeal was rejected and the sentence was to go through as scheduled.

On April 12, 2012, at 6:59 p.m., it was announced that David Alan Gore's death sentence had been carried out by lethal injection. The execution took nearly ten minutes, and it was witnessed by almost two-dozen people, including police officers and Lynn Elliot's father.

A police officer who'd discovered Elliot's body on the scene stated that it was time for Gore to pay for his crimes. He also said that when he'd found the girl lying dead, his worst fears had come true. When Gore had been previously let out on parole for an armed trespassing conviction, he had apprehensions and feared that a situation like this may present itself. Gore had been caught by a deputy police officer lying in wait in the backseat of a girl's car with a handgun on him. He served just two years for that crime.

However, with his sentencing coming through, it was time for Gore to be held accountable properly. The officer also went on to describe that the entire process, with all the execution delays, had not only been frustrating and emotional for the victims' families but also the authorities involved.

David Alan Gore and Fred Waterfield committed heinous and completely sickening acts of brutality. Analysts and experts have not been able to pinpoint any concrete reason for their behavior and aggression towards women and girls. Gore's letters from the prison were dissected and observed in detail to identify the trigger behind his acts of violence. However, not much could be determined. Most of the experts concluded that Gore had acted out under the influence of his dominant cousin, Fred Waterfield, while some just believed that he was a mentally unstable and twisted man who liked torture and killing.

In one of his letters, Gore said that women to him were just like objects and nothing more.

If it hadn't been for the sheer courage on the part of Lynn Elliot, who'd tried to escape and lost her life in the process, Gore might have never been caught. Perhaps his rampage may have gone on for a longer period of time with many other innocent girls becoming his victims. With a stroke of luck, Gore's plan went awry. He made the wrong move and the entire shooting was witnessed.

Other Victims

The killing cousins deserved what they got when the judicial courts sentenced them for life and handed out a death penalty for David Alan Gore. Fred Waterfield was sentenced for his part in the murder of the two girls, Barbara Ann Byer and Angelica LaVallee. His sentence carried two consecutive life terms with no possibility of parole while Gore was put on death row for the murder, rape and torture of six victims.

The murder victims were not Gore's only targets. When he was caught and the police officials conducted an extensive investigation, they discovered that David Alan Gore had attempted to rape and assault more than a dozen other women.

These other victims were fortunate enough to escape captivity and abduction. Some even got away before Gore could execute his attack. In his statements, the serial killer and rapist confessed about his targets who'd somehow evaded him. One of his attempts had led to his previous arrest, when he was caught by a police officer for armed trespassing. His sentence at the time was for five years; however, he was released on parole after spending just two years in jail.

It has been reported that Gore and Waterfield had already been under suspicion quite a few times since 1976. There had been a few assaults and disappearances in which the killing cousins might have been involved. However, the investigating authorities could not incarcerate either of them or even charge them with anything, due to lack of evidence.

There was that one rape victim who did come forward, but she'd dropped all the charges due to fear of humiliation in court. Another girl reported being raped at gunpoint by Waterfield and Gore, which had briefly led the police officers to detain and question the two. The cousins insisted that everything that had happened was consensual, and since nothing could be proved, they were released without being charged.

The killing cousins also targeted other girls who, with some stroke of luck, managed to escape unharmed.

Dana Sturgis

Eighteen-year-old Palm Bay resident, Dana Sturgis, was targeted by Gore when he was still an auxiliary deputy sheriff. At the time, Gore was already under suspicion for his behavior, and the Indian River County Sheriff's Department was about to open an investigation.

David Alan Gore approached her car and signaled her to pull over, feigning a traffic stop. She, believing that he was just a police officer, followed him and came to a halt.

He pretended that there had been a burglary in the neighborhood and asked a few fake questions about it. In his confession statement to police later, he said that his intent was to kidnap and rape the girl after luring her over to a deserted area.

Dana was able to narrowly avoid that after some fishermen spotted them both on the road. Gore had managed to trick her into following him on to a dark, desolate road, but his plan failed when the passing fishermen saw them. He abandoned his plan to abduct her and let her go unharmed. However, Dana found his behavior suspicious and narrated the incident to her family. It was then brought to the attention of sheriff officials, who opened up an investigation.

This investigation ultimately led Gore to quit the job at the Sheriff's office on account of "suspicious and improper conduct." In July of 1981, David Alan Gore had been released from duty, amidst an internal affairs investigation.

Marilyn Holland Owens

Marilyn was a twenty-three-year-old girl who Gore targeted just a couple of weeks after quitting his job. On July 31, 1981, he saw her in Vero Beach and started following her. In his confession statement, he said that he had seen her in the parking lot of a former doctor's clinic and was going to abduct her from there.

Upon seeing her car parked, he decided to break in and wait until she came back. This was when he was arrested by a police officer for trespassing. When he was caught, he had a .357 handgun along with a police scanner and a big glass jar filled with vodka.

The deputy police officer arrested him and charged him with armed trespassing. He was incarcerated and sentenced to a five-year imprisonment. However, in just two years, on March 15, 1983, he was released on parole.

Gore's statement said that he would have probably kidnapped her if he hadn't been caught by the police. He had broken into her car and was settling in her back seat when the deputy officer came and found him with the weapon and alcohol. Gore also stated that he was going to call his cousin Fred Waterfield "on that one."

Owens was fortunate enough to avoid the ordeal. Gore was caught and put away in jail for some time, hence, the killing cousins were unable to wreak any more havoc for the time that Gore was behind bars. However, he was let out and soon enough, the rampage began again, resulting in the deaths of the three other girls: Angelica LaVallee, Barbara Ann Byer, and then Lynn Elliot.

Diane Sullivan Smalley

According to court records, Smalley, aged twenty-seven, was targeted when she was driving up to Lake Wales. There was a gas station at a junction on State Road 60, and Diane Smalley had just driven out of there when the tires of her car were shot at.

In June of 1976, the cousins, David Alan Gore and Fred Waterfield followed the secretary from Miami when she was driving up to the lake. They shot out the tires of her Datsun 240Z, resulting in two of them going flat. Smalley had just left the gas station when she heard the 'pop' sound of her tires getting punctured. Upon realizing that she would be unable to go any farther like that, she pulled over to the side of the road.

This was when the cousins drove by and approached her under the pretense of offering help. She really thought that they were going to assist her and got out of the car.

As soon as she was outside, Waterfield pulled out his gun and shoved it into her ribs. Then both the men forced her to get into their car, a 1967 Chevrolet. Diane Smalley testified in court in 1985 and stated that she was in the backseat of their car and was looking for a way to escape.

She saw another car's headlights coming towards them and decided to make a run for it. In her testimony, she said that she took the chance, thinking that if they had already planned to kill her, then they might as well do it while she was "trying to get away."

Her escape was successful; she got away and luckily came across another couple that was driving by. They offered her a lift and she got into their car.

Upon reaching her home safely, she reported the incident to the authorities. At the time, Smalley did not know that the two men who had almost kidnapped her were serial killers and rapists. It was after their arrest in 1983, when she heard about Lynn Elliot's murder, that she realized who her abductors were.

Lynn Autrey
David Alan Gore saw Lynn Autrey in June of 1981 at Sebastian Inlet Beach. He told the investigating officials in his statements that he had targeted her for rape and murder. His plan was to kidnap her, assault the girl, and then possibly murder her after.

According to plan, he slashed the tires of her car, and then approached her, pretending to offer assistance with changing them. However, Gore couldn't go through with his plan when he realized that he actually recognized the girl.

In his statement, he said that Lynn Autrey also recognized him, as she had seen him on patrol before as an auxiliary deputy sheriff with the Indian River County Sheriff's Office.

Although Gore knew that his intended target was an acquaintance, he still came up with a fake story in order to get her to follow him to a nearby restaurant. He told Autrey that her boss, who was a police officer in Fellsmere, wanted to see her. Hence, she followed him into Stuckey's restaurant under the impression that her boss needed to meet with her.

Gore said that they met at the restaurant, situated near the Interstate 95 and the Country Road 512. After chatting with her for nearly an hour, the serial killer decided to let her go unscathed. He told the authorities that after getting to know her, he'd changed his mind about raping or murdering her.

Later on, when he was asked why he had left his victim unharmed, he said that it was "harder to do it to somebody you know."

Angela Hommell Austin

Austin, a resident of Colorado, was twenty years old when she became a rape victim of the cousins in 1976. Later on, she stated that she might have been the last woman whom the cousins raped but did not murder. Luckily enough, she somehow escaped death at the hands of the killing cousins.

Court records state that Austin, a German native, was sexually assaulted in June of 1976. In a statement, she said that Waterfield was friends with her ex-husband, which is why she asked him for help when she discovered her car outside her home with two flat tires.

Austin, thinking that Waterfield and Gore were acquaintances, asked them for a ride to work since her car could not be repaired in time. She said in an interview that what she thought was a friendly ride to work turned out to be the most harrowing and life-altering experience ever.

In an armed encounter, she was raped by both Gore and Waterfield, who pointed a gun at her. The incident occurred inside Fred Waterfield's vehicle, a Lincoln Continental, which the cousins parked in a desolate citrus grove.

During a deposition, Gore gave a sworn statement, saying that both he and Waterfield took turns raping Austin at gunpoint. However, they did not murder her, and they let her go when she promised that she wouldn't tell anybody or go to the police.

Austin, upon being released, went to the hospital and ultimately reported the encounter to the authorities. The cousins were detained in jail very briefly and questioned about it. They were let go when no charges could be pressed due to lack of evidence. Both Gore and Waterfield had insisted that there was no rape and everything was consensual.

Since the authorities were unable to prove otherwise, the case was unable to go any further and the killing cousins walked away free.

Unreported incidents

These were just the incidents that were recorded through Gore's statements. Experts and analysts did not rule out the possibilities of more victims who never came forward. There were speculations that Gore may have murdered more than the six victims found. During the investigation, the authorities did suspect that the killing cousins could have targeted other girls or women along the way as well.

The murderous spree that forever changed the quaint county around Vero Beach shook not only the people living there, but terrified everyone across the state of Florida.

Different people who lived in the area and knew the cousins came forward with their narratives. When Fred Waterfield was arrested, a woman who lived across the street from him couldn't believe that someone like him might have committed such heinous crimes. According to her, Fred Waterfield seemed like a "nice and polite guy." She said that he was "good-looking and always had a girlfriend with him."

Earlier on, she thought that his cousin David Gore was the one responsible for all the crimes and Waterfield may have been wrongly accused. However, a surprising revelation changed her entire perception.

She was in the car with her daughter, talking about Waterfield, when her daughter suddenly revealed that Fred Waterfield had raped her at the age of fourteen. Stunned into silence by her daughter's revelation, she didn't know what to say. In an interview later, she said that all she did after that was cry. Her daughter had kept it a secret for more than ten years and only came forward with this after Waterfield's arrest because she wanted her mother to know to truth.

The victim felt that she did not want to be silent anymore. She wanted people to know the truth. However, it was very difficult to deal with, as the lingering scars of the incident were always going to remain no matter what. In order to deal with the emotional stress, she underwent rape counseling years after the encounter took place.

The victim said that she was fourteen years old when Waterfield lured her over to a remote place under the pretense of showing her a flower field. She was a naïve child at the time and Waterfield was a high school football star.

After the incident, she was traumatized but didn't tell anyone. Her father was very proud of their family name, so to avoid bringing shame to the family, she preferred to remain quiet. Her mother later said that she should have confided with someone instead of staying silent and going on with life, pretending everything was fine. The mother also admitted to feeling bad about not being there for her daughter or knowing what was going on with her.

Finally, after coming forward with the incident, the victim said that she is trying to let go of what happened. Her focus is now towards her art, which has provided her with freedom and escape from the trauma in her life. She also said that she was going to forgive Waterfield as he was a "sick man and needed help."

The incident brought to light another very unpleasant encounter that her sister had to face. The victim learned that even her sister had to go through a violent experience when she was babysitting at Waterfield's house. She said that Waterfield had tried to make a move two or three times with the intent of molestation, and she had barely managed to avoid his advances. During one of his attempts, he even ripped out the phone when she tried calling for help. The woman admitted later on that she had never told anyone because he had apologized for what happened and she believed that he was being sincere.

Her younger sister, the rape victim, also admitted to feeling very guilty when reports of the heinous crimes committed by Waterfield and Gore made the rounds. In an interview, she said that maybe if she had reported the incident, the murderers might have been caught earlier on and it could have prevented the cousins from murdering all those innocent women.

When these reports came forward, Waterfield was sent a letter in prison, inquiring about them, but he refused to either confirm or deny the allegations.

***

A number of experts and analysts have tried to figure out what prompted David Alan Gore to go on a murderous spree. Many of them communicated with him in prison, writing letters to the serial killer, in order to get a closer look inside his mind.

Some of his letters were bone chilling, blood curdling accounts of how and what he had done to the girls who became his victims. In the letters that he wrote to an author, he revealed some very disturbing details about how he lured over his victims and what he did to them in captivity. These letters were brought to the attention of Governor Rick Scott, who eventually signed his death warrant in 2012, and saw that justice was served.

Despite everything Gore has provided, experts still haven't figured out what triggered the psychopathic tendencies within the serial killer. In his letters, he appeared remorseless, ruthless and a man who was ruled by his urge to kill.

In fact, in one of the letters, he even described that he kept on killing these girls because he could not control the urge that overpowered him. He wrote that the more he did it, the more he wanted to do it again. He wrote that, at that time, a woman was merely an object to him and that he "literally hunted" them.

Experts who analyzed his letters were actually left quite baffled. In his letters, he was almost polite and never seemed as violent as he could be. In a particular letter that he wrote to a female writer, he even admitted to being protective towards women that he "liked." Gore wrote to her saying that if he knew someone personally or liked her, she would be "off-limits."

***

Perhaps the greatest tribute that could have been given to the victims was justice being served. When David Alan Gore was executed, almost all of the victims' families drove over to see the death penalty carried out by lethal injection.

All the families were united in seeing that justice was served to the serial killer and rapist. Finally, after a delay of many years, they believed that they could now be at peace.

Chapter 9
ERIN CAFFEY
Child Killer
By Sylvia Perrini

Erin Caffey was just sixteen when she planned the shocking murders of her parents and two younger brothers at the familial home. What, people ask, could possibly make a child wish to annihilate her family?

Her parents, Penny Lynn Daily and Terry Caffey, met at a revival meeting in the city of Garland Texas, when he was 24 and she was 21. They were immediately attracted to each other, and their equally strong faith in the Baptist Church tied them closer together. In 1989, within eight months of knowing each other, they married. Penny was blonde, pretty and had a captivating smile. They lived at first in the small town of Celeste in Hunt County, Texas, where they had three children, Erin, Matthew (Bubba) and Tyler. Erin was born on July 27, 1991, Bubba in 1994 and Tyler in 1999.

In 2004, when Erin was 13, they moved to the rural farming community of Alba, with little more than four hundred inhabitants. Here they moved into a property that was reached by a narrow gravel road at the 1800 block on County Road 2370. The house sat on twelve acres of land in a remote dusty strip of pine-canopied woodland.

They moved here to be closer to the Miracle Faith Church, Emory where they served as the church's youth ministers. Emory, six miles from Alba, was another small town with one supermarket, 17 churches, and a population of around 1,200.

In Alba, Terry had a job delivering medical supplies to home health care patients, and Penny began to home school the children in a Bible-based curriculum. It was an isolated existence for children who had been used to attending school, and their only social life involved the church. On Wednesday evenings, they attended Bible study, and on Sundays they went to church. Members of the church congregation had to agree to a number of rules, one of them being a complete abstinence from alcohol.

Penny was musical and an accomplished pianist and, apart from playing for the church, she also joined a gospel band. She passed her musical talent on to Bubba, who became proficient at playing the harmonica and guitar, while blonde, blue-eyed Erin sang moving vocals with the voice of an angel for the church choir.

Above the family home doorway, a polished tree plank hung with the message inscribed upon it: "The Caffeys—Joshua 24:15." "If it seem evil unto you to serve the Lord, choose you this day whom ye will serve . . . as for me and my house, we will serve the Lord."

One day during a social gathering at the Miracle Faith Church, shortly before Erin's sixteenth birthday, she met another young teenager, Michael Washburn. They started talking, and he began to drop by her house to visit. Erin viewed him as her boyfriend. This relationship was abruptly halted by her parents when the two teenagers were spotted kissing behind the church with Michael's hand under her shirt, caressing a breast. Terry and Penny were deeply mortified by Erin's behavior and forbade them to see each other again.

When Erin turned sixteen and got her driver's license, her father bought her an old Chevy pickup. She took a day job at the Sonic in Emory, a burger fast-food joint and drive-in. From the beginning, she was a hit with the boys with her gentle, softly spoken voice, blue eyes, blonde hair, sweet pretty face, flirtatious smile and diminutive height of 4 feet, 11 inches. She sped around the drive-in cars, delivering her orders on roller skates. Many of the local boys would only visit the Sonic when they knew she was on duty, and Erin seemed to thrive on the attention and the effect she had.

At the beginning of the academic year of 2007-2008, Bubba and Tyler said they wanted to go back to public school as they missed their friends and sports. This suited Penny as financially the family was struggling, and she got a job as a driver for Meals On Wheels, delivering food to the elderly and disabled.

Eighteen-year-old Charlie Wilkinson had just arrived back in the Emory area after attending a boot camp with his Texas National Guard unit at Fort Sill, Oklahoma. He was about to start his senior year of high school when one afternoon he spotted Erin at the Sonic. He was immediately smitten with the petite blonde and would drive to the Sonic in his beat-up 1991 Ford Explorer on an almost daily basis to see her.

Charlie lived out in the country with his dad, stepmom, stepsister, stepbrother and, half-sister. He rarely saw his mom since his parents had divorced as she had moved to Del Rio. His father worked at a paper mill near Dallas. Like many of the other kids in the area, he enjoyed outdoor pursuits such as fishing and hunting wild hogs and, like the other kids, he was adept with a firearm. Although only an average student he was never any trouble at school and had never been in trouble with the law.

It did not take Erin long to notice the attractive sandy-haired, light blue-eyed boy who turned up almost daily and when he asked her out on a date, she immediately accepted as she had instantly been taken with him in his black cowboy boots, Wranglers, and large Western hat.

When Erin took Charlie home to meet her parents, they were not impressed with him. In particular, Terry disliked him as he thought he was a disrespectful young man. But Penny, who was more tolerant, accepted him into the family home. They would not, however, allow the two teenagers to be alone together. Nor was Erin allowed to talk to Charlie after her phone curfew of 9:30, 10:00 on weekends.

As the weeks wore on, Erin and Charlie seemed to become more and more infatuated with each other and considered each other to be soul mates. Charlie talked about Erin to his friends almost endlessly, and every afternoon he would join Erin for her half-hour break. In the evenings, he would frequently spend it at the Caffeys' house until nine when her parents would tell him it was time to leave. Charlie also began to attend the Miracle Faith Church. The pastor of the church, Pastor McGahee, would later say, "He seemed like a nice boy."

In December of 2007, Erin asked Terry and Penny if she could re-enroll in school with her brothers. Her parents agreed. Once Erin was back at school, she and Charlie would spend all their spare time together and would walk down the school corridors hand in hand, or slip out to Erin's pickup to make out. Occasionally her parents would allow them to eat out together as long as Charlie had her home by nine-thirty.

On one of their nights out, Charlie went down on his knee and presented Erin with a promise ring he said had belonged to his grandmother. As he slipped it on her finger, he vowed to be faithful to Erin forever and promised to always take care of her. Erin was delighted with the ring and proudly displayed it to her girlfriends.

When her mother spotted the ring on her finger, she was furious and demanded that she remove it immediately. When Terry returned home from work later that evening, Penny gave it to him. Both parents were alarmed at the speed and intensity of the relationship. A couple of days later, Terry spotted Charlie playing basketball and confronted him with the ring.

"This is totally out of order," he shouted as he waved the ring in Charlie's face. "Erin is only sixteen years old. I'm not having it."

Terry and Penny then gave Erin a new set of rules that she was to obey if she wanted to continue her relationship with Charlie. From that point on, they told her, she was only to see Charlie once a week at their house under their supervision. Erin was furious with her parents and told her school friends and aunt that when she turned seventeen, she was going to leave home to live with Charlie.

The relationship of the Caffeys and Erin deteriorated further when Penny overheard her teenage daughter giggling one night on her phone at eleven in the evening—one-and-a-half hours past her permitted phone time. Penny was incensed and grounded her, confiscated her phone and car keys, and forbade Charlie's weekly visits. For the next several weeks, Penny drove her daughter to and from school.

Erin was distraught and felt trapped. She began to hate her parents with a vengeance and wished them dead. She told Charlie the only way they could be together was if they killed her parents. She became obsessed with the idea and talked about it relentlessly. Charlie was not happy with the situation either as he missed hanging out with Erin. Even when she finally got her car keys back, Charlie's visits were still not permitted.

In February, Charlie turned nineteen, and he suggested that if he got Erin pregnant, then her family would have to accept him. Erin, however, scoffed at that idea as she said she was far too young to have a baby. He then suggested that they just run away together, but Erin told Charlie her father would only come after them and separate them again. She insisted that the only way they could be together was by killing her parents. Charlie, who was totally wrapped around her finger, told her he would do whatever he had to do to make her happy. He talked to a few of his friends about killing Erin's parents but seemed ambivalent about the idea, preferring the idea of running away with her.

In February, close friends of Terry and Penny sensed that not all was right with the Caffey family. Penny seemed withdrawn and depressed, and Erin was unfriendly and appeared preoccupied. On February 27, Penny's sister, Mandy, phoned her and suggested she that she go to the library and check out Charlie's MySpace profile, where he went by the name 'Hillbilly.' Penny did as Mandy suggested and was absolutely horrified with what she found. She was so upset that she phoned Terry at work and demanded that he leave work early and join her at the library.

What they had found on Charlie's profile was comments about getting drunk and having sex.

When Erin arrived home from school that day, she found her parents sitting stony-faced in the living room waiting for her.

"It's over," her father thundered at her. "You are not to have anything to do with that boy again. Your mom and I didn't raise you to be this way. He's no good for you. You will end your relationship today."

***

In the early hours of March 1, 2008, as Terry and Penny were sleeping in their ground-floor bedroom, two gunmen burst into their room with guns and a samurai sword and began shooting at them. Terry recalls that as he lay there, the right side of his body felt paralyzed. He couldn't make a sound and felt like he'd been shot in the face. As he lay there in fear, one of the men took the sword to Penny, aged 37, and began stabbing her in the neck, almost decapitating her. As Terry, aged 41, lay in his bed drifting in and out of consciousness, he felt panicked about the thought of his children sleeping peacefully in their beds upstairs. He heard his 13-year-old son Bubba cry out. "No, Charlie. No, don't! Why are you doing this?"

It was then that Terry realized who was in his family home and why. He then heard more gunfire before once again drifting into unconsciousness. The gunmen had shot Bubba and then took turns stabbing 8-year-old Tyler with the samurai sword where he tried to hide in a cupboard.

When Terry next regained consciousness, the house was on fire. He realized his wife was dead, and he was unable to make it upstairs because of the intensity of the flames. Somehow he dragged himself out of the bed and crawled into the bathroom and out of the window and away from the house.

Slowly, Terry crawled 300 yards, bleeding profusely, through the woods to Tommy Gaston's house, his neighbor and friend—a journey that normally took him about five minutes had taken him nearly an hour to complete. He reached his neighbor's house and banged on the door.

Tommy was horrified by the state of his friend as he stumbled and crawled in through his front door shortly after 4:30 in the morning, leaving a trail of blood across the floor.

"What's happened?" Tommy asked.

"I've been shot."

"Where's Penny and the kids?" Tommy asked.

"They're all dead. Charlie shot them all," he gasped before collapsing.

Tommy immediately rang 911 and told the operator his friend had been shot and was bleeding.

"Where is he bleeding from?" asked the operator.

"Where isn't he bleeding from?" Tommy replied. "It's a miracle he's here at all."

After putting the phone down on Tommy, the operator immediately alerted the Rains County Sheriff's Office. Officer Charles Dickerson took the call and immediately made his way over to Tommy's house and arrived at the same time as an ambulance with flashing lights brightened up the darkness of the cold, gloomy night. In Tommy's living room, he could see the bloodied body of Terry Caffey lying in a pool of blood on the living room floor. The paramedics immediately made their way over to Terry and placed him on a gurney and carried him out to the waiting ambulance. Terry had been shot five times: twice in the back, once in the head, and twice by his right shoulder.

As he was carried out to the ambulance, he managed to splutter to Charles Dickerson, "They're all dead. Charlie Wilkinson shot my family."

Terry was rushed off to the critical care unit of the East Texas Medical Center in Tyler. As the ambulance left Tommy's house, Richard Almon, the sheriff's investigator, and chief deputy Kurt Fischer arrived just as Charles Dickerson was asking Terry who Charlie Wilkinson was.

Tommy explained to the three men that Charlie Wilkinson was Terry and Penny's daughter Erin's boyfriend who neither

Terry nor Penny approved of, and they had recently forbidden Erin from seeing him. As the men listened, Kurt Fischer said that he knew Charlie; he was a friend of his two sons. Given how small the community was, there was nothing surprising in this. He went on to say that he had noticed, on the way over to Tommy's, Charlie's car parked outside Matthew Waid's trailer. Matthew was another local young man, a couple of years older than Charlie, whose younger brother Charles also hung out with his sons.

"I guess you better stop by the trailer then, Kurt, and have a word with him," said Richard Almon.

While Terry was in the hospital, he learnt that Erin was still alive. He thought that maybe she had managed to survive like him. It gave him a sense of hope again, something worth living for. That hope was short-lived.

***

After her parents forbade her any further contact with Charlie, Erin insisted that Charlie kill them. He still just wanted to run away with her, but she eventually persuaded Charlie it was the only way forward. They enlisted two friends to help them: Charles Waid, a twenty-year-old hunting buddy of Charlie's, and his animated high school senior girlfriend, Bobbi Johnson.

Erin had told Charlie that there was a lockbox in the house containing $2,000 that they could pay Charles with. This seemed to be enough to persuade Charles Waid to take part in the killings. They decided to carry out the plan on the night of February 29–March 1, after Erin's parents had gone to bed.

That evening, the two young men started drinking heavily, contemplating the night ahead. As it approached midnight, Erin phoned Charlie on his cell phone from the family home wanting to know what was keeping them. Between midnight and 1 a.m., she made a total of six calls to him, urging him to hurry up.

The boys finally decided to follow through with their plan. Charles Waid, driving his girlfriend's car, a silver Dodge Neon, went to the Caffey home. Bobbi insisted on going with them. At 1.15 a.m., as the two young men got out of the car to approach the Caffey's house, the family dog barked so much they bottled out and turned back.

Moments later, Erin called Charlie, wanting to know where they were and what was keeping them. When Charlie told her it was the dog's barking, she promised to keep it quiet when they returned. Charlie said he was no longer sure and why didn't they just run away. Between 1:22 to 1:58, Erin called Charlie seven times. Eventually, Charlie told Charles to turn the car around and return to Erin's family home.

Erin was waiting at the end of the driveway and climbed into the rear seat of the Dodge Neon next to Bobbi Johnson. They sat in the car for about an hour arguing about the murders; Charlie was still trying to persuade her to just run away until Erin, tired and irritated by all the bickering said, "Just do it."

Charlie and Charles climbed out of the car and made their way to the Caffey's house where Erin had left the front door open for them. They entered Terry and Penny's bedroom on the first floor, armed with a samurai sword and a .22-caliber gun and shot them while they lay in bed. Before they left the room, Charlie cut Penny's throat as she was still making sounds.

The noise of the gunfire had woken Tyler and Bubba, who cried out for their parents. They, then realizing something was seriously amiss, ran to Erin's empty bedroom and locked themselves in.

Charlie and Charles then made their way upstairs to take care of the boys. Charlie talked to the boys through the door and persuaded Bubba to come out, the young boy came out and pleaded with Charlie and asked him why he was doing this. Charles then shot the boy in the face. He immediately fell down and never moved again. Tyler, meanwhile, had hidden in a closet where Charles hunted him down, and the two young men then took turns in stabbing the young child.

Following the killing spree, Charlie collected Erin's previously packed suitcase, located the lockbox and emptied it with the combination number Erin had provided him with, along with any other cash they could find in the house. They then set fire to the house, and returned triumphantly to the car and the waiting girls.

As Erin sat in the backseat of the car and watched her home burn with her family confined within it, Charlie noted she looked happy.

"Holy shit, that's awesome," she said as the two boys climbed back into the front seats. After driving around back streets for a bit to calm down, Charles Waid took them all to his older brother's Matthew's trailer to spend the night. Here, Charlie and Erin had sex, free, they mistakenly thought, of any repercussions from her family or anyone else.

***

After leaving Tommy Gaston's house, Kurt Fischer and an officer stopped by Matthew Waid's trailer home. It was shrouded in darkness and no lights were on. Kurt knocked on the door and a bleary-eyed Matthew groggily answered.

"Is Charlie Wilkinson here?" Kurt asked.

"I've no idea, man. But feel free to take a look," Matthew answered, not wanting to be bothered with any trouble his kid brother's friend may have gotten into.

Kurt wandered through the empty-beer-can strewn, messy trailer. He opened one door and saw Charles Waid and his girlfriend and quickly closed the door. He walked down a hallway and opened another door to see Charlie Wilkinson, bare-chested but wearing jeans lying awake in bed, with a semiautomatic gun lying beside him.

"Hi, Charlie," said Kurt.

"What's up?" Charlie asked.

"The Caffey family has been murdered and I need to ask you some questions."

The other officer accompanying Kurt had his gun trained on him, and Charlie obediently got out of bed. Kurt turned the half-naked teenager around and handcuffed him before leading him out onto the porch and reading him his Miranda rights. Charlie was silent.

"Did you have anything to do with it?" Kurt asked.

"No, sir, I got drunk last night and passed out," Charlie said, as he hung his head. Kurt sent the officer with him to fetch Charlie a t-shirt and his boots. The officer went to Charlie's room and retrieved the items off the floor. As he held them up, he noted that they were splattered with blood.

With Charlie in custody, Kurt returned to the trailer with a search warrant. By the time he got back there, Matthew, Charles Waid, and Bobbi Johnson had left. In the living room of the trailer, he found a purse containing Erin Caffey's driver's license. In the back bedroom, spent shell casings lay strewn across the floor, and a box of ammunition was on a table next to the bed. As he pulled the sheet off the bed, a recently used condom fell to the floor.

In a corner near to a closet, a blanket covered a shape on the floor. He lifted the blanket and was shocked to see a small blonde girl curled up in the fetal position. She opened her eyes and stared up at him.

"What's your name?" Kurt asked.

"Erin Caffey," she stuttered. Kurt held his hand out and helped her to her feet and led her to a sofa in the living room. Kurt thought she seemed disorientated and wondered if she was on some kind of drug.

"How did you get here?" Kurt asked.

"I don't know," she stammered with wide eyes. "Where am I?"

Kurt thought she looked sweet and candid with her hair tied back off her face into a ponytail and dressed in flower-print pajamas.

"Can you tell me what happened?" Kurt asked.

"Fire," she told Kurt; her voice a mere whisper. An ambulance was called for and she was taken to a hospital in Sulphur Springs and given a full medical assessment.

Detective Almon decided that she should be interviewed in the trauma room at the hospital. At this point, the police thought Erin was a victim who had been kidnapped after the murders, and they felt profoundly sorry for her, as she had just lost her mother and two brothers. Erin was unaware at this point that her father had survived.

During the interview she spoke in a soft, childlike, timid voice. She said she had woken up in her house, which was full of smoke, and saw "two guys with swords." They had been dressed all in black with masks and ordered her to lie on the floor. She said she couldn't remember how she got to the trailer, but when she got there, she was given something to drink and couldn't remember anything else, except at some point trying to phone her friend Charlie.

Her grandmother, Virginia Daily, came to visit her at the hospital and told Erin that her father had, amazingly, survived the attack. Two other police officers, Chief Sanders and Deputy Booth, remained at the hospital, waiting for Erin to be released.

Meanwhile, down at the sheriff's office in Emory, Charlie Wilkinson was being interviewed. At first he was reluctant to cooperate, but when Detective Almon informed him that Terry Caffey had survived and had identified him as one of the attackers, Charlie made a full confession and identified Erin as being the instigator of the attack.

Charles Waid and Bobbi Johnson were arrested and brought in for questioning. They too made full confessions, which mirrored Charlie's and implicated Erin as the mastermind.

The hospital in Sulphur Springs sent Detective Almon Erin's medical report. Her toxicology test was negative, and she displayed no symptoms of smoke inhalation.

Erin, meanwhile, was released from the hospital and was being driven by Chief Sanders and Deputy Booth, and followed by her grandparents Larry and Virginia Daily, to visit her father in the intensive care ward in Tyler. As they were driving Chief Sanders's cell phone rang. She listened to the voice on the other end of the phone in shocked silence and then handed the phone to Deputy Booth.

"You want us to do that now?" asked Deputy Booth.

Chief Sanders pulled the squad car into a parking lot followed by Larry and Virginia Daily.

Sanders got out of the car and told the grandparents that they had been ordered to place Erin under arrest as she had been implicated in the murders of her family. Chief Sanders then returned to the squad car and requested Erin to step out of the car. When she stepped out of the car, Deputy Booth handcuffed her while Chief Sanders read Erin her Miranda rights.

Erin's grandmother became hysterical and clutched hold of her granddaughter's face. "Did you have any part in this?" she demanded.

"No, Grandma," Erin replied, crying. She was then driven to Greenville and the juvenile detention center where she was held on three capital murder charges.

Less than twenty-four hours after the murder and arson attack, Charles Waid, Charlie Wilkinson, Bobbi Johnson, and Erin Caffey were all in custody.

***

Erin, during further questioning while in custody, stuck to her original story.

During the ongoing investigation, detectives interviewed her school friends who corroborated that Erin had talked about killing her parents and frequently wished they were dead. The boy whom Erin was caught kissing at Miracle Faith, months before she began dating Charlie, told detectives that

Erin had told him about her wish to have them killed—and that she thought about hiring a hit man.

Terry Caffey was discharged from the hospital several days later and went to stay with his sister in the town of Leonard, about an hour's drive from Alba. He suffered from severe depression and thought about suicide.

Despite this, twice a week he drove to Greenville to visit his daughter. Erin's lawyer warned him that all their conversations were recorded and anything his daughter might say to him could be used against her at trial. Thus their conversations tended to be very mundane. All the questions he wanted to ask her, he couldn't. He found the visits excruciatingly difficult as detectives tried to convince him that Erin was the mastermind behind the murders, but she was his only surviving child and he always ended each visit by telling her he loved her.

The prosecutors in the cases of Charlie Wilkinson and Charles Waid wanted the death penalty. And in Erin's case, they wanted her to be tried as an adult. If she was tried as an adult, she could be imprisoned for life without parole; as a juvenile, she would not be eligible for the death penalty.

After various court appearances, a judge in Rains County agreed that Erin should be tried as an adult, and she was transferred from juvenile detention in Greenville to Sulphur Springs, Hopkins County Jail.

Despite the overwhelming evidence against Erin, Terry supported her at every court appearance, holding her hand when allowed, and continued to visit her at the County Jail.

Terry forgave his daughter, along with Charlie Wilkinson and Charles Waid. In an interview, he said that he realized that in order to move on with his life and not become embittered, "he had to forgive those who took the lives of his family."

He wrote a letter to Robert Vititow, the district attorney of Rains County, in which he said, "My heart tells me there have been enough deaths. I want them, in this lifetime, to have a chance for remorse and to come to a place of repentance for what they have done. Killing them will not bring my family back."

He asked that Charles Waid and Charlie Wilkinson instead be given sentences of life in prison with no parole and be spared the death penalty. The district attorney granted Terry his wishes and offered the two young men a plea deal. As part of the deal, Waid and Wilkinson had to face Terry and elucidate their actions.

In October 2008, Charles Waid and Charlie Wilkinson each pleaded guilty to three counts of capital murder. In November 2008, they were each sentenced to life in prison without the possibility of parole.

Terry also pleaded to the district attorney on behalf of his daughter Erin. He asked that she be given a sentence less than life without parole. He wanted her to have something to live for. Once again, the attorney general honored his request in a plea deal with Erin.

In January 2009, Erin Caffey and Bobbi Johnson both pleaded guilty to murder. Bobbi Johnson was sentenced to two 40-year concurrent sentences, and Erin Caffey was given two consecutive life sentences, plus an additional 25 years.

Bobbi Johnson will be eligible for parole in 2028. Erin will not be eligible for parole until she is around 59 years old. Erin was sent to the high-security prison in Gatesville, Texas, where she still remains.

Terry Caffey has since remarried but makes a three-hour trip once a month to visit his daughter. He hopes to still be alive when she walks out of prison. Since she's been sentenced, he has been able to ask her all the questions he'd longed to ask her while awaiting trial.

She told him she had known of the plan and had thought about running away that night, but she'd changed her mind and decided to stay and persuade Charlie to change his mind, and that was what the phone calls were all about. It was Charlie who'd wanted the family dead, and when he arrived at the house, she had gone out to stop him but had been forced to wait in the car with Bobbi and had been powerless to stop Charlie or Charles.

Terry said, "Charlie tried to pin it on her, claiming she was the mastermind and he was only going along with it because she had brainwashed him, but I know that's not true. That's not Erin. She was a vulnerable 16-year-old girl with a controlling, psychopathic boyfriend."

Piers Morgan interviewed Erin Caffey for a TV series, *Killer Women,* which was broadcast in the U.K. in May 2016. In an interview after the broadcast he said, "Erin Caffey is the most dangerous woman I have met in my entire life."

This statement was echoed by Israel Lewis, a criminal therapist who worked with Erin after her arrest. She said, "I've never come across anyone as dangerous as Erin, and I hope I never do again. She was the best liar I've encountered in my career."

Chapter 10
KENNETH ALLEN McDUFF
The Broomstick Killer
By JJ Slate

If ever there was a time you could say the justice system truly failed to protect the citizens of a community, surely the case of Kenneth Allen McDuff would be that time. This is the story of a man with a criminal past who received a death sentence for the murder of three innocent people, but was later paroled (yes, you read that correctly—paroled after being sentenced to death) and released back into the general population where he went on to kill at least a half-dozen more times.

Born in 1946 in Rosebud, Texas, Kenneth Allen McDuff lived anything but an ordinary childhood. His father, John Allen McDuff, was a successful businessman, running his own concrete pouring company at the height of the construction boom in the 1960s. His mother, Adilee "Addie" Howard McDuff, was a tough old bird, gaining the nickname of the "pistol packing momma" after she threatened a bus driver one day for kicking Kenneth's older brother, Lonnie, off the bus. Though Kenneth wasn't quite the baby of the family, his mother doted on him like he was and later described him as "the tenderest-hearted of my children."

The fifth of six children (two boys, four girls), Kenneth grew up pretending to be tougher than he really was. His hulking stature helped him appear intimidating, and he often bullied younger, weaker kids at school, stealing their lunch money. But after he picked a fight with a kid tougher than him—and lost—Kenneth dropped out of school to work alongside his brother, Lonnie, in his father's business.

At the age of eighteen, Kenneth just couldn't keep himself out of trouble. He loved drinking, doing drugs, and engaging the local police in high-speed car racing. Those who knew him called him "Mac" or "Cowboy," referencing the cowboy hat and boots he often wore. It wasn't long before Mac started burglarizing homes nearby.

In March of 1965, Mac was sentenced to thirteen four-year prison terms (a total of 52 years) for burglary, but instead of serving them consecutively, the judge ordered that his sentences be served concurrently. This meant Mac was paroled less than two years later. Prison toughened him up, and he emerged an angrier, more dangerous man than when he went in.

The Broomstick Murders

August 6, 1966, started out as a typical Saturday in Texas. Mac asked one of his friends, eighteen-year-old Roy Dale Green, to help him pour some concrete that day for his father's business. They finished up around noon, had some lunch, and then headed to Fort Worth, Texas, where Mac said he knew some girls they could meet up with for a little fun. They stopped off for some beer along the way and headed north in Mac's Dodge Coronet.

Around ten o'clock that evening, the two were still aimlessly driving around the Texas dark roads. Mac noticed a pretty girl standing next to a car with two male teens at a baseball field near Everman High School. He cut the lights, pulled the car over, and instructed Roy to stay out of sight until he told him to come out.

"What are you gonna do?" Roy asked him nervously.

Mac reached over his friend and pulled a .38 Colt revolver from the glove compartment. "I'm gonna get me a girl."

The three teens didn't see Mac until he was standing right next to them, pointing a gun at their heads. He ordered them to give him all their wallets, the keys to the car, and to get into the trunk of their 1955 Ford. The trio quickly complied and Mac closed the trunk, locking them inside. Then he called out for Roy and told him he'd locked all three in the trunk.

Mac ordered Roy to get in the Dodge and follow him in the Ford. Roy complied and followed the vehicle to a secluded area next to a pasture.

After looking through the wallets, Mac opened the trunk slowly and ordered the girl out of the car. A young sixteen-year-old named Edna (who went by her middle name, Louise) Sullivan cautiously stepped out of the trunk and looked at the two men with fear in her eyes. Mac told his friend to put the girl in the trunk of the Dodge, which he did.

When Roy turned back, Mac stood over the two teens, holding the gun steadily. Mac told Roy the two had gotten a good look at his face, and he needed to kill them. Roy would later testify that he'd only met Mac a month earlier, and though he'd listened to his new friend brag about times he'd committed rape and murder, he wasn't exactly sure if he was actually capable of something like that. Until that moment.

While the boys pleaded with their captor for their lives, Mac began shooting. The first two shots went directly into seventeen-year-old Robert Brand's head. He then turned the gun on fifteen-year-old Marcus Dunnam, shooting him several times in the head, including once between the eyes. In all, six shots had been fired into the trunk, killing the two teens.

Roy couldn't comprehend what he'd just seen. He stared at his friend and asked him why he'd killed those boys.

Mac just shrugged. "I had to."

The two folded up the limbs of the dead kids and closed the trunk on them one last time. Then Mac ordered Roy to find something to wipe the car down with. Almost zombielike, Roy pulled a clean shirt out of the backseat of the Ford and began wiping the trunk, trying to remove any fingerprints from the vehicle. He then entered the driver's side and wiped down the steering wheel and gearshift before exiting the car and wiping the door handle. The two then used the shirt to try to cover up the tire tracks in the dirt before driving away in Mac's Dodge with Louise in the trunk.

The two drove in silence for a while. Eventually, Mac pulled over on a deserted dirt road with tall grass on either side and ordered Louise out of the trunk. He ordered her to take her clothes off and forced her into the backseat, where he raped her. Mac then offered the girl to Roy, who at this point was still coming to grips with the events of the past few hours. Roy declined to take over, which only enraged Mac.

Thinking about the gun and how his life might be in danger too, Roy quickly changed his mind and told his friend he would like a turn after all. Mac relinquished the backseat and Roy climbed on top of the terrified girl and had his way with her. He later testified that he couldn't get fully aroused during the rape and had kept his eyes on Mac the entire time, worried about what might happen next.

After Roy was finished, Mac climbed back into the backseat and continued to molest Louise while Roy drove. At one point, Mac used the jagged edge of a broken broomstick in the backseat to rape the girl. Roy remembered hearing her cry out in pain at that point, "Stop! I think you ripped something!"

Eventually, Mac lost interest in Louise and ordered Roy to pull over onto a rocky road. He pulled Louise out of the car and told her to put her clothes on. Towering over the quivering girl, still holding the broken broomstick, Mac yelled at Roy to get him some rope to tie her up with.

There was no rope in the car, Roy told him, and offered him his belt.

Mac ordered Louise to sit on the ground and suddenly lunged at her. Straddling her hips, he held the broomstick against her throat and pushed her into the rocky ground. Louise's legs kicked and splayed out in every direction as she tried to push the stick away from her neck, gasping for air.

"Hold her legs!" Mac grunted at Roy as he continued to push on the stick.

"No!" Roy yelled and pleaded with his friend to leave her alone. Hadn't he done enough?

"It has to be done," Mac replied, matter-of-factly.

Reluctantly, Roy grabbed Louise's legs and held them until she stopped moving.

The two then carried Louise's lifeless body to a nearby

fence and hurled her over it into some bushes. Then, almost like an afterthought, Mac jumped the fence, ripped a necklace of a German cross off her neck, and shoved it into his pocket.

Once they were back in the car, with Roy in the passenger's seat, Mac pulled the necklace out of his pocket and told his friend to get rid of it.

Roy rolled down his window and tossed the chain onto the road. As they began driving, they threw other incriminating items out the window—the broomstick, a soda bottle that Mac had used to rape Louise, and the spent shell casings from the gun. At some point, they pulled over and buried the boys' wallets before heading back to Roy's house, where they spent the night.

Roy later claimed that Mac told him, "Keep your mouth shut. If the police beat on you, it's better than what'll happen if you tell them. They'll put you in the electric chair."

The next morning, Mac buried his gun next to Roy's garage, and the two spent some time cleaning out the interior of the car. After Mac left, Roy confessed what they had done the night before to his friend's parents. They called Roy's mother, who encouraged him to call the police. By then, the bodies of the two teens had already been discovered in the trunk of their car, but Louise was still considered missing.

After his arrest, Roy led two sheriff's deputies to the spot where Mac had buried the gun. But when they tried to dig it up, they found someone had already beaten them to it. The gun was never recovered. When the deputies showed up to arrest Mac, they found he too had vanished.

Roy spent several days trying to help the police find Louise's body. Since he'd never really been in the area before, he couldn't be sure exactly where they'd left her that night. Days after the murder, her body was finally discovered and identified.

Dead Man Walking

Mac was eventually caught, and the two were put on trial. During the trial, Mac remained adamant that Roy had killed the three teens, not him. Mac took the stand in his own defense and claimed the gun had been Roy's and he'd let his friend borrow his car that night. But the jury did not agree. On November 5, 1966, he was found guilty of capital murder and was later sentenced to death by electric chair.

Roy pleaded guilty to murder without malice in the death of Marcus Dunnam, for which he received a five-year sentence. He also pleaded guilty to murder with malice in the death of Edna Louise Sullivan, for which he received an additional twenty-five-year sentence. He ended up getting paroled in 1979, after serving just thirteen years for his part in the crimes.

Mac, on the other hand, continued to vie for his release, steadfastly claiming his innocence. His first execution date was set for December 3, 1968. Just days before that date, he received a stay of execution, and his new date was set at January 2, 1969. Unbelievably, he received three more stays of execution over the next several years until the Supreme Court ruled that death by electric chair was considered "cruel and unusual punishment." On September 18, 1972, Mac's death sentence was commuted to life in prison with the possibility of parole. (In 1976, the Supreme Court reinstated the death penalty, but Mac's sentence remained unchanged.)

From that day forward, Mac's demeanor changed. He was no longer a man who knew the date of his execution. He was now a man who did everything possible to secure his release from prison. He was on his best behavior and began taking college courses in prison for credit—anything he could do to prove he was a hardworking, well-behaved man who could continue to contribute to society upon his release.

In 1977, Mac's family paid an attorney to write a lengthy petition detailing how Roy had committed the crimes and not Mac. The attorney also subjected Mac to a polygraph test, which he passed. Finally, he insisted Mac had been denied the right to a speedy trial due to a clerical error that had occurred years ago. His lawyer had filed a *Writ for a Quick and Speedy*

Trial in 1970, but for some reason, the paperwork was treated as a *Writ of Habeas Corpus* and denied. Essentially, that meant the courts had denied Mac the right to a quick and speedy trial, something that violated his constitutional rights.

A judge agreed. On March 8, 1978, the rape and capital murder charges in regards to Edna Louise Sullivan's case were dismissed, though the other murder charges still stuck. He was eventually released on parole on October 11, 1989, after serving twenty-three years in prison for the broomstick murders. Just one day later, it is believed, he had already killed his next victim.

Zero Remorse

On October 14, 1989, the body of twenty-nine-year-old Sarafia Parker was found in the town of Temple, just fifty miles south of Waco. She had last been seen in a pickup truck driven by a man, later identified by the witness as Kenneth McDuff, on October 12, the same day he'd traveled to Temple to visit his parole officer. While he has never been charged with her murder and the eyewitness testimony is all the evidence police had against Mac, to this day many believe Sarafia's murder was the spark that reignited the killing frenzy in a deeply disturbed killer's mind.

People who had followed the broomstick murder case for years were astonished to learn that the courts had let a convicted murderer—one who'd been on death row for his actions—just walk out of prison. Those who'd worked so hard to convict him were disgusted with a legal system that had let them down. Many assumed bodies would start to turn up, and several people in the community admitted to keeping a loaded gun ready in their homes, just in case.

One year after gaining his freedom, Mac violated one of his parole conditions and was sent back to prison. Just two months later, he walked out a free man once again. The return to prison did not scare him straight. As soon as he was released, he quickly returned to his old practices of drinking heavily, doing drugs, and picking up prostitutes. To avoid living with his parents, he took advantage of Project RIO (Re-Integration of Offenders), a program that provided grants to convicts seeking college or trade school education. The forty-five-year-old received an eight-hundred-dollar loan for his studies at Texas State Technical College and was placed in student housing. All he had to do to keep his new place of residence was show up for class.

One night in October of 1991, Mac picked up thirty-seven-year-old Brenda Thompson in Waco, Texas, presumably for a sexual encounter. At some point, he tied her up and began to drive her to a different location. He soon realized he was driving right into a police checkpoint and slowed down to contemplate his next move. One of the officers running the checkpoint began to walk toward Mac's red pickup truck when he saw a female in the passenger seat start screaming and repeatedly kicking at the front windshield. Spider-web cracks appeared in the glass before Mac stepped on the gas and drove directly toward the officer and his colleagues, who were forced to leap out of the path of the oncoming vehicle.

The officers piled into their patrol cars and tried to track him down, but Mac turned off his lights and took several dark, one-way streets, managing to shake his tail. He eventually parked his truck near a secluded wooded area and killed Brenda before burying her body in a shallow grave. Her body remained there until she was discovered in 1998.

Just a few days after Brenda's disappearance, one of her friends, seventeen-year-old Regenia Moore, also disappeared. She was last seen in Kenneth McDuff's red pickup truck as he was driving around his usual parts, looking for cocaine to buy. Her body also wasn't found until 1998.

A week after Regenia's disappearance, police interviewed Kenneth McDuff, who indeed admitted picking up the missing girl in his father's red pickup truck that day, but also told police he "dated" many women in the area and dropped her off in the same area he picked her up after their "date" that day. He stressed the word "date" as if to imply the encounter was strictly sexual and not romantic or friendly in nature. Police also noted that Mac's truck was the same truck involved in the police checkpoint incident just weeks earlier, but he was not questioned about it, nor was he issued a ticket or arrested for reckless driving, evading the police, endangering an officer's life, or kidnapping. Another missed opportunity. Mac was free to continue on his way.

Weeks later, Mac returned the red pickup truck with the cracked windshield to his father in exchange for a beige Thunderbird one of his sisters had driven for years before buying something new.

An Unrelated Crime?

On December 6, 1991, four teenage girls were found dead in an Austin, Texas, yogurt shop after it was set on fire. Three of the four girls were found naked and stacked on top of each other. They were tied up with items of their own clothing. The other teen had been raped and strangled, and all four had been shot in the head before they were set on fire.

In the years since the murders, police claim over fifty people have confessed to the Yogurt Shop Murders, including two teen suspects who were charged with the murders in 1999. Two of their friends were also charged, but those charges were later dropped due to lack of evidence. The two teens recanted their confessions before their trials, claiming they'd been coerced by detectives who'd interrogated them for hours on end. A jury convicted Robert Springsteen of capital murder in 2001 and sentenced him to death. A year later, his friend, Michael Scott, was also convicted and sentenced to life in prison. An appeals court later overturned both convictions due to unfair trials. The prosecutors had used pieces of each of the other teen's confession in both trials and did not allow for cross-examination of those witnesses, which denied each defendant the right to face his accuser.

After DNA evidence excluded Springsteen and Scott from

samples taken from the crime scene, the two were released from prison in 2009, after ten years of incarceration. The state dismissed all charges against both men a few months later, and no new charges have been filed in the case.

While it would seem to many as if the case has gone stone cold, it's interesting to note that we now know a well-known serial killer was actively murdering young women in the Austin, Texas, area in this same time period. Not only did he shoot two of his Broomstick Murder victims in the head, but he also raped the female teen and strangled her to death. He also liked to tie his victims up with articles of their own clothing, something investigators would learn in later years. Another interesting fact? Kenneth McDuff allegedly confessed to the Yogurt Shop Murders several years later, but police still insist he is not the killer.

Déjà vu?

On December 29, 1991, while cruising around the streets of Austin, Texas, with his friend, Alva Hank Worley, Mac suddenly turned down a street and pulled into a carwash where a young woman was washing her Mazda Miata in one of the stalls. He casually walked up to the petite woman and grabbed her by the throat with one hand, easily lifting her off the ground, pinning her arms behind her back with his other hand. He carried her back to the car, where Hank stood waiting.

Hank's story, similar to Roy Dale Green's account twenty-five years earlier, would be he initially had no idea why Mac had stopped the car that night. But when he saw his friend walking toward him, carrying a screaming woman by the throat, he acted out of fear when he helped get her in the backseat of the Thunderbird and tried to restrain her while Mac drove away.

At an exit, Mac pulled over and ordered Hank to switch places with him in the vehicle. As soon as he was in the backseat, he ordered Colleen Reed to take her clothes off before he began his brutal assault on her. Colleen was raped vaginally, anally, and forced to perform oral sex before Mac began to beat her and burn her with a cigarette. "Her screams were so loud they hurt my ears," Hank later told the police.

Hank finally pulled over on a service road in Salado, over sixty miles away from the Austin carwash where they'd abducted Colleen. In a scene straight from the Broomstick Murders, Mac got dressed and asked Hank if he'd like to have a turn. Hank agreed and also raped Colleen, but he later told police he only did so to keep Mac away from her and hopefully protect her from him.

Mac drove for another twenty-five miles while Hank raped Colleen in the backseat. She tried to tell him details about her life and she begged him to protect her from Mac. He later told police he'd even started to like her.

Mac pulled the car over near his parents' house in Temple, in an area where overgrown grass hid them from the nearby road. He pulled Colleen out of the car by her hair and raped her on the hood of the vehicle. When he was finished, he demanded more oral sex and threw the trembling woman to her knees.

Hank later testified he believes Colleen may have bitten Mac at that moment because he heard his friend let out a loud scream before letting fly a single punch that knocked the woman to the ground, dead.

After smoking a cigarette, Mac threw Colleen's body into his trunk and warned his friend not to talk about what they'd just done. The two drove home in silence.

Unbeknownst to Mac and Hank, witnesses near the carwash had heard a woman screaming for help and rushed over, only to find a soapy, abandoned vehicle with the keys still in the ignition and a woman's purse sitting on the passenger seat. They immediately called the police. Newly purchased groceries had been also left behind, as well as all the money and credit cards in her wallet. Her license and car registration gave detectives a name to work with—Colleen Reed, a twenty-eight-year-old accountant. Police knew they had an abduction on their hands.

Colleen's family, especially her older sister, Lori, immediately began searching for her. They put up hundred of fliers all over Austin while police checked out thousands of tips as they poured in each day.

The Bodies Start Piling Up

On February 24, 1992, Valencia Joshua knocked on the window of a dormitory in Texas State Technical College, looking for her friend, Mac. She knocked on at least one wrong window before she found Mac's room. That was the last time she was ever seen alive. Her body was found partially buried in a wooded area at a nearby golf course. She had been strangled to death.

In the early hours of March 1, after a long day of drinking and smoking crack, Mac's Thunderbird broke down just south of Waco, Texas. A nearby Quik-Pak gas station loomed in the distance. Working behind the counter that night was twenty-two-year-old Melissa Northrup, a petite brunette who was two-and-a-half months pregnant. Melissa's husband, Aaron, also a Quik-Pak employee, typically hung out at the store with his wife when she worked the graveyard shift, but he'd left her alone earlier that evening after visiting her.

Exactly what happened in the gas station that morning is unknown. Around four in the morning, Aaron called the store to check on his wife, but no one picked up the phone. He tried calling a few more times, and when he still did not get an answer, he drove to the gas station to check on her.

When Aaron pulled into the parking lot, he immediately noticed Melissa's car was missing. A customer standing at the checkout counter turned to him as he walked in and told him no one seemed to be working. Aaron went behind the counter and spotted Melissa's purse in her usual spot, but when he opened the register, he could see all of the money had been removed. Sitting next to the register was a pad of paper with a list of baby names in his wife's handwriting. After searching the entire building, Aaron called 911.

About a half hour earlier, a witness later reported seeing a man using one car to push a Thunderbird down the road near the Quik-Pak. The witness told police the man would use the car to push the Thunderbird a few feet, get out of the first car, straighten the wheel of the Thunderbird, and get back in to push again. The man got the car into a vacant lot nearby and turned down help when the witness approached him.

After hearing this account days later, and locating the Thunderbird, police believed the witness saw Kenneth McDuff using Melissa Northrup's vehicle to hide his Thunderbird from view. When they processed the vehicle, they found Mac's wallet, along with several items of paperwork with his name on it. They also found a receipt from the Quik-Pak station earlier in the night, before Melissa had shown up for work.

Melissa's body was discovered by a fisherman nearly eight weeks later in a flooded gravel pit in a small town called Combine, over a hundred miles away. She was nude from the waist down and her hands were tied behind her back with her shoelaces. Her feet were also bound. Due to the advanced state of decomposition in her body, an exact cause of death could not be determined. Her car was found abandoned in a muddy bog about a mile and a half away.

The Manhunt

On March 3, just two days after Melissa's abduction, Mac's mother, Addie, called police to report her son missing. She claimed the last time she'd seen him was on February 29 when he'd gone to Victoria to see about a machinist job. She insisted that, since he'd missed his final test at school, he must be dead. She claimed there was no other explanation. Police didn't believe Addie's account and thought she might be trying to cover for her son while he tried to go on the run.

Detectives all across Texas were starting to put the pieces together and suspected Kenneth McDuff in several murder-abductions. But because the victims were spread out across different counties, none of them had all the facts. They suspected they were dealing with a skilled and dangerous killer, but few of them really understood just exactly what Kenneth McDuff was capable of. Eventually, due to some quick thinking by U.S. Marshals who realized that some of Mac's crimes involved drug dealing and possession of an illegal firearm, a federal warrant was issued for his arrest.

In April, after several visits from detectives, Hank Worley's conscience got the better of him. He broke down and told police about that night with Colleen Reed. After a long night of interrogation, police arrested Hank and used his statements to put together a probable cause affidavit for Kenneth McDuff's arrest. The media got ahold of the story, and suddenly the entire country knew the Broomstick Killer was on the loose, snatching up women, torturing them, raping them, and killing them.

The TV shows *Unsolved Mysteries* and *America's Most Wanted* aired episodes describing Kenneth McDuff's crimes and explaining he was a wanted man. On May 1, after watching one of the shows, a man named Gary Smithee in Kansas City, Missouri, made the connection. He thought the man on the TV show resembled one of his coworkers, but the guy went by the name Richard Dale Fowler, not Kenneth McDuff. He called the police anyway and they pulled Richard Fowler's records—who'd just recently been arrested for soliciting prostitutes downtown. When they compared Fowler's fingerprints with McDuff's prints, they realized they had their man. On May 4, 1992, Kenneth McDuff was pulled over in Kansas City and arrested by a team of six officers.

The End for McDuff

On June 26, 1992, Mac was indicted on one count of capital murder in regards to Melissa Northrup. Hair samples taken from Melissa's body and vehicle matched that of the defendant. After the judge allowed evidence to be presented from

Colleen Reed's case, Hank Worley also took the stand and described in detail what had happened the night he and Mac had stopped at that carwash in Austin. Finally, against the advice of counsel, Kenneth McDuff took the stand in his own defense.

Most of what came out of Mac's mouth was lie after lie, and the jury saw through it. He was convicted after they deliberated for just four hours, and on February 18, 1993, that same jury sentenced him to death by lethal injection. He was the first prisoner in United States history to be sent back to death row after being paroled from death row, and he's the only prisoner to have ever been sentenced to death by two different means—the electric chair in 1966 and the needle in 1993.

McDuff through the years.

In January of 1994, the trial for Colleen Reed's murder began. Despite searching many sites, police still hadn't found where Mac had ultimately dumped Colleen's body. The last time Hank Worley had seen her was right after his friend had killed her and put her in the trunk of his Thunderbird. Essentially they were charging him with capital murder without a body.

Five hairs found in the Thunderbird matched hairs taken from Colleen's belongings. The hairs had been forcibly ripped from her head—the roots were still found intact.

Just like he did in Melissa Northrup's trial, Hank Worley

testified about that horrible night. Mac's defense attorneys tried to imply Hank was the real killer and he was only testifying to make himself a deal to get out of prison early, but Hank assured the court he had made no such deal. He was facing his own capital murder charges himself.

In the end, the jury took just over two hours to convict Kenneth McDuff on all three counts—capital murder, aggravated sexual assault, and aggravated kidnapping. As he was being led into court to hear the verdict, Mac told reporters Hank Worley couldn't be trusted and had confessed to him that he'd killed the four teens in the Austin yogurt shop in December of 1991. Hank Worley angrily denied the accusation and even offered to take a polygraph test to prove his innocence. Neither man was ever charged with those murders.

In spring of 1998, after several stays of execution and still awaiting his death sentence to be carried out, Mac finally gave up the location of Regenia Moore's body. Police located her body buried under some chunks of concrete and an old carpet in a wooded area off the Tehuacana Creek near State Highway 6. Regenia's hands had been tied behind her and her feet were tied with her stockings. Finally, after seven years, Regenia's family had closure.

Shortly after, detectives were also able to locate Brenda Thompson's body using directions given to them by McDuff. Brenda was found in a shallow grave in a wooded area on Ghoulson Road, just a few miles north of Waco, Texas. Mac later described how after he'd eluded the police at that checkpoint, he'd taken Brenda to a field where he had raped her for hours. Finally, he'd strangled her using his hands, put her back in his pickup truck and drove to the site where he buried her.

Finally, in October of 1998, McDuff gave up the location of Colleen Reed's body. He led police to another shallow grave in a wooded area just off a bridge on the Brazos River. Days later, a federal judge lifted all stays of execution and rescheduled McDuff's final day on earth to be November 17, 1998. No more stays would be granted.

On the day of his scheduled execution, McDuff confessed to killing the girls at the yogurt shop in Austin. But he got several of the details wrong, even at one point claiming there were five girls, not four, who were killed that night. Police still maintain Kenneth McDuff is not a prime suspect in the Yogurt Shop Murders. The crime remains unsolved to this day.

As the poisonous solution began flowing into his veins at 6:10 that evening, Mac stared at the ceiling and announced, "I am ready to be released. Release me." The family members of his victims watched the scene from behind a two-way mirror. They were more than happy to release Kenneth McDuff from their lives that day.

Meet the Authors

Dr. Peter Vronsky

 **Peter Vronsky, Ph.D.** is a criminal justice historian, filmmaker, and the author of two bestselling definitive histories of serial homicide, *Serial Killers: The Method and Madness of Monsters* and *Female Serial Killers: How and Why Women Become Monsters.* He teaches in the history department of Ryerson University in Toronto where he lectures on the history of terrorism and espionage in international relations. The third volume of his serial killer history books explores in depth serial killers before Jack the Ripper and the years before the 1970-1980 "serial killer epidemic" era. *Serial Killer Chronicles: An Early History of Monsters* is scheduled to be published by Berkley Books - Penguin Random House in 2017.

Peter Vronsky books can be found at:
www.petervronsky.com
Websites: www.petervronsky.org and
www.SerialKillerChronicles.com
Facebook: www.facebook.com/killersbypetervronsky

Sylvia Perrini

Sylvia Perrini is an author, historian, wife and mother.

Sylvia studied history and law at Manchester University and developed a particular interest in women who live outside the common boundaries of society.

Sylvia lives with her husband and children in the New Forest, Hampshire, UK. Here she spends her time reading, writing and painting.

Author Page: www.amazon.com/SYLVIA-PERRINI/e/B007WRWEI0
Facebook: www.facebook.com/AuthorSylviaPerrini
Website: www.sylviaperrini.goldmineguides.com/

Michael Newton

Michael Newton has published 311 books under his own name and various pseudonyms since 1977. He began writing professionally as a "ghost" for author Don Pendleton on the best-selling Executioner series and continues his work on that series today. With 104 episodes published to date, Newton has nearly tripled the number of Mack Bolan novels completed by creator Pendleton himself. While 221 of Newton's published books have been novels—including westerns, political thrillers and psychological suspense—he is best known for nonfiction, primarily true crime and reference books. He has written many books on serial killers including:

Silent Rage: Inside the Mind of a Serial Killer
The Encyclopedia of Serial Killers (Facts on File Crime Library)
Hunting Humans: An Encyclopedia of Modern Serial Killers
Daddy Was the Black Dahlia Killer: The Identity of America's Most Notorious Serial Murderer—Revealed at Last

Website: www.michaelnewton.homestead.com/
Author Page: www.amazon.com/Michael-Newton/e/B001IXMYNO
Facebook: www.facebook.com/MichaelNewtonAuthor

RJ Parker

RJ Parker, Ph.D., is ranked in the Top 100 authors list on Amazon and a member of Amazon's Smile program. He donates to Wounded Warriors Project and Victims of Violent Crimes.

He has written 22 true crime books, which are available in eBook, paperback, and audiobook editions and have sold in over 100 countries. He holds certifications in Serial Crime and Criminal Profiling.

"Parker amazes his readers with top notch writing and idealist research. The Canadian writer has a better grasp of criminology and the psyche of a serial killer's mind than most people who spend a lifetime in a professional field chasing criminals and diabolic fiends." -- John Douglas (Retired FBI Agent - Behavioral Science)

RJ Parker Publishing represents several authors in the genres of True Crime and Crime Fiction.

CONTACT INFORMATION
Email: AuthorRJParker@gmail.com
Website: http://m.RJPARKERPUBLISHING.com/
Twitter: www.Twitter.com/realRJParker
Facebook: www.facebook.com/RJParkerPublishing
Author's Page: rjpp.ca/RJ-PARKER-BOOKS

JJ Slate

 **JJ Slate** is a bestselling true crime author and blogger. Born in Massachusetts, she has always been fascinated with true crime stories, especially those dealing with missing persons and cold cases. This is JJ's sixth book with **RJ Parker Publishing, Inc**. Her first, *Missing Wives, Missing Lives*, a compilation of true cases about wives that have gone missing, published in June of 2014 and quickly became an Amazon bestseller.

JJ currently lives in New England with her husband. When she isn't writing or researching her next book, she is usually investigating and blogging about current cases in the media.

CONTACT INFORMATION
Blog: www.jenniferjslate.com
Email: JJSlate@RJParkerPublishing.com
Amazon: www.amazon.com/author/jjslate
Twitter: www.twitter.com/jenniferjslate
Facebook: www.facebook.com/JJSlate

Recent Releases by RJ Parker Publishing, Inc.

Crimes Canada: True Crimes That Shocked the Nation

By VronskyParker Publications, an imprint of RJ Parker Publishing, Inc.

An exciting 24-volume series collection, edited by crime historian Dr. Peter Vronsky and true crime author and publisher RJ Parker. Each month we will publish a book of some of Canada's most notorious shocking criminals, written by various authors, and published under VP Publications. Collect them all!

Robert Pickton: The Pig Farmer Killer (Volume 1)
By Chris Swinney
Marc Lépine: The Montreal Massacre (Volume 2)
By RJ Parker
Paul Bernardo and Karla Homolka: The Ken and Barbie Killers (Volume 3)
By Peter Vronsky
Shirley Turner: Doctor, Stalker, Murderer (Volume 4)
By Kelly Banaski
Canadian Psycho: The True Story of Luka Magnotta

Forensic Analysis and DNA in Criminal Investigations: Including Solved Cold Cases
By RJ Parker and Peter Vronsky
Released October 15, 2015

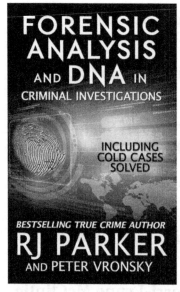

With its clear explanations, this 400-page entertaining book is intended as an introductory guide and reference to forensic techniques for mystery fans, armchair sleuths, front-line police officers, criminal attorneys, journalists, and crime authors. This encyclopedic book is a must read for any true crime aficionado.

Parker and Dr. Vronsky provide real cold case examples where forensic science was key in, not only identifying the guilty, but also in clearing the innocent and freeing the wrongly convicted. Thanks to DNA analysis and new forensic techniques, many cases once thought hopeless are being resolved.

Till Death Do Us Part:
A Collection of Newlywed Murder Cases
By JJ Slate
Released February 28, 2015

Studies have shown that marriages typically thrive the most in the months after the wedding, a period known as "the honeymoon period."

Not these marriages.

Spousal murder is never acceptable, but newlywed murder seems to be on a completely different level. It is unconscionable to think someone could stand in front of his family and friends, pledging to honor and cherish another person for the rest of his life, and then kill his spouse in cold blood just months, weeks, or even days later. It happens more than you'd think—and, contrary to popular belief, it's not always the husband who acts as the aggressor.

In her third true crime book, bestselling author JJ Slate examines more than twenty true stories of newlywed murders, delving into the past of the victims and aggressors, searching for answers to the question everyone is asking: How does this sort of thing happen? These shocking cases of betrayal and murder might just make you think differently about those five sacred words, "till death do us part."

The Basement

By RJ Parker

Released October 4, 2016

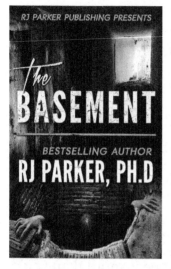

This is a shocking story of kidnapping, rape, torture, mutilation, dismemberment, decapitation, and murder.

Warning: The subject matter in this book is graphic.

On March 24, 1987, the Philadelphia Police Department received a phone call from a woman who stated that she had been held captive for the last four months. When police officers arrived at the pay phone from which the call was made, Josefina Rivera told them that she and three other women had been held captive in a basement by a man named Gary Heidnik. He imprisoned women in chains, in the filth and stench of a hole dug under his home.

Missing Wives, Missing Lives
By JJ Slate
Released June 16, 2014

When a wife goes missing, her husband is often the prime suspect in her disappearance. But what happens when she is never found? In some of the cases profiled in this chilling book, their husbands were found guilty of murder, even without a body.

Missing Wives, Missing Lives focuses on thirty unique cases in which a missing wife has never been found and the undying efforts of her family as they continue the painful search to bring her home. The book covers decades old cases, such as Jeanette Zapata, who has been missing since 1976, to more recent and widely known cases, such as Stacy Peterson, who has been missing since 2007. Keeping these women's stories alive may be the key to solving the mystery and bringing them home to their family.

Revenge Killings

By RJ Parker

Released January 28, 2016

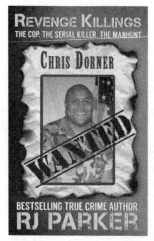

Chris Dorner was a cop with the LAPD who was fired after reporting that his training officer beat up a handcuffed, non-resisting suspect. He appealed. Lost. Then snapped. In his manifesto that he posted on Facebook, he vowed to kill those associated with him being fired as well as their families. His first victims were the daughter of the LAPD lawyer who represented him and her fiancé. This recent case from 2013 includes several pictures, some of which are quite graphic, including the all-out manhunt for Dorner and his controversial death.

Did the LAPD blow the whole scenario way out of proportion? Keeping in mind the fact that the LAPD is one of the most militarized police forces in America, one man's attempts to clear his name should not have sent the whole LAPD into the frenzy that it went into after Dorner's manifesto and statement came to light.

This is the first book in a new 'Recent True Crime Cases' series by Peter Vronsky and RJ Parker, VP Publications, an imprint of RJ Parker Publishing.

Serial Killers True Crime Anthology: Vols I - IV

Collect them all!

Including case files written by Katherine Ramsland, Sylvia Perrini, Kelly Banaski, Michael Newton, Peter Vronsky, RJ Parker, Dane Ladwig, and Kelly Banaski

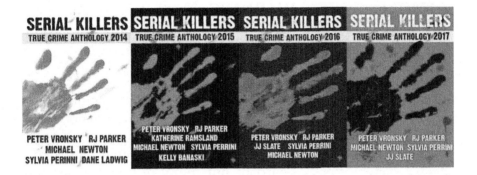

You've read Volume IV, now go back and read the first three volumes!

Serial killers: they cross the bounds of evil. They murder at random without logic or reason other than the one twisting in their sick and evil minds. They are diabolical vile creatures devoid of morality or pity. You will meet a chosen few of them in these pages. You will see that serial killers are roaming among us all, from small towns to big cities. They are not limited to a particular place, gene pool, culture, social class or religion. They are not restricted to any particular demographic, political propensity and they can be of any gender.

Serial Killers Abridged: An Encyclopedia of 100 Serial Killers
By RJ Parker
Released May 31, 2014

WARNING: There are dramatic crime scene photos in this book that some may find very disturbing

The ultimate reference for anyone compelled by the pathologies and twisted minds behind the most disturbing homicidal monsters. From A to Z, there are names you may not have heard of but many of you are familiar with, including the notorious John Wayne Gacy, Jeffrey Dahmer, Ted Bundy, Gary Ridgway, Aileen Wuornos, and Dennis Rader, just to name a few. This reference book will make a great collection for true crime enthusiasts. Each story is in a Reader's Digest short format.

Parents Who Killed their Children: Filicide

By RJ Parker

Released April 30, 2014

What could possibly incite parents to kill their own children?

This collection of "filicidal killers" provides a gripping overview of how things can go horribly wrong in once-loving families. *Parents Who Killed their Children* depicts ten of the most notorious and horrific cases of homicidal parental units out of control. Included are the stories of Andrea Yates, Diane Downs, Susan Smith, and Jeffrey MacDonald, who received a great deal of media attention. The author explores the reasons behind these  murders—from addiction to postpartum psychosis, insanity to altruism.

Each story is detailed with background information on the parents, the murder scenes, trials, sentencing and aftermath.

Radical Islamic Terrorism in America Today
By RJ Parker
Released May 26, 2016

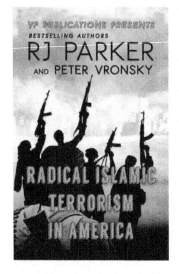

This book depicts the rise of ISIS and how these savages have infiltrated America.

Today's radical Islamist terrorist could be just a breath away from any of us: a fellow student, an employee, or even the soldier in the next bunk. We could be attacked at a park, a mall, or a dance club.

Americans today are facing an alarming new terrorist threat: the 'Self-Radicalized' Terrorist. Unlike previous 'sleepers' like the 9/11 hijackers who infiltrated the United States from abroad, this new breed of 'Terrorist' comes from within. Many are natural born Americans or immigrants to the U.S. who, over time, 'Self-Radicalized' themselves through radical Islamist internet propaganda and undertook terrorist action on their own initiative with little or no guidance from overseas terrorist groups.

Unpredictable and often disguised in their previous identities as loyal American university students, government employees, or even members of the U.S. military, this new 'franchise style' of terrorist is difficult to detect.

RJ Parker, Ph.D., documents in a single volume some of the prominent and frightening recent cases of self-radicalized terrorist strikes in the United States.

References

Chapter 1:

Associated Press. "Innocent Couple Released. Man, Woman Served 4 Years in 'Happy Face Killer' Case." *The Spokesman Review*. November 28, 1995. http://www.spokesman.com/stories/1995/nov/28/innocent-couple-released-man-woman-served-4-years/.

Associated Press. "Murderer threatens to run up legal tab." *The Spokesman Review*. Sunday, December 31, 1995. https://news.google.com/newspapers?nid=1314&dat=19951231&id=F6QpAAAAIBAJ&sjid=ZfEDAAAAIBAJ&pg=6571,5154550&hl=en.

"Evidence Clears Two. The Law Doesn't." The New York Times. November 26, 1995. http://www.nytimes.com/1995/11/26/us/evidence-clears-two-the-law-doesn-t.html.

Fuoco, Michael. "Touching Evil: Serial killer's need to control shows in letters to students." *Pittsburgh Post-Gazette*. December 17 2007. http://www.post-gazette.com/frontpage/2007/12/17/Touching-Evil-Serial-killer-s-need-to-control-shows-in-letters-to-students/stories/200712170224.

Gomez, Mark. "Detective embarks on final hunt for slain woman's identity." *The Mercury News*. June 23, 2007. http://www.mercurynews.com/2007/06/23/detective-embarks-on-final-hunt-for-slain-womans-identity/.

Grollmus, Denise. "'Happy Face Killer' Keith Hunter Jesperson Racks Up More Victims." *True Crime Report*. December 22, 2009. http://www.truecrimereport.com/2009/12/happy_face_killer_keith_hunter.php.

More, Melissa G. & M. Bridget Cook (2009). *Shattered Silence: The Untold Story of the Daughter of a Serial Killer*. Cedar Ford. ISBN 978-1-59955-238-5.

Olsen, Jack (2002). *I: The Creation of a Serial Killer*. St Martin's Press. ISBN 978-0-312-24198-8.

Chapter 3:

Associated Press. "Killer Nurse Gets 360 Years," November 15, 1999.

—. "Nurse's Hospital Murder Trial Begins," August 30, 1999.

Borg, Gary. "Nurse Linked To Deaths, Supervisor Tells Board," *Chicago Tribune,* September 19, 1995.

Dedman, Bill. "Trial Opens for Ex-Nurse Charged in Indiana Deaths," *New York Times,* August 31, 1999.

—. "Nurse Guilty Of Killing Six Of His Patients," *New York Times,* October 18, 1999.

"Ex-nurse pleads not guilty to 6 murder charges," CNN, December 30, 1997.

"Jury In 6-murder Case Prayed, *Chicago Tribune,* October 19, 1999.

"Jury Pool Hears Of Sacrifice," *Chicago Tribune,* July 13, 1999.

"Jury Weighs Case Of 7 Hospital Deaths." *Chicago Tribune,* October 15, 1999.

Orville Lynn Majors v. Katie Engelbrecht et al., U.S. Court of Appeals for the Seventh Circuit, 149 F.3d 709 (7th Cir. 1998).

Orville Lynn Majors v. State of Indiana, Supreme Court of Indiana No. 11S00-0004-CR-239 (2002).

Pasternak, Judy. "Deaths at Hospital Roil Rural County," *Los Angeles Times,* December 31, 1997.

"Patient's Last Minutes At Issue," *Chicago Tribune,* September 22, 1999.

"Police: 100 Hospital Deaths May Be Murder," *Chicago Tribune,* December 17, 1996.

Robinson, Bryan. "Majors sentenced to 360 years in prison for patients' deaths," CourtTV.com, November 15, 1999.

Rogers, Abby. "What It's Like To Be In The Same Room With A Convicted Serial Killer," *Business Insider,* January 8, 2013.

"2nd Exhumation Ordered," *Chicago Tribune,* June 10, 1997.

Yorker, Beatrice, Kenneth W. Kizer, Paula Lampe, A.R.W. Forrest, Jacquetta Lannan, and Donna Russell. "Serial Murder by Healthcare Professionals." Forensic Science 51.6 (2006): 1362-1371.

Chapter 4:

https://en.wikipedia.org/wiki/Sara_Aldrete

https://en.wikipedia.org/wiki/Adolfo_Constanzo

http://www.sfgate.com/news/article/Woman-called-priestess-of-satanic-cult-says-she-s-2774267.php

http://murderpedia.org/female.A/a/aldrete-sara.htm

https://www.bizarrepedia.com/el-padrino-de-matamoros/

http://truecrimecases.blogspot.com.es/2012/08/adolfo-constanzo.html

https://books.google.co.uk/books?id=DwNVbOcTncwC&pg=PA54&lpg=PA54&dq=Sara+Aldrete&source=bl&ots=B2BGuqWq8H&sig=vUsezaEfid1ghis3T_VvJZPQ3Cw&hl=en&sa=X&ved=0ahUKEwjWnJvBivTPAhUHtRQKHSFCAPg4FBDoAQgvMAQ#v=onepage&q=Sara%20Aldrete&f=false

http://archivo.eluniversal.com.mx/ciudad/53172.html

http://articles.latimes.com/1989-05-16/business/fi-385_1_mexico-massacre-jesus-constanzo-mass-suicide

Chapter 5:

[1] Stella Sands, *The Dating Game Killer: The True Story of a TV Dating Show, a Violent Sociopath, and a Series of Brutal Murders*, New York: St. Martin's True Crime Library, 2011. Kindle Edition.

[2] https://www.youtube.com/watch?v=12PXvKfWdZs

[3] http://articles.latimes.com/2011/jan/28/local/la-me-alcala-20110128

[4] Dan Logan, "Rodney Alcala: Orange County's Murderer Behind Bars," *Orange Coast Magazine*, Vol.15, No. 6, June 1989, pp. 105-106; see also, *People v. Alcala* , 36 Cal.3d 604 available at: (http://scocal.stanford.edu/opinion/people-v-alcala-23258)

[5] http://www.ocregister.com/news/alcala-243387-photos-detectives.html?graphics=1#graphics1

[6] https://krazykillers.wordpress.com/2015/12/19/the-dating-game-killer/

[7] http://stevehodel.com/

[8] https://www.fbi.gov/wanted/topten/topten-history

[9] Stella Sands, (Kindle Locations 645-646).

[10] Peter Vronsky, *Serial Killers: The Method and Madness of Monsters,* New York: Berkley Books-Penguin Random House, 2004, pp.262-263

[11] http://www.disastercenter.com/crime/nycrime.htm

[12] http://christineruththornton.blogspot.ca/2014/09/chrisare-you-out-there.html

[13] http://kgab.com/dating-game-killer-wont-face-murder-charge-in-wyoming/

[14] http://articles.latimes.com/2011/jan/28/local/la-me-alcala-20110128

[15] United States Sentencing Commission, *The History of Child Pornography Guidelines,* Washington DC, 2009; *New York vs Ferber,* 458 U.S. 747; 102 S. Ct. 3348; 73 L. Ed. 2d 1113; 1982 U.S. LEXIS 12; 50 U.S.L.W. 5077; 8 Media L. Rep. 1809

[16] Sands, (Kindle Locations 4947-4949)

[17] Sands, Kindle Locations 2877-2878

[18] http://www.ocregister.com/articles/-291041--.html

[19] http://www.laweekly.com/news/seinfeld-actor-jed-mills-met-creepy-alleged-dating-game-serial-killer-rodney-alcala-in-abcs-green-room-2392831

[20] http://www.10news.com/news/local-man-discusses-game-show-appearance-with-serial-killer

[21] http://www.heraldsun.com.au/ipad/my-dream-date-with-a-serial-killer/story-fnbzs1vo-1226406771022

[22] http://www.cbsnews.com/videos/extra-i-could-have-been-next/

[23] *People v. Alcala* , 36 Cal.3d 604 available at: (http://scocal.stanford.edu/opinion/people-v-alcala-23258)

Chapter 6:

Altman, Larry. "A Teen's Terrifying Days with a Killer in 1984, an L.A.-area Girl Became One of the Targets of a Hunted Man who Took Her on a Cross-Country Nightmare. *Daily News.* May 28, 2008. https://www.thefreelibrary.com/A+TEEN%27S+TERRIFYING+DAYS+WITH+A+KILLER+IN+1984,+AN+L.A.-AREA+GIRL...-a0179511757.

Bearak, Barry and Eric Malnic. "Christopher Wilder a real 'killer'

with the ladies." *The Tuscaloosa News*. April 26, 1984.
https://news.google.com/newspapers?nid=1817&dat=19840
425&id=cDodAAAAIBAJ&sjid=76UEAAAAIBAJ&pg=6904,7
213272.

Bovson, Mara. "'Beauty Queen Killer' and race car driver Christopher Bernard Wilder takes a bloody ride through the states, kidnapping, raping and murdering 8 women in short 1984 span." *New York Daily News*. September 19, 2015.
http://www.nydailynews.com/news/crime/beauty-queen-killer-takes-bloody-ride-1984-article-1.2366878.

Brown, Anne-Louise. "Double killing DNA sample lost." *The Sydney Morning Herald*. July 6, 2014.
http://www.smh.com.au/nsw/double-killing-dna-sample-lost-20140703-zsuxv.html.

Gibney, Bruce (1984). *The Beauty Queen Killer*. Pinnacle Books, New York. ISBN: 0-205-42380-2.

Johns, Loujane. "Nothing Ever Happens Here." The Chronicle-Express. May 6, 2009. http://www.chronicle-express.com/article/20090506/NEWS/305069999.

King, Jonathon. "The Mystery of Beth Kenyon." *The Sun-Sentinel*. April 24, 1988. http://articles.sun-sentinel.com/1988-04-24/features/8801250922_1_new-hampshire-car-gun.

Nightingale, Tom. "DNA advances may solve brutal murders." *ABC News*. February 27, 2012.
http://www.abc.net.au/news/2012-02-27/dna-advances-may-solve-cold-case-murders/3855916.

Chapter 7:

Anonymous. "Hugh G. Aynesworth." http://spartacus-educational.com/JFKaynesworth.htm.

Aynesworth, Hugh. Various articles, *Dallas Times-Herald,* April 1985.

Call, Max. *Hand of Death: The Henry Lee Lucas Story*. Vital Issues Press, 1985.

Cox, Mike. *The Confessions of Henry Lee Lucas*. Pocket Books, 1991.

DiEugenio, Jim. "Hugh Aynesworth: Refusing a Conspiracy is his

Life's Work," http://www.ctka.net/aynesworth.html.

Draper, Robert. "The Twilight of the Texas Rangers," *Texas Monthly*, February 1994.

Gilmore, Tim. *Stalking Ottis Toole: A Southern Gothic*. CreateSpace, 2013.

Harris, Arthur Jay. *Jeffrey Dahmer's Dirty Secret: The Unsolved Murder of Adam Walsh*. CreateSpace, 2013.

Jones, Malcolm. "Hugh Aynesworth Has Spent His Career Debunking JFK Conspiracy Theories." *The Daily Beast,* November 22, 2013.

Knox, Sara. "The Productive Power of Confessions of Cruelty" http://pmc.iath.virginia.edu/issue.501/11.3knox.html.

London, Sondra. *True Vampires: Blood-sucking Killers Past and Present*. Feral House, 2003.

McGowan, David. "There's Something About Henry," http://whale.to/b/henry.html.

Newton, Michael. *Raising Hell: An Encyclopedia of Devil Worship and Satanic Crime*. Avon Books, 1993.

Norris, Joel. *Henry Lee Lucas: The Shocking True Story of Americas Most Notorious Serial Killer*. Pinnacle Books, 1991.

Sonnenschein, Allan. "Serial Killers." *Penthouse,* February 1985.

Standiford, Les, and Joe Matthews. *Bringing Adam Home: The Abduction that Changed America*. Ecco, 2011.

Chapter 9:
http://murderpedia.org/female.C/c/caffey-erin.htm
http://www.mirror.co.uk/news/world-news/killer-women-teen-who-masterminded-7953911
https://www.youtube.com/watch?v=NY2AHhPMc7Q
http://lifestyle.one/closer/news-real-life/in-the-news/devestated-dad-daughter-murdered-wife-sons-ve-forgiven/

Chapter 10:
Cartwright, Gary. "Free to Kill." *Texas Monthly*. August, 1992. http://www.texasmonthly.com/articles/free-to-kill-2/.

Cartwright, Gary. "The End. Kenneth McDuff, Do Not Rest In Peace." *Texas Monthly*. December, 1998.

http://www.texasmonthly.com/articles/the-end/.

Cochran, Mike. "McDuff likely to take grisly secrets to grave." *Associated Press*. November 24, 1996. http://lubbockonline.com/news/112496/mcduff.htm.

Kendall, Pete. "Dead man prime suspect in Gonzalez murder." *Cleburne Times Review*. March 30, 2009. http://www.cleburnetimesreview.com/archives/dead-man-prime-suspect-in-gonzalez-murder/article_b92553d5-cfeb-5cdc-b425-02bd8c4f4032.html

Lavergne, Gary M. *Bad Boy: The True Story of Kenneth Allen McDuff, The Most Notorious Serial Killer in Texas History.* 1999. St. Martin's Paperbacks. ISBN: 0-312-98125-2.

Steward, Bob. *No Remorse*. Pinnacle Books. 1996. ISBN: 0-7860-0231-X.

Turner, Allan. "Eternity's gate slowly closing at Peckerwood Hill." Houston Chronicle. August 3, 2012. http://www.chron.com/news/houston-texas/article/Eternity-s-gate-slowly-closing-at-Peckerwood-Hill-3761731.php.

CPSIA information can be obtained
at www.ICGtesting.com
Printed in the USA
BVOW06s1913301117
501654BV00013B/503/P